M. Iroshnikov. D. Kovalenko. V. Shishkin

Genesis of the Soviet Federative State (1917-1925)

Progress Publishers
Moscow

Translated from the Russian by *Aini Lehto* and *Albert Zdornykh*
Designed by *Alexander Shafransky*

М. Ирошников, Д. Коваленко, В. Шишкин

СТАНОВЛЕНИЕ СОВЕТСКОГО СОЮЗНОГО ГОСУДАРСТВА

(1917-1925)

На английском языке

Printed in the Union of Soviet Socialist Republics

И $\dfrac{10604-695}{014(01)-82}$ 62—82   0505000000

2

CONTENTS

INTRODUCTION

The Constitution of the USSR states that "the Union of Soviet Socialist Republics is an integral, federal, multinational state formed on the principle of socialist federalism as a result of the free self-determination of nations and the voluntary association of equal Soviet Socialist Republics".

This definition summarises the development of the multinational federal state over the past 60 years.

The formation and development of the multinational Soviet state was an achievement of great complexity. This process began with the victory of the Great October Socialist Revolution which enabled the workers and peasants of Russia to start "building a proletarian socialist state".[1] "The October Revolution rent the chains of social and national oppression and raised all the peoples of our country to independent historical creativity."[2]

The programme for this construction was outlined by Lenin in his pre-revolutionary works and in his initial speeches to the representatives of the working people of Russia after the triumph of the October armed uprising.

Among the programme documents of the new state, Lenin's speeches at the All-Russia Congress of Soviets, and the first decrees of the Soviet government drawn up under his guidance, most of which bear his signature, are of particular importance, as are the numerous decisions taken by the meetings and congresses of working people who for the first time ever were able to put into practice their right to administer the state.

---

[1] V. I. Lenin, "Meeting of the Petrograd Soviet of Workers' and Soldiers' Deputies, October 25 (November 7), 1917", *Collected Works*, Vol. 26, Progress Publishers, Moscow, 1964, p. 240.

[2] "Resolution of the Central Committee of the Communist Party of the Soviet Union on the Sixtieth Anniversary of the Formation of the Union of Soviet Socialist Republics", *Pravda*, 21 February 1982.

The establishing of the Soviet government, which was a government of the working people without any bourgeois participation whatsoever, permitted the working people to establish their own power, to demolish the old state apparatus, and to create "a new administrative apparatus set up in the form of the Soviet organisations".[1]

Lenin had already defined the content of the new stage of Russia's development in his first speech at the meeting of the Petrograd Soviet on October 25 (November 7), 1917: "From now on, a new phase in the history of Russia begins, and this, the third Russian revolution, should in the end lead to the victory of socialism."[2]

If socialism was to be built successfully, a dictatorship of the proletariat had to be set up and workers' control established over production and distribution, there had to be fundamental socialist transformations in industry, finance, banking, transport, and trade on the basis of nationalisation, the big landed estates had to be abolished and the national question solved.

The new state was founded on an alliance of the working class and the peasantry, which realised that only through such an alliance would it escape from the imperialist world war, and the domination of landowners, money-lenders and kulaks.

"A decisive role in the creation of the single union state was played by the RSFSR, around which all the Soviet republics joined together at their own wish."[3]

At the Third All-Russia Congress of Soviets, held in January 1918, Lenin said with the utmost conviction that "more and more diverse federations of free nations will group themselves around revolutionary Russia. This federation is invincible and will grow quite freely, without the help of lies or bayonets."[4]

---

[1] V. I. Lenin, "Meeting of the Petrograd Soviet of Workers' and Soldiers' Deputies, October 25 (November 7), 1917", *Collected Works*, Vol. 26, p. 239.

[2] Ibid.

[3] "Resolution of the Central Committee of the Communist Party of the Soviet Union on the Sixtieth Anniversary of the Formation of the Union of Soviet Socialist Republics", *Pravda*, 21 February 1982.

[4] V. I. Lenin, "Third All-Russia Congress of Soviets of Workers', Soldiers' and Peasants' Deputies", *Collected Works*, Vol. 26, p. 481.

Five years had passed after the victory of the socialist revolution before a federal Soviet state, the Union of Soviet Socialist Republics, was formed in December 1922.

Mikhail Kalinin, a prominent leader of the Soviet state, said in his closing speech at the First All-Union Congress of Soviets: "For thousands of years forward-looking human thought has wrestled with the theoretical problem of how to find forms enabling peoples to live in friendship and brotherhood without inflicting incredible suffering on each other, without fighting against each other. Only now, today, is the first stone in that direction being laid."[1]

After the First All-Union Congress of Soviets an enormous amount of work went into drafting the legislation for a single federal state based on the voluntary union of the Soviet republics. The Second Congress of Soviets held in January 1924 adopted the Constitution of the USSR, which was based on Lenin's principles of voluntary state association of equal peoples, their equality and sovereignty.

Towards the end of 1925 the USSR already counted six Union republics, 15 autonomous socialist republics, and 16 autonomous regions. Many nations and nationalities acquired, for the first time in history, an independent statehood in tune with their national interests.

The single federal state made it possible to solve the national question. "The peoples of former tsarist Russia, for the first time, had had a possibility of making a historical choice, the right to determine their own destiny,"[2] said Leonid Brezhnev, General Secretary of the CPSU Central Committee and Chairman of the Presidium of the USSR Supreme Soviet, in his speech on the occasion of the 60th anniversary of the October Revolution.

The formation of the USSR was an enormously important historical and international example of how fraternal friendship grew between peoples in the struggle for a better future for

---

[1] M. I. Kalinin, *Articles and Speeches (1919-1935)*, Gospolitizdat, Moscow, 1936, p. 95 (in Russian).

[2] L. I. Brezhnev, *Our Course: Peace and Socialism*, Novosti Press Agency Publishing House, Moscow, 1978, p. 172.

all mankind. The construction of socialism in the new federal state led to the formation of a new international historical community, the Soviet people, and of a developed socialist society, the foundations of which were consolidated in the 1977 Constitution of the USSR.

The authors, in selecting the years 1917-1925 for their study of the genesis of the Soviet federal state, were prompted by several considerations.

These years saw both the establishment of the Soviet state of the dictatorship of the proletariat, formalised in the first RSFSR Constitution of the 1918, and the shaping of the basic forms of co-operation between the independent Soviet republics.

Between 1918 and 1920, following the initial period (November 1917—mid-1918) of liberation of the peoples, many of which gained national statehood for the first time, this took the form of a military and political alliance. After the end of the Civil War it was replaced by treaty relations between the individual republics.

During the period of the 1922 Genoa Conference, the Soviet republics co-operated as diplomatic allies. Then, in order to rehabilitate the economy, which had been disrupted by the war, a closer economic, political and diplomatic unity had to be established between all the Soviet republics; without this it would have been impossible to safeguard the freedom and independence of the world's first proletarian state, as the country was encircled by hostile capitalist states. The formation of the USSR in 1922, adoption in 1924 of the first Union Constitution, and admission into the federation of new Union republics (Turkmenia and Uzbekistan) strengthened the Soviet state, thus helping to rehabilitate the economy, and enhance the USSR's international prestige.

The genesis of the Soviet federal state has been thoroughly studied by Soviet historians, jurists, economists, and philosophers. Hundreds of books, documents and symposia have been printed in Russian and in the languages of the other peoples of the USSR.[1] The authors see the present volume as summarising the vast amount of factual material examined by Soviet scholars.

---

[1] See, for example, *History of National-State Development in the USSR, 1917-1978* in two volumes, 3rd ed., Mysl Publishers, Moscow,

Introducing this book on the genesis of the Soviet federal state to foreign readers, the authors hope that a knowledge of how the Soviet Union solved the national question will help to expand mutual understanding between peoples and reinforce the principles of the peaceful coexistence of states with different social systems.

The solving of the national question, the levelling out of economic, political and cultural development, the achievement of true equality within the USSR, and the formation of a new historical community, the Soviet people, are of enormous historical and international importance for all the peoples which have chosen the road of national liberation and social progress. As stressed in the Resolution of the CPSU Central Committee:

"The formation and successful development of the USSR is of permanent international significance and heralds an important historical milestone in the centuries-old struggle of progressive mankind for equality and friendship among peoples, for the revolutionary renewal of the world."[1]

1979; *National Relations and the State in the Contemporary Period,* Nauka Publishers, Moscow, 1972; *The USSR—a Great Community of Fraternal Nations,* Nauka Publishers, Moscow 1972; M. I. Kulichenko, *National Relations in the USSR and Their Development Tendencies,* Mysl Publishers, Moscow, 1972; S. I. Yakubovskaya, *Development of the USSR as a Federal State,* Nauka Publishers, Moscow, 1972; D. A. Chugayev, *The Communist Party Is the Organiser of the Union of Soviet Socialist Republics,* Mysl Publishers, Moscow, 1972; A. V. Likholat, *The Community of the Peoples of the USSR in the Struggle to Build Socialism. 1917-1937,* Politizdat, Moscow, 1976; V. E. Malanchuk, *Historical Experience of the CPSU in Solving the National Question in the USSR,* Vysshaya Shkola Publishers, Moscow, 1972; T. U. Usubaliyev, *Leninism Is the Great Source of the Friendship and Brotherhood of the Peoples,* Nauka Publishers, Moscow, 1972; *Leninism and the National Question in Present-Day Conditions,* Politizdat, Moscow, 1972; *Triumph of Lenin's Ideas on Proletarian Internationalism,* Nauka Publishers, Moscow, 1974; *The Soviet People as a New Historical Community,* Nauka Publishers, Moscow, 1975; *The Communist Party Is the Inspirer and Organiser of the Ukrainian People's Unification Movement for the Formation of the USSR,* Politizdat, Kiev, 1972 (all in Russian).

[1] "Resolution of the Central Committee of the Communist Party of the Soviet Union on the Sixtieth Anniversary of the Formation of the Union of Soviet Socialist Republics", Pravda, 21 February 1982.

Chapter I

THE OCTOBER REVOLUTION AND THE BIRTH OF THE SOVIET STATE

The National Question in Russia at the Turn of the Century

In the early 20th century the centre of the world revolutionary movement shifted from Western Europe to Russia, which had become the weakest link of world imperialism and the focal point of its contradictions. The development of monopoly capitalism was tied up with diverse remnants of feudalism and serfdom, and the dominance of the tsarist autocracy. At the same time Russia, which tsarism considered "integral and indivisible", was a multinational power: it was inhabited by about 100 nations, nationalities and ethnic groups.

This huge country, comprising almost half of Europe and a third of Asia, was a major colonial power. Of the 75 million square kilometres of colonial territories at the turn of the century, 65 million, or 86 per cent, were in the hands of six states: Great Britain, Germany, Russia, France, the USA, and Japan. Tsarist Russia controlled 17.4 million square kilometres and a population of 33,200,000 in the colonies, itself covering 5.4 million square kilometres with a population of 136,200,000.[1]

This vast colonial empire had, under the tsars, become a real "prison of the peoples", where a large number of non-Russian nations and nationalities, comprising almost half of its population in 1913, suffered from cruel social, class, and national and colonial oppression.[2] Hence the particularly acute nature of the

---

[1] See V. I. Lenin, "Imperialism, the Highest Stage of Capitalism", *Collected Works*, Vol. 22, Progress Publishers, Moscow, 1964, p. 258.
[2] See *History of National-State Development in the USSR. 1917-1978*, Vol. I, p. 20.

national question, which in the age of imperialism developed into a *"world-wide* phenomenon".[1] *"Over one-half, almost three-fifths (to be exact, 57 per cent)* of the population of Russia is subject to national oppression; they are not even free to use their native language, they are forcibly Russified."[2] For this reason the solution of the national question within Russia was of such importance both for that country and for the whole world.

To eliminate definitively both class and national-colonial oppression it was essential first of all to demolish the system of bourgeois and landlord rule and tsarism, on which it was based. The revolutionary proletariat of Russia was the sole social force capable of cutting through this "Gordian knot" of imperialist contradictions. Significantly, it was in tsarist Russia that the revolutionary struggle reached its peak, as shown by the increasing strength of the three Russian revolutions, the major revolutionary events of the two decades of this century.

In the course of class conflicts the Russian proletariat, led by Lenin, created in 1903 a new type of proletarian party, the Bolshevik Party, which was a truly communist, truly internationalist party, as distinct from the social-democratic parties of the Second International, which leaned increasingly towards opportunism, social-chauvinism and reformism.

The Nationalities Programme of the Bolsheviks

Lenin began elaborating a theory of the national question and a programme for its solution long before the triumph in October 1917 of the proletarian revolution in Russia. Developing the teaching of Karl Marx and Frederick Engels in the new historical conditions of the age of imperialism, the age of revolutionary storms and social upheavals, he made a searching study of and drew conclusions from not only the class struggle of the

---

[1] V. I. Lenin, "Theses for a Lecture on the National Question", *Collected Works,* Vol. 41, Progress Publishers, Moscow, 1969, p. 313.
[2] V. I. Lenin, "Lecture on the 1905 Revolution", *Collected Works,* Vol. 23, Progress Publishers, Moscow, 1974, p. 249.

multinational proletariat of Russia, but also the entire world working-class movement, and the national liberation struggle of the oppressed colonial peoples.

Lenin's theory of the national question, based on the objective law, outlined by Marx, of the unification of nations in the course of capitalism's economic development and the forcible form of this unification through the domination of weaker nations by the big powers, took account also of the following two trends in world history that are peculiar to capitalism. First, the growing desire among peoples to throw off the shackles of colonial and semi-colonial dependence, the growing strength of the national liberation movements and the struggle to create national states. The second trend is the movement, under developed capitalism, towards the international unity of capital and distribution of labour, towards the creation in this context of interdependence between peoples, and towards the removal of national barriers.

The increasing international spread of capitalist domination in the age of imperialism made it inevitable that the working class of the advanced countries should work out and implement an ideology and policy of international solidarity to ensure the international unity of proletarian forces and all working people, and the oppressed masses of the colonies and dependent countries. "Capital," Lenin stressed, "is an international force. To vanquish it, an international workers' alliance, an international workers' brotherhood is needed.

"We are opposed to national enmity and discord, to national exclusiveness. We are internationalists."[1]

Posing the national question in this way was characteristic of the Leninist Bolshevik Party, which emphasised the exceptional importance of uniting the proletarians of all the nationalities of Russia if a socialist revolution was to be successful in the country.

A genuine, absolutely consistent proletarian internationalism was a fundamentally important feature of the Party created under Lenin's guidance. This was clearly stated in the Programme

---

[1] V. I. Lenin, "Letter to the Workers and Peasants of the Ukraine Apropos of the Victories over Denikin", *Collected Works*, Vol. 30, Progress Publishers, Moscow, 1965, p. 293.

of the Russian Social-Democratic Labour Party (RSDLP) and recorded subsequently in other Party documents, particularly in the resolutions of the Cracow and Poronin meetings of the RSDLP Central Committee with Party workers in 1912-1913. The Party Programme adopted at the Second Congress of the RSDLP in 1903 proclaimed "the right of all nations in the state to self-determination" and the equality of all citizens irrespective of race or nationality.[1] The proletariat of Russia and its Bolshevik Party stressed thereby the Marxist conclusion that a nation which oppresses other nations cannot be free.

Along with the proclamation of the right of nations to self-determination, including seccession and the formation of an independent state, another central factor of a genuinely internationalist policy was, in Lenin's view, the correct combination of the struggles for national liberation and social emancipation. This implied that the national liberation movement should be approached as part of the general question of socialist revolution, as that of the allies of the working class in the struggle to overthrow the bourgeois-landlord regime and establish socialism, which alone can ensure a just and final solution to the national question.

Lenin invariably emphasised the exceptional importance of the slogan "Workers of All Countries, Unite!" advanced by Karl Marx and Frederick Engels, and vigorously countered the Jewish Bundists' and other nationalists' demands that the party be built on a federal principle and that it be an association of national organisations independent of a common Party centre, as was then the case in many parties of the Second International. The congress adopted the Marxist principle of building the Party as an integral centralised organisation incorporating all the national contingents of Russia's working class, and supported the Party's Leninist programme on the national question which was aimed at eliminating national and colonial oppression, and at establishing the equality, friendship and brotherhood of all the peoples. The RSDLP, founded on the principles of proletarian internationalism, within a few years had attracted the progressive work-

---

[1] *The CPSU in Resolutions and Decisions of Its Congresses, Conferences and Central Committee Plenary Meetings*, 8th ed., Vol. 1, Politizdat, Moscow, 1970, p. 63 (in Russian).

ers of no less than 24 nations and nationalities within the country.[1]

"In Russia and in the Caucasus," Lenin wrote to Maxim Gorky in 1913, "the Georgian+Armenian+Tartar+Russian Social-Democrats have worked *together,* in a *single* Social-Democratic organisation *for more than ten years.* This is not a phrase, but the proletarian solution of the problem of nationalities. The only solution."[2] The same was true of other ethnic regions of the Russian empire. In accordance with Lenin's formulation of the national question as a worldwide phenomenon and part of the general question of the socialist revolution, the content of proletarian internationalism in the changed conditions of the age of imperialism was expressed in the call: "Working men of all countries and all oppressed peoples, unite!"

The Bolshevik Party, implementing its first Programme under Lenin's guidance, confidently led the working class and all the working people of multinational Russia in the struggle against the tsarist autocracy and the bourgeois-landowner system, for the power of the proletariat. The first Russian bourgeois-democratic revolution of 1905-1907 and the February bourgeois-democratic revolution of 1917 greatly promoted the national consciousness of the working people in the outlying ethnic regions, helping their struggle against national and social oppression.

The national liberation movement expanded greatly at the time of the February revolution. Along with the Soviets of Workers', Soldiers' and Peasants' Deputies various national institutions and committees were formed in the great majority of the ethnic regions, such as the Central Rada in the Ukraine, the Byelorussian Rada, the National Councils in Latvia, Lithuania, Georgia, Armenia, and Azerbaijan, the *kurultais* in Bashkiria and the Crimea, the Zemstvo Council in Estonia, the Sfatul-Tseria in Moldavia, the National Committee in Buryat-Mongolia, the Alash and Shuro-i-islamiya in Central Asia, and the Alash-orda in Kazakhstan. All these organisations, which were initiated

---

[1] See *The Heroic Road of the CPSU,* Politizdat, Moscow, 1973, p. 16 (in Russian).

[2] V. I. Lenin, "To Maxim Gorky", *Collected Works,* Vol. 35, Progress Publishers, Moscow, 1966, pp. 84-85.

by the nationalistic bourgeois and petty-bourgeois parties after the overthrow of tsarism, sought to pose as representatives of the interests of their people, to blunt class contradictions, and, as a rule, advocated the right to national and territorial autonomy within the framework of a bourgeois-democratic republic of Russia.

The Nationalities Policy of the Provisional Government

The February revolution, however, did not liberate the oppressed peoples. This was due to the imperialist content of the foreign and domestic policies of the Provisional Government of Russia, which zealously championed capitalist interests as regards the national question as well. While formally promulgating certain national liberties as part of a programme of free cultural self-determination advanced by the Cadets (Constitutional-Democratic Party) who were the chief political force of the bourgeois counter-revolution, in practice the Provisional Government continued the reactionary, colonialist policy of tsarism.

While proclaiming the abolition of "religious and national restrictions" in March 1917, the Provisional Government failed to come to terms with fundamental aspects of the self-determination of the numerous peoples who had been part of the former empire. The Central Committee of the Cadet Party, which played a leading role in determining the Provisional Government's political course and action programme, in effect advocated an "integral and indivisible" Russia, and urged the population to set aside "all the differences between parties, classes, estates and nationalities". More, the Eighth Congress of the Cadet Party openly declared that self-determination of the peoples would lead to the disintegration of the state. At the same time in a telegram dispatched on March 4, 1917 to the Russian diplomats assigned to the Entente* governments, P. N. Milyukov,

---

* *The Entente*—a World War I alliance of imperialist states comprising Britain, France and Russia.

a Cadet leader, who had become the Minister of Foreign Affairs, declared that Russia would honour its commitments to its allies in the imperialist war for the redivision of the world and the conquest of colonies. The telegram also hypocritically referred to the new regime's resolve to be "guided by democratic principles of respect for both small and big nations, their free development and concord between the peoples".[1]

The Provisional Government's sweeping statements contrasted sharply with its practical activity. Let us take its attitude towards the people of Finland. In a special declaration on this question (March 7, 1917) the government of the new regime confirmed the old tsarist constitution, limiting itself to recognising the Finnish people's right to "domestic self-determination, and the right to their national culture and languages".[2] When, at its opening session on June 18, the Finnish Parliament adopted the law declaring its supreme power in all spheres of life, with the exception of foreign policy, military legislation and administration, the Provisional Government immediately dissolved it and dispatched troops to take over the premises.

Practically no changes were introduced in the old administrative appartus of the other ethnic regions of the former empire, with the exception of purely formal changes in some of the names. Thus, in Bukhara it was decided to change the official name of the representative of the central power, which had been that of "political agent", into "representative of Russia," and to set up indigenous commissions for improving administration along the lines of that in Algeria, Egypt, Morocco, and Tunisia, all of which were then colonies of the big imperialist powers. As before, Turkestan's affairs were administered by the tsarist Governor-General Kuropatkin, who was replaced only at the end of March by the Turkestan Committee made up of representatives of the Russian and local bourgeoisie headed by N. Shchepkin, a Cadet. The Special Transcaucasian Committee was formed under the chairmanship of V. Kharlamov, yet another representative of the Cadets, to administer the Caucasus.

---

[1] *The Revolutionary Movement in Russia after the Overthrow of the Autocracy.* Documents and Materials, Nauka Publishers, Moscow, 1957, p. 423 (in Russian).

[2] Ibid., pp. 427-28.

This organ of power took the place of the vicegerent of the Russian tsar, and was guided in all its activity by the tsarist law on vicegerency in the Caucasus and from the outset protected landed estates against seizure by the peasantry, and opposed the creation of political organisations within the army. And in all the other ethnic regions of the country—the Ukraine, Byelorussia, Estland, and others—the Provisional Government, regarding these provinces no different from those of Russia, left practically everything unchanged.

Developments after the February revolution clearly showed that the new regime had no intention of solving such vital issues as bringing about a just peace, and abolishing landed proprietorship, and national and colonial oppression. As pointed out by Lenin, the government chose a very peculiar way of solving these major problems confronting the working people: "promising everything without fulfilling any of its promises".[1] The capitalists and Menshevik and Socialist-Revolutionary conciliators sought to convince the people that only the All-Russia Constituent Assembly was competent to meet all their needs. Yet, they delayed its convocation indefinitely.

The Bolshevik Programme for the Solution of the National Question as Formulated on the Eve of the October Revolution

In these conditions the Bolsheviks, with Lenin at their head, came out vigorously against supporting the Provisional Government, and for transferring power to the Soviets and promoting the bourgeois-democratic revolution into a socialist one.

The Bolshevik Party countered the bourgeois-nationalistic programme of cultural and national autonomy with a Marxist-Leninist programme for solving the national question, based on the principles of proletarian internationalism, the key provision of which was recognition of the right of nations to free develop-

---

[1] V. I. Lenin, "Lessons of the Revolution", *Collected Works*, Vol. 25, Progress Publishers, Moscow, 1974, p. 235.

ment and self-determination, up to and including secession. At the same time the Bolsheviks' programme, as outlined by Lenin in his "Critical Remarks on the National Question", "The Right of Nations to Self-Determination", "Materials Relating to the Revision of the Party Programme" and in other works, included a demand for regional autonomy for areas with a distinct national composition and life style. *"The republic of the Russian nation must attract other nations or nationalities not by force," wrote Lenin, "but exclusively by voluntary agreement on the question of forming a common state."*[1]

During the transition from a bourgeois-democratic to a socialist revolution in 1917 the Seventh (April) Conference of the Bolshevik Party advanced a number of democratic demands: broad regional autonomy for the peoples remaining within the confines of Russia; recognition of their sovereignty in determining their frontiers; inclusion in the constitution of a law ruling out the extension of privileges to any one nation and violation of the rights of the national minorities. Simultaneously the conference stressed the need for the workers of all nationalities inhabiting Russia to unite in the struggle against international capital and bourgeois nationalism. Only by recognising the right of nations to self-determination, including secession, could the proletariat of Russia win the approval and friendship of the working masses of the oppressed nations.

Lenin vigorously opposed those who denied the right of nations to self-determination by claiming that in the age of imperialism this demand was reactionary and belonged to the past, or on the pretext that a given nation was, for a number of reasons, under the sway of chauvinism. When G. Pyatakov declared at the April Party Conference that he was against the right of nations to self-determination, advancing the slogan "Down with frontiers", Lenin replied: "We maintain that the state is necessary, and a state presupposes frontiers. The state, of course, may hold a bourgeois government, but we need the Soviets. But even Soviets are confronted with the question of frontiers. What

---

[1] V. I. Lenin, "Materials Relating to the Revision of the Party Programme", *Collected Works*, Vol. 24, Progress Publishers, Moscow, 1974, p. 472.

does 'Down with frontiers' mean? It is the beginning of anarchy. . ."[1]

The Bolshevik Party, in working for the right of nations to self-determination, for their sovereignty and equality, brought about in practice the domination of the proletariat in the national liberation movement. At this time, when the bourgeois-democratic revolution was developing into a socialist one, the complex national question could only be solved by the unity of the liberated peoples and the class unity of the proletariat, achieved through democracy and self-determination. Addressing the April Conference, Lenin said: "We are for a fraternal union of all nations. If there is a Ukrainian republic and a Russian republic, there will be closer contact and greater trust between the two. If the Ukrainians see that we have a Soviet republic, they will not secede, but if we have a Milyukov republic, they will."[2] Recognition of the right of nations to self-determination helped to accelerate class differentiation within nations, to separate the working people from the bourgeoisie.

"The Party of Lenin and the working class vigorously championed the equality of all nations and nationalities, the right of nations to self-determination, up to and including the formation of independent states in the name of establishing a close voluntary alliance of equal peoples," states the resolution of the CPSU Central Committee entitled "Preparations for the 50th Anniversary of the Formation of the Union of Soviet Socialist Republics".[3]

The Bolsheviks, by condemning the chauvinistic stand of the Provisional Government with which the Mensheviks and Socialist-Revolutionaries sided, and by upholding the right of nations to self-determination, helped to lay bare the demagogy of the bourgeois nationalists, and to establish a genuine alliance between the workers and peasants of all nations. Lenin used the example of defence of the Ukraine's right to self-determination to make

---

[1] V. I. Lenin, "The Seventh (April) All-Russia Conference of the R.S.D.L.P.(B.)", *Collected Works*, Vol. 24, pp. 299-300.

[2] Ibid., p. 301.

[3] *The CPSU in Resolutions. . .*, Vol. 11, Politizdat, Moscow, 1978, p. 48.

this clear. He wrote: "We do not favour the existence of small states. We stand for the closest union of the workers of the world against 'their own' capitalists and those of all other countries. But for this union to be voluntary, the Russian worker, who does not for a moment trust the Russian or the Ukrainian bourgeoisie in anything, now stands for the right of the Ukrainians to secede, *without imposing* his friendship upon them, but *striving to win* their friendship by treating them as an equal, as an ally and brother in the struggle for socialism."[1]

The fraternal alliance of the future proletarian-peasant republic of Russia with any national republic was dependent on its democratic administration and its recognition of the non-Great Russian nations' freedom to secede. Lenin predicted that the more consistently this was implemented, "the more strongly will other nations be *attracted* towards an alliance with us, the less friction will there be, the more rarely will actual secession occur".[2] The future state system of the republic of Soviets was thus of great importance. The Bolsheviks were fundamentally opposed to federation, and called for a democratic unitary state with individual regions having autonomy. The Bolsheviks' negative attitude towards federation as a form of state unification did not imply, of course, that they rejected it out of hand in every case. In 1903, upholding the provisions on the national question in the first Party Programme, Lenin wrote: "We must always and unreservedly work for the *very closest* unity of the proletariat of all nationalities, and it is only in isolated and exceptional cases that we can advance and actively support demands conducive to the establishment of a new class state or to the substitution of a looser federal unity ... for the complete political unity of a state."[3] In his letter to S. G. Shahumyan of December 6, 1913, Lenin expounded in greater detail the Bolsheviks' attitude towards federation.[4] The changed conditions of social development, the necessity of fighting the annexationist policy of the

---

[1] V. I. Lenin, "The Ukraine", *Collected Works,* Vol. 25, p. 92.

[2] V. I. Lenin, "Finland and Russia", *Collected Works,* Vol. 24, p. 338.

[3] V. I. Lenin, "The National Question in Our Programme", *Collected Works,* Vol. 6, Progress Publishers, Moscow, 1964, p. 454.

[4] See V. I. Lenin, "A Letter to S. G. Shahumyan", *Collected Works,* Vol. 19, Progress Publishers, Moscow, 1973, p. 500.

imperialist states with which Russia was allied, the development of the socialist revolution in the ethnic regions, which made an alliance with the Russian people more attractive to the formerly oppressed nations, and the threat of the single state disintegrating into small states with the nationalist bourgeoisie in control, necessitated a changed attitude to a federal pattern for the Soviet state. In May 1917, Lenin formulated the possibility of forming a union (federal) state. He wrote: "The Great Russians offer a fraternal union to all the nations and propose the formation of a common state by voluntary consent of each individual people, and under no circumstances by means of violence, direct or indirect."[1] The same idea was expressed by Lenin at the First All-Russia Congress of Soviets of Workers' and Soldiers' Deputies. He exposed the annexationist policy of the Provisional Government and the attitude of the Socialist-Revolutionaries and Mensheviks towards the Ukraine and Finland, saying: "It amounts to a mockery of the rights of a nationality which was tormented by the tsars because its children wanted to speak their mother tongue. That means being afraid of separate republics. From the point of view of the workers and peasants, there is nothing terrible about that. Let Russia be a union of free republics."[2]

Lenin also expressed the idea of recognising a federation in *The State and Revolution*, which he wrote in August 1917.

The Bolsheviks fought against the annexationist policy of the Provisional Government and the bourgeois nationalists by implementing the principles of Lenin's programme on the national question and rallying the working people of different nations. "On the eve of the October Revolution more than 100,000 Bolsheviks were active among the working people of the ethnic regions trying to merge the revolutionary action of the Russian proletariat with the struggle of the oppressed nations."[3] An important role in promoting the nationalities programme of Lenin's

---

[1] V. I. Lenin, "Mandate to Deputies of the Soviet Elected at Factories and Regiments", *Collected Works*, Vol. 24, p. 355.

[2] V. I. Lenin, "First All-Russia Congress of Workers' and Soldiers' Deputes", *Collected Works*, Vol. 25, p. 37.

[3] *History of the Communist Party of the Soviet Union*, Vol. 3, Book I, Politizdat, Moscow, 1967, p. 273 (in Russian).

Party was played by his articles: "Finland and Russia",[1] "A Mote in the Eye",[2] "It Is Undemocratic, Citizen Kerensky!",[3] "The Ukraine",[4] "The Ukraine and the Defeat of the Ruling Parties of Russia".[5] With the aim of awakening the class consciousness of the workers, soldiers and peasants, and achieving united action with the workers and peasants of Russia, the Bolsheviks exposed the chauvinism of the Provisional Government, the Menshevik and Socialist-Revolutionary parties, and the nationalism of the local petty-bourgeois parties by intensifying their work in the Soviets, trade unions, and factory committees, by speaking at rallies and meetings and publishing articles in the press. In each region this work was adapted to the specific conditions there. In the Ukraine, which was closely linked with Russia, the local Bolshevik organisations strove to show the masses the essential demagogy of the Central Rada, which through its slogans and promises had succeeded in strengthening its influence among the working masses. In this context it is worth noting the appeal issued by the regional Party conference of the Bolsheviks of the Southwestern Territory (July 1917): "To conduct work among the Ukrainian masses, splitting them in terms of the class struggle and separating the revolutionary elements from the chauvinistic influence of the Ukrainian Social-Democracy."[6]

Although the Ukrainian Bolsheviks underestimated the strength of the national movement in individual provincial organisations, they were successful in winning the masses over to the revolution, and in exposing the bourgeois-nationalistic nature of the Central Rada. Up to October 1917, however, the Ukrainian bourgeois nationalists maintained a strong influence on the soldiers of the Southwestern and Romanian fronts, on the peas-

---

[1] See V. I. Lenin, *Collected Works*, Vol. 24, pp. 335-38.
[2] Ibid., pp. 565-67.
[3] Ibid., pp. 568-69.
[4] V. I. Lenin, "The Ukraine", *Collected Works*, Vol. 25, pp. 91-92.
[5] Ibid., pp. 99-102.
[6] *The Bolshevik Organisations in the Ukraine in the Period of Preparation for and Accomplishment of the Great October Socialist Revolution (March-October 1917)*. Compilation of Documents and Materials, Politizdat, Kiev, 1957, p. 668 (in Russian).

antry and even on sections of the Ukrainian workers. The process of converting the masses of peasants and soldiers and the Soviets that represented them to Bolshevism had not been fully completed by the time of the armed uprising in the Ukraine.

In Byelorussia the Bolsheviks also sought to counter the influence of the local nationalists and conciliators, and worked to bring the socialist revolution to victory. The First Northwestern Regional and Front Conference of the Bolsheviks, held on September 15, 1917, discussed key aspects of promoting the revolution and elected the Western regional Party committee headed by A. F. Myasnikov. The Second Northwestern Regional Conference, held on October 5-7, 1917, concentrated on preparing for the armed uprising. The fact that in the 20 days that elapsed between the first and second conferences the number of Bolsheviks in the region increased five-fold shows the Bolshevik Party's impact on the masses. The conference discussed the elections to the Soviets and the soldiers' committees, and preparations for the Second All-Russia Congress of Soviets, which was authorised to take power into its hands. The Bolsheviks' policy was supported by the workers and peasants of Byelorussia, and also the Conference of the Soviets of the Western Region, held on October 16, 1917.

The Minsk Soviet and the Minsk Bolshevik Committee became the centres for preparing for an uprising in Byelorussia. The Minsk Bolsheviks thwarted the counter-revolutionaries' attempts to overcome the Minsk Soviet and the revolutionary forces of the garrison and prepared the masses for a triumphant armed uprising.

Complex conditions surrounded the development of the national liberation movement in the Baltic region—Estonia, Latvia and Lithuania. The German barons and Russian tsarism were responsible for oppression in the first two, and Polish landlords and Russian tsarism, in Lithuania. During the First World War a part of the territory of Latvia and Lithuania was seized by German troops. The national movement, particularly in Latvia and Estonia, developed amidst sharp class battles. After the February revolution the local bourgeoisie attempted to take over the leadership of the national liberation movement and to rally the working masses under nationalistic slogans. The Estonian bourgeoisie, for instance, taking advantage of the fact that there was no distinct self-administration in the Estland Province, seized the apparatus of local power. The Provisional Government appointed Poska, the mayor of Tallinn, Provincial Commissar of the Estland Province, and Krastkalns, the mayor of Riga, Provincial Commissar in the Lifland Province; the district as well as the city power apparatus fell into the hands of the bourgeoisie. The bourgeoisie succeeded in separating southern Estonia from the Lifland Province and in uniting all the Estonians in one province. Attached to the Provincial Commissar's office was the Provincial Zemstvo Council—a consultative body for self-government. With these "successes" behind them, the Estonian bourgeoisie considered the revolution complete and urged the masses to submit to the Provisional Government pending the convocation of the Constituent Assembly. The Socialist-Revolutionary and Menshevik Soviets essentially upheld bourgeois positions. This policy did not suit the working masses, who came out against the anti-democratic elections to the Provincial Council in May 1917. But because they failed to seek a revision of the election results, the Provincial Council fell into the hands of the Estonian bourgeoisie. In July 1917 the latter attempted to set up a so-called people's congress with the aim of electing Poska, who had already been appointed to the post, Provincial Commissar, and of enhancing his authority. The withdrawal from the congress of the workers' and peasants' representatives (at the call of the Bolsheviks), and the frustration of Poska's "election" was a sign of the deepening class differentiation within the Estonian nation. This was borne out also by the demonstration of the Tallinn workers against the so-called people's congress on July 4, 1917. The demonstrators forced the congress participants to declare it a private meeting, which passed a resolution demanding autonomy for Estonia within the framework of a bourgeois federation.

The national rights of the Estonian working people could be ensured only by transferring all power in the land to the Soviets, the fate of which depended on the outcome of the struggle of the proletariat and its vanguard, the Bolshevik Party, to further promote the revolution and change the composition of the Soviets and their policy.

The Bolsheviks' authority grew with every passing month. The Second Conference of the North-Baltic Organisation of the RSDLP(B), held in mid-August 1917, upheld Estonia's right to self-determination, to autonomy and the democratisation of the local government bodies, but was against its secession from Russia.[1] By the autumn of 1917 the Bolsheviks and their followers received a majority at the elections to the Soviets. The large meeting of representatives of the Soviets, trade unions, soldiers and sailors, held in Reval on September 27, vigorously supported the establishment of Soviet power in the country.

The Estonian Soviets and the Revolutionary Military Committee formed by them played an important part in the victory of the October armed uprising in Petrograd, and the establishment of Soviet power in Estonia.

Similar events took place in Latvia and Lithuania. The struggle of the working class in alliance with the working peasantry to solve the national question was closely linked with that of promoting the socialist revolution.

In multinational Transcaucasia the national liberation movement developed in extremely complex conditions.[2] The peoples of the region had fought for centuries against Turkish and Persian invaders, as well as against the brutal national oppression and despotism of Russian tsarism, for their national liberation and social emancipation; there was much hatred there for the Great-Russian oppressors—the landlords and tsarist officials—and it was often directed against the Russians in general. In some backward areas with a small number of proletarians the process of class differentiation within nations developed very slowly. This largely accounted for the bourgeois nationalists' influence.

There were about 20 bourgeois-nationalist parties, tendencies and groups in the Caucasus. Foremost and most influential among them were the Mensheviks, Dashnaks, Musavatists, and Social-Federalists. The Dashnaktsutyun—a bourgeois-nationalist party— had organisations in many towns and villages. Its demands were

[1] See *The Struggle for Soviet Power in the Baltic Region,* Politizdat, Moscow, 1967, pp. 101-102 (in Russian).
[2] See *The Victory of Soviet Power in Transcaucasia,* Politizdat, Moscow, pp. 97-107 (in Russian).

restricted to self-government for Western Armenia within the framework of Russia; it advocated that all the Armenian people in the Caucasus unite in the general national interest. The Armenian Cadet Party, which essentially adhered to liberal-populist and Cadet views, was formed in May 1917.

In Georgia the Social-Federalists demanded autonomy within the framework of a bourgeois republic; they exhorted the masses to refrain from class conflict. The National-Democrats were even opposed to autonomy for the national minorities and small nations. The Georgian Mensheviks and Socialist-Revolutionaries, who commanded a majority in the Soviets, demanded only "national cultural autonomy"; it was only after the victory of the October Revolution that the Mensheviks, with N. Jordania at their head, called for the creation of an independent "Georgian Democratic State".

In Azerbaijan the Musavat (Equality) party sought control of the Muslim national councils, which did not represent the interests of the workers and peasants. The Musavatists were in favour of "defending Muslim rights" in general, irrespective of class distinctions. Under this slogan they held a Muslim congress in Baku in April 1917, where representatives of the bourgeoisie, bourgeois intelligentsia and the clergy were in the majority. In March the "Turkic Federalist" party was formed, which advocated "defending the national rights and unity" of the Turkic peoples; in June the Musavatists and the Federalists combined forces. After the victory of the October Revolution the Musavatists called for the independence of Azerbaijan under the protectorate of Turkey.

Lenin's thesis on the objective nature of the national liberation movement among the peoples of Transcaucasia helps us to assess it correctly. In his article "A Caricature of Marxism and Imperialist Economism" Lenin wrote: "All national oppression calls forth the resistance of the *broad masses* of the people; and the resistance of a nationally oppressed population always *tends* to national revolt. Not infrequently (notably in Austria and Russia) we find the bourgeoisie of the oppressed nations *talking* of national revolt, while in practice it enters into reactionary compacts with the bourgeoisie of the oppressor nation behind the backs of, *and against*, its own people. In such cases the criticism of revolutionary Marxists should be directed not against the national movement, but against its degradation, vulgarisation, against the tendency to reduce it to a petty squabble."[1] The Bolsheviks were aware of the complexity of the national question, but at the same time they approached it from a class viewpoint: the tasks where the national question was concerned were always subordinated to the primary issue of ensuring the victory of the socialist revolution in the country. The least departure from this principle jeopardised the Bolsheviks' struggle for the masses. The complexity and acute nature of the national question occasionally led to local Bolshevik organisations making mistakes. As A. I. Mikoyan subsequently wrote, "among the Bolsheviks of the Caucasus there was much confusion as to how to solve the national question for the peoples of the Caucasus. This circumstance affected the entire course of struggle for Soviet power in the Caucasus and undoubtedly facilitated the creation by the bourgeois chauvinists of a barrier between workers of different nationalities and between the revolutionary proletariat and the peasantry".[2]

The resolutions passed by the First Congress of the Bolshevik Organisations of the Caucasus also underestimated the importance of the national question. The congress was held in Tiflis (now Tbilisi) early in October 1917 and it elected the RSDLP(B) Territorial Committee in the Caucasus. Some delegates opposed the right of nations to self-determination. A congress resolution stated: "Bearing in mind the great variety and numerical strength, as well as the intermingling of nations and tribes in our territory, and, on the other hand, proceeding from the interests of the unity of the working-class movement in the Caucasus, we call for the closest unity and convergence of the democrats of the Caucasus irrespective of their nationality."[3] Thus the congress did not mention the recognition of the right of nations to self-determination, including secession and the formation of independent state entities, which was subsequently used to ad-

---

[1] V. I. Lenin, "A Caricature of Marxism and Imperialist Economism", *Collected Works,* Vol. 23, p. 61.

[2] *Krasny arkhiv,* Nos. 4-5, 1938, p. 8.

[3] Quoted in *The Struggle for the Triumph of Soviet Power in Georgia (1917-1921),* Gosizdat of Georgia, Tbilisi, 1958, p. 106 (in Russian).

vantage by the Georgian Mensheviks, Musavatists, Dashnaks and other nationalists. The congress's appeal for the unity of "democrats" in the Caucasus was also a mistake, for it concealed the fact that at the time the Mensheviks, Socialist-Revolutionaries and bourgeois nationalists were advancing slogans of democracy and socialism. It was also obviously affected by the lack of clarity on the question of who expresses a nation's will to self-determination. In its first programme the Bolshevik Party advanced this slogan in general terms, for its primary aim was to oppose the great-power chauvinists' annexationist policy, and the inequality of peoples under tsarism. The Party's goal was to unite the workers of all nations and nationalities. To reach this goal the workers had to surmount the formidable difficulties standing in the way of the right of nations to self-determination and equality.

In 1914 Lenin wrote on the question of future relations between Russia and the Ukraine: "Whether the Ukraine, for example, is destined to form an independent state is a matter that will be determined by a thousand unpredictable factors. Without attempting idle 'guesses', we firmly uphold something that is beyond doubt: the right of the Ukraine to form such a state. We respect this right; we do not uphold the privileges of Great Russians with regard to Ukrainians; we *educate* the masses in the spirit of recognition of that right, in the spirit of rejecting *state* privileges for any nation."[1]

The question of the right of nations to self-determination was given concrete form in the drafting of the second Party Programme (1919). Criticising Bukharin, who advanced an erroneous thesis on the self-determination of the working people, but not of nations, Lenin declared: "We hold a strictly class standpoint. What we are writing in the programme is a recognition of what has actually taken place since the time we wrote of the self-determination of nations in general. At that time there were still no proletarian republics."[2] Lenin insisted on a concrete historical approach to the question of who expresses the will of a

---

[1] V. I. Lenin, "The Right of Nations to Self-Determination", *Collected Works*, Vol. 20, Progress Publishers, Moscow, 1964, p. 413.

[2] V. I. Lenin, "Eighth Congress of the R.C.P.(B.)", *Collected Works*, Vol. 29, Progress Publishers, Moscow, 1977, p. 172.

nation for secession—the proletariat or the bourgeoisie. The crucial factor was how class differentiation took place in a nation. Lenin stressed: "Our programme must not speak of the self-determination of the working people, because that would be wrong. It must speak of what actually exists. Since nations are at different stages on the road from medievalism to bourgeois democracy and from bourgeois democracy to proletarian democracy, this thesis of our programme is absolutely correct. With us there have been very many zigzags on this road."[1] Lenin backed up his theory of how the "self-determination of the working people" or class differentiation in nations takes place by citing data on Germany, Finland and Poland. About the composition of the Warsaw Soviet of Workers' Deputies, the majority of whom adhered to social-defencist positions, he noted: "We cannot speak here of the self-determination of the working people. We must carry on propaganda in behalf of this differentiation. This is what we are doing, but there is not the slightest shadow of doubt that we must recognise the self-determination of the Polish nation now. That is clear." [2] Thus the second Party Programme gave a comprehensive, substantiated reply to the question of the right of nations to self-determination, taking account of what had already been learned about solving the national question in Soviet Russia.

The Bolshevik organisations in the Caucasus revised their attitude to the right of nations to self-determination only after their First Congress. The fact that the Bolsheviks did not win a single seat even in the Tiflis Soviet shows how weak class differentiation was among the Caucasian nations in 1917. The Soviet was dominated by the Mensheviks and Socialist-Revolutionaries. In complex and difficult conditions, the Bolsheviks of Azerbaijan, Armenia and Georgia endeavoured to correct their mistakes, working to consolidate the forces of the proletariat and the revolutionary soldiers, and to gain a Bolshevik majority in the Soviets. They were most successful in the industrial centres: in the Baku Soviet they commanded half the seats. On August 30 the Baku Soviet adopted its first Bolshevik resolution; shortly afterwards

---

[1] Ibid., p. 174.
[2] Ibid., p. 175.

the Socialist-Revolutionary and Menshevik Executive Committee of the Soviet resigned and was replaced by a newly-elected Provisional Executive Committee headed by S. Shahumyan, a prominent leader of the Bolshevik Party. On October 15, 1917 the Baku Soviet called for the convocation of the Second All-Russia Congress of Soviets and elected delegates to it.

With the approach of the socialist revolution the workers' strikes gained in intensity; the peasantry stepped up its fight for land, but the industrial proletariat of Baku failed to win the peasantry over to its side. Nor had the influence of the nationalists and the petty-bourgeois Menshevik and Socialist-Revolutionary parties among the Transcaucasian working people and soldiers of the Caucasian Front been surmounted by the time of the triumph of the socialist revolution, as the results of the elections to the Constituent Assembly show. Of the 2,445,000 votes cast in the Transcaucasian District, the Georgian Mensheviks polled 622,000; the Musavatists, 616,000; the Dashnaks, 560,000; the Socialist-Revolutionaries, 170,000; the Muslim socialist bloc, 160,000, and the Bolsheviks, 93,000, or 4 per cent. All this could not but complicate the struggle for the victory of the socialist revolution in Transcaucasia.

The Internationalist Cohesion of the Working People

The Provisional Government's failure to solve the question of peace and land, and its persistence in the policy of oppressing the non-Russian peoples strengthened the leading role of the proletariat in the general democratic and national liberation movements of Russia. The mass strike movement that swept the Urals, Ivanovo-Kineshma district, the Baltic region, the Ukraine, Byelorussia, Transcaucasia, Central Asia, Kazakhstan, and Yakutia in the spring and summer of 1917, involved over 200,000 Uzbeks, Kazakhs, Turkmens, Kirghiz and Buryats, who had been mobilised for work on the home front, along with the Russian, Ukrainian and other workers in the major industrial areas.[1] The

---

[1] See G. F. Dakhshleiger, *The October Revolution and the Oppressed Peoples of Tsarist Russia*, Politizdat, Moscow, 1967, p. 9 (in Russian).

strikes held by the workers in Riga and Tallinn, the miners and railway workers of the Donbas and Kharkov, the workers at the Baku oil fields and the ginneries and creameries of Khodzhent (Samarkand region) combined with the large-scale peasant actions in Central Russia, the Ukraine, Azerbaijan and Georgia and with the strikes of the agricultural workers and landless peasants of Latvia and Estonia.[1]

The growing strength of the national liberation movement played an important role in the mounting nationwide revolutionary crisis which had gathered force in Russia by the autumn of 1917, and in increasing the number of and enhancing the influence of the Soviets. On the eve of the October Revolution 41,6 per cent of the total number of Soviets were in the non-Russian ethnic regions, which accounted for about 57 per cent of the country's population. This included 51.6 per cent of the Soviets of Workers', Soldiers' and Peasants' Deputies, 39.4 per cent of the Soviets of Workers' and Soldiers' Deputies, and 32.6 per cent of the Soviets of Peasants' Deputies. By this time approximately two-thirds of the 383 towns and cities in the non-Russian territories came under the sphere of influence of the Soviets.[2]

Another graphic example of the working masses of the oppressed nations siding with the revolutionary proletariat were the results of the votes cast by the delegates of the non-Russian group at the Democratic Conference held from September 14 to 22, 1917. With the growing influence of the Bolsheviks and the massive conversion to Bolshevism of the Soviets after the defeat of the Kornilov revolt,* the Socialist-Revolutionary and Menshevik leaders resorted to direct forgery in a desperate attempt to retain the confidence of the masses. In violation of the resolution of the First All-Russia Congress of Soviets of Workers' and Sol-

---

[1] See I. I. Mintz, *History of the Great October Revolution*, Vol. 2, Nauka Publishers, Moscow, 1968, pp. 873, 875, 880, 889 et al (in Russian).

[2] See D. A. Chugayev, *The Communist Party Is the Organiser of the Union of Soviet Socialist Republics*, p. 78.

* The Kornilov revolt was an attempt in August-September 1917 by the counter-revolutionary forces led by General Kornilov to overthrow the Provisional Government and to reinstate the monarchy.

diers' Deputies on the convocation in mid-September 1917 of the Second All-Russia Congress of Soviets, they organised instead a Democratic Conference with hand-picked representatives from local councils, city bodies of self-government, conciliatory Soviets, trade unions, army committees and other organisations still under the influence of the Socialist-Revolutionaries and the Mensheviks.

However, the conciliatory leaders' attempt to thwart the mounting revolutionary wave and to buttress the imperialist bourgeois dictatorship under the pretext of setting up the so-called pre-parliament (Provisional Council of the Republic) appointed by the conference, was exposed by Lenin's working-class party. As a result even at the Democratic Conference the representatives of 43 provinces and four armies, and the delegates of the ethnic regions condemned by a clear majority (40 against 15) the Menshevik and Socialist-Revolutionary policy of coalition with the bourgeoisie.

The historical experience gained by the Bolshevik Party at various stages of the struggle to promote a bourgeois-democratic revolution to a socialist one and to implement the key political slogan "All Power to the Soviets!" confirmed the validity and correctness of the Bolsheviks' Leninist aim for a proletarian revolution and showed that the objective prerequisites for its success existed.

"As matters stood in October," Lenin subsequently wrote, "we had made a precise calculation of the *mass* forces. We not only thought, we *knew* with certainty, from the experience of the *mass* elections to the Soviets, that the overwhelming majority of the workers and soldiers had *already* come over to our side in September and in early October. We knew, even if only from the voting at the Democratic Conference, that the coalition had also lost the support of the peasantry—and that meant that our cause had *already* won."[1]

In the joint struggle for a cardinal solution to major issues such as that of power, the agrarian and national questions, and withdrawal from the war, the internationalist unity of the coun-

---

[1] V. I. Lenin, "The Revolutionary Phrase", *Collected Works*, Vol. 27, Progress Publishers, Moscow, 1977, p. 25.

try's working people grew stronger. In this way the national liber-ation movement among the oppressed nationalities, the peasants' democratic movement for land, the working masses' general democratic struggle for peace, and the socialist working-class movement to overhrow the power of the bourgeoisie merged into a single, powerful revolutionary process.

The Bolshevik Party created by Lenin, steeled in battles against the class enemies and armed with the Marxist-Leninist doctrine on the general laws of social development, steered, like an experienced helmsman, the proletariat and all peoples of Russia through the formidable trials of three revolutions to the triumph of the Great October Revolution.

"All Power to the Soviets!"
The First Revolutionary Acts
of Soviet Power

At the time of the October armed uprising in Petrograd there were in the whole of Russia about 1,400 Soviets, which expanded and gained in strength throughout the summer and autumn of the revolutionary year of 1917. The regional and provincial congresses of the Soviets, which were held throughout the country in the autumn of 1917, pointed clearly to the major change that had occurred in the correlation of forces: the overwhelming majority of the Soviets of Workers', Soldiers' and Peasants' Deputies now supported transferring all power to the Soviets. The Soviets of the Northern Industrial Region and Petrograd, of the Central Industrial District and Moscow, of Minsk and the Western Region, the Baltic area, the Urals, Siberia, Northern Caucasus, and a larger part of the Ukraine, voted for Soviet power. The representatives of the Soviets followed Lenin's Bolshevik Party in an organised and active manner.[1] The American writer and publicist Albert R. Williams, who was with John Reed in revolutionary Petrograd in 1917, wrote: "From the depths now lifted up a mighty cry: 'All power to the Soviets!' The de-

---

[1] See I. I. Mintz, *History of the Great October Revolution*, Vol. 2, p. 971.

mand of the capital in July became the demand of the country."[1]

Lenin's well-known appeal "To the Citizens of Russia!" put out by the Petrograd Revolutionary Military Committee on the morning of October 25, 1917, announced the victory of the October armed uprising and the overthrow of the Provisional Government. At 10:40 p.m. on that day the Second All-Russia Congress of Soviets of Workers' and Soldiers' Deputies opened in the Smolny. In the white-columned assembly hall were gathered delegates of the broad masses of the working people of Russia—representatives of the Soviets of the central regions, the Urals, Siberia, the Far East and outlying ethnic regions, and 199 delegates from the army and navy. The available congress documents do not give any information about the participation of delegates from only two provinces and one region (Yelizavetpol and Kutaisi provinces and Trans-Baikal Region) out of the 80 administrative units existing in Russia in October 1917.

The Soviets of all the provinces (with the exclusion of those occupied by German troops) in the major ethnic regions were represented at the congress. The Ukrainian delegates comprised one-fifth of the overall number of delegates, 51 delegates came from Byelorussia, Latvia was represented by the delegates of its central organ—the District Congress of Soviets, and also delegates from Lifland, Smiltene District, Venden District, the towns of Valka, Dvinsk and Rezhitsa. The delegates of Central Asia, Azerbaijan, Armenia, Lithuania, Estonia, Georgia, Moldavia, Tataria, Karelia, the Crimea, Ufa Province, Izhevsk, Saransk, and other places also attended.[2] In addition to the delegates, numerous guests were present at the congress sessions—representatives of the press, delegations from factories, the revolutionary troops of the Petrograd garrison and the battleships of the Baltic Fleet.

This is how John Reed, the American publicist who attended the congress sessions, describes these historic days: "A thousand chairs are ranked in the space between the columns. Most of

---

[1] A. R. Williams, *Through the Russian Revolution*, The Labour Publishing Company Ltd., London, 1923, p. 93.

[2] See *History of National-State Development in the USSR. 1917-1978*, Vol. I, pp. 22-23.

the delegates are in the uniform of private soldiers. The rest wear the plain black blouse of the Russian workers, with a few colored peasant blouses. All around, in the spaces between the columns, on the window-ledges, massed on the steps of the stage and on its edge, are the public—also common workers, common peasants, and common soldiers. Bayonets bristle among them. Exhausted Red Guards, girdled with cartridge-belts, sleep at the base of the columns."[1]

The Second All-Russia Congress of Soviets, which was a vivid illustration of the bankruptcy of the Mensheviks and the Right Socialst-Revolutionaries, demonstrated at the same time how the masses were being converted to Bolshevism and clearly confirmed the correctness of the Bolshevik Party's Leninist course towards a socialist revolution. Of the 649 delegates registered before the opening of the congress, 390 were Bolsheviks, who together with the Left Socialist-Revolutionaries (160 mandates) held a large majority among the delegates, thereby controlling the entire work of the congress and the nature of its decisions. Under the leadership of the Bolsheviks, 14 of whose representatives (V. I. Lenin, V. A. Antonov-Ovseyenko, A. M. Kollontai, N. V. Krylenko, A. V. Lunacharsky, V. P. Nogin, P. I. Stučka, and others) were elected to the congress presidium, the Second All-Russia Congress began immediately to pass revolutionary legislation.

Its first act was adopted at 5 a.m. on October 26, after the delegates had been told of the seizure of the Winter Palace and the arrest of the ministers of Russia's last bourgeois government. This act, which made the triumph of the socialist revolution official, was the appeal "To Workers, Soldiers and Peasants!" written by Lenin. Having unanimously approved the appeal, the text of which was read out by A. V. Lunacharsky, the congress proclaimed the transition of all central and local power to the Soviets of Workers', Soldiers' and Peasants' Deputies. The appeal was signed: "The All-Russia Congress of Soviets of Workers' and Soldiers' Deputies." On the proposal of a peasants' representative at the congress, the words: "The Delegates from the Peas-

---

[1] John Reed, *One Year of Revolution*, issued by the Socialist Publication Society, Brooklyn, N. Y., 1918.

ants' Soviets" were added to it. The Soviets, created in revolutionary fashion by the masses, and profoundly democratic in their content and tasks, became the sole organs of the new, proletarian power.

The congress also defined the urgent tasks facing that new, proletarian power. "The Soviet government will propose an immediate democratic peace to all the nations and an immediate armistice on all fronts," the appeal said. "It will secure the transfer of the land of the landed proprietors, the crown and the monasteries to the peasant committees without compensation; it will protect the rights of the soldiers by introducing complete democracy in the army; it will establish workers' control over production; ... it will guarantee all the nations inhabiting Russia the genuine right to self-determination."[1] This crucial document was adopted at the close of the first session of the congress. In the evening of October 26, at its second and conlusive session, the congress began the practical implementation of the programme.

That peace be immediately concluded was the first insistent demand of the working people, exhausted by the war. It was precisely to the question of peace that Lenin, the leader of the victorious proletarian revolution, devoted his first report.[2]

Lenin read out his draft Decree on Peace that was submitted to the congress by the Bolshevik Party and which stressed that peace was the most urgent question of the time. This historic document proclaimed Soviet Russia's refusal to take part in the imperialist war and simultaneously formulated the fundamental principles of the foreign policy and diplomacy to be conducted by the new, socialist type of state: strong condemnation of war as a means of solving disputed issues; genuine peaceableness and desire for friendly relations with all states; full equality of all, big and small nations; respect for the sovereignty of other states and non-interference in their internal affairs.

---

[1] V. I. Lenin, "Second All-Russia Congress of Soviets of Workers' and Soldiers' Deputies", *Collected Works*, Vol. 26, p. 247.

[2] Lenin was entrusted with preparing the theses on the question of war and peace, and on land and power by a special decision of the RSDLP(B) Central Committee of October 21, shortly before the opening of the congress.

The decree also proclaimed the right of each people, irrespective of size and economic and cultural development level, to self-determination, up to and including secession and the setting up of an independent state, and, moreover, contained a comprehensive definition of annexation, which created an international legislative basis for the nations' struggle for self-determination and independence.

Lenin's Decree on Peace was the first practical step towards a universal, just, democratic peace. It expressed the Soviets' readiness to conduct talks on peace by any method—by telegram or telephone, as well as negotiations between representatives of various countries, or at joint conferences. At the same time it was stressed that the proposed conditions were not in the nature of an ultimatum and that Soviet power was willing to examine any other proposals advanced by any of the belligerent states. The decree insisted only that the talks must be conducted openly in front of all the peoples, thereby ensuring "the complete absence of all ambiguity and secrecy". Soviet power announced the abolition of secret diplomacy and declared its intention of making known to all the peoples the secret agreements concluded by the tsarist and Provisional governments before October 25, 1917, and began the immediate publication of all secret diplomatic papers.

A fundamentally important feature of the Decree on Peace was the fact that it was simultaneously a Declaration addressed both to governments and to all peoples, and particularly the workers of the belligerent countries. "We cannot ignore the governments," Lenin said to the congress delegates as he reported on the draft Decree, "for that would delay the possibility of concluding peace ... but we have no right not to appeal to the peoples at the same time. Everywhere there are differences between the governments and the peoples, and we must therefore help the peoples to intervene in questions of war and peace."[1]

In conclusion the decree expressed deep conviction in the unshakeable international cohesion of the world working-class movement, in the fact that the politically aware workers of the

---

[1] V. I. Lenin, "Second All-Russia Congress of Soviets of Works' and Soldiers' Deputies", *Collected Works*, Vol. 26, pp. 250, 252.

countries taking part in the First World War, and above all the workers of the three major belligerent states: Britain, France and Germany, would do all they could to vigorously support the proletariat of Russia in their work to "conclude peace successfully".

The discussions following Lenin's report on the draft Decree on Peace showed that the stand of the Bolshevik Party was universally approved. F. E. Dzerzhinsky, P. I. Kulinichenko, V. S. Mickevičius-Kapsukas, P. I. Stučka and other congress delegates declared their support for Lenin's Decree on Peace and noted its exceptional importance. "The decree is enthusiastically hailed by the Social-Democrats of Poland and Lithuania," said Dzerzhinsky, "we know that the only force capable of liberating the world is the proletariat, which is fighting for socialism"[1]

The Second All-Russia Congress of Soviets unanimously adopted Lenin's Decree on Peace. The approval of this historic document set the tone of the general foreign policy to be conducted by the Soviet state, which from the outset aimed to ensure peace and the security of nations, to develop and strengthen good-neighbourly and friendly relations between states. It expressed Lenin's idea on the possibility of the peaceful coexistence of states with different social systems. "We reject all clauses on plunder and violence," noted Lenin, "but we shall welcome all clauses containing provisions for good-neighbourly relations and all economic agreements; we cannot reject these."[2] The Decree on Peace, which revealed to the working people of all countries the real essense of imperialist wars, was at once the first law in history to vigorously condemn aggressive war and declare it the greatest crime against humanity.[3] It was not by chance that shortly after the adoption of the decree a group of professors from the University of Istanbul stated that "Mr. Lenin is the primary and the most honoured political figure in the world",

---

[1] *Second All-Russia Congress of Soviet of Workers' and Soldiers' Deputies,* Gosizdat, Moscow-Leningrad, 1928, p. 65 (in Russian).

[2] V. I. Lenin, "Second All-Russia Congress of Soviets of Workers' and Soldiers' Deputies", *Collected Works,* Vol. 26, p. 255.

[3] It should be noted that in the Soviet Union propaganda of war is forbidden and considered a criminal offence (See, for instance, Article 28 of the USSR Constitution and Article 71 of the Criminal Code of the RSFSR).

and the Social-Democratic Party of Norway submitted to the Nobel Prize Committee a proposal that Lenin be awarded the peace prize for 1917. "Up until the present," the proposal read, "Lenin has done more than anyone else to make possible the triumph of the ideas of peace; he not only promotes peace in every possible way, but is taking concrete measures to bring it about."[1]

In the early hours of October 27 the Second All-Russia Congress of Soviets resolved another crucial question of the proletarian revolution, that of land. For centuries the peasantry of multinational Russia had fought to abolish the big landed estates. From the outset Soviet power put into effect the revolutionary will of the country's many millions of peasants. Lenin delivered a report on land at the Congress of Soviets. "Then Lenin was at the podium again. The seething hall became silent, the provincial delegates leaned forward, faces stern. He was reporting on the next item, land."[2]

The key provision of the Bolshevik Party's agrarian programme in the October Revolution was the demand for the immediate abolition of landed proprietorship and the transfer of land to the peasantry, which Lenin had stated already in the April Theses, on the basis of which the Seventh (April) All-Russia Conference of the RSDLP(B) adopted a resolution on the agrarian question, and later in his notable speech at the First All-Russia Congress of Soviets of Peasants' Deputies on May 22, 1917. Parallel with this, Lenin's article "From a Publicist's Diary. Peasants and Workers", of August 1917, focussed attention on the "Model Mandate Compiled on the Basis of 242 Mandates Submitted by Local Deputies to the First All-Russia Congress of Peasants' Deputies". Lenin analysed the peasants' demands where the question of land was concerned as outlined in the "Model Mandate", and concluded that this important document should be used in drawing up a revolutionary law on land so as to strengthen the alliance of the working class and

[1] *Vladimir Ilyich Lenin. Biographical Chronicle,* Vol. 5, Politizdat, Moscow, 1974, p. 68 (in Russian).
[2] Albert Rhys Williams, *Journey into Revolution. Petrograd, 1917-1918,* Quadrangle Books, Chicago, 1969, p. 132.

the working peasantry and to ensure the success of the socialist revolution.

Lenin's intensive work on formulating a fundamental legislative act of proletarian power with respect to land was concluded during the October armed uprising in Petrograd. On October 26, Lenin finished writing the draft of the historic Decree on Land. V. D. Bonch-Bruyevich, an active participant in the October uprising in Petrograd, recalled that on reading out the text of the decree in the morning, Lenin turned to those present with the words: "Now to announce it, publish and distribute it far and wide. Then let them try to reverse it! No, nothing doing, there is no power on earth that can take this decree away from the peasants and return the land to the landlords. This is a very important gain of our October Revolution. The agrarian revolution will be concluded and formalised this very day. . ."[1]

The draft Decree on Land, which Lenin submitted to the delegates of the Second All-Russia Congress of Soviets late in the evening of October 26, formed the basis for fundamental agrarian transformations. The decree immediately abolished without compensation the big landed estates. The lands of the landlords, the crown, the monasteries and church, including their livestock, equipment and buildings, were put at the disposition of the *volost* land committees and district Soviets of Peasants' Deputies, which were also charged with ensuring strict revolutionary order in confiscating the landlords' estates. The lands of ordinary peasants and ordinary Cossacks were not be confiscated.

In accordance with the decree, the peasants received for their free use over 150 million dessiatines* of crown, landed proprietors' and church lands. The peasants' debts to the Peasant Land Bank, which back in 1914 were about 1,500 million roubles, were cancelled. The peasants were also released from paying annual rent to the landed proprietors and capitalists and from expenditure in buying new land to a sum of more than 700 million gold roubles, and about 300 to 350 million roubles' worth of the landlords' agricultural equipment was transferred to them. Factory

[1] V. D. Bonch-Bruyevich, *At the Fighting Posts of the February and October Revolutions*, Sotsekgiz, Moscow, 1931, p. 119 (in Russian).

* A dessiatine=2.7 acres.

owners and merchants, who prior to the revolution had owned around 19 million dessiatines of land, were also denied the right to land ownership.

An inalienable part of the decree was the peasants' mandate on land, which Lenin included in full and without a single change in Article 4 of the decree. In line with this mandate, the right to use land was granted to all citizens who wished to work the land themselves or in an association based on the equitable use of the land, i.e., the land being distributed between the working people, in accordance with local conditions, by labour or consumer norms.

The Bolsheviks did not support the petty-bourgeois idea of equalitarian distribution of land contained in the Socialist-Revolutionaries' "land socialisation" programme. But since the broad peasant masses of Russia then saw equalitarian use of land as the fairest solution to the agrarian question, the Bolshevik Party advocated that it be drafted into law. The practical changes brought about by the revolution in the countryside were bound to convince the peasants of the disadvantages of equalitarian land use and of the need for socialised forms of agricultural production. As far back as August 1917 Lenin wrote: "The peasants want to keep their small farms, to set equal standards for all, and to make readjustments on an equalitarian basis from time to time. Fine. No sensible socialist will differ with the peasant poor over this. If the land is confiscated, that *means* the domination of the banks has been undermined, if the implements are confiscated, that *means* the domination of capital has been undermined—and in that case, *provided the proletariat rules centrally,* provided political power is taken over by the proletariat, the rest will come *by itself,* as a result of 'force of example', prompted by experience."[1]

The peasants' mandate contained another provision which the Bolsheviks considered much more important: the right to private landownership was abrogated for all time, the sale of land or any other form of its alienation was forbidden, all land became the property of the whole people, that is, state property.

---

[1] V. I. Lenin, "From a Publicist's Diary. Peasants and Workers", *Collected Works,* Vol. 25, p. 285.

It meant, in fact, the nationalisation of land. With political power in the hands of the proletariat, the implementation of this important part of the Bolsheviks' agrarian programme created in Russia, as Lenin emphasised, "an agrarian system which is the *most flexible* from the point of view of the transition to socialism".[1]

The overwhelming majority of the delegates voted for the adoption of Lenin's Decree on Land. The congress loudly applauded the impassioned speech of an old peasant from the Rzhev District in Tver Province, K. G. Zhegunov, who said: "I bring compliments and greetings to this meeting", and on behalf of his peasant-electors conveyed "greetings and thanks to Comrade Lenin, the staunchest defender of the poor peasants".[2]

The Decree on Land was crucial in winning over the peasantry of Russia to the side of the working class and consolidating the victory of the socialist revolution. "That is exactly how the Russian proletariat *won the peasantry* from the Socialist-Revolutionaries, and won them literally *a few hours after* achieving state power; a few hours after the victory over the bourgeoisie in Petrograd, the victorious proletariat issued a 'decree on land', and in that decree it entirely, at once, with revolutionary swiftness, energy and devotion, *satisfied* all the most urgent economic needs of the *majority* of the peasants, it expropriated the landowners, entirely and without compensation."[3]

The Bolshevik Government

After adopting the historic Decree on Peace and Decree on Land, the Second All-Russia Congress of Soviets examined the question of a new power of workers and peasants. This fundamental question of the socialist revolution was dealt with by

---

[1] V. I. Lenin, "The Proletarian Revolution and the Renegade Kautsky", *Collected Works*, Vol. 28, Progress Publishers, Moscow, 1977, p. 314.

[2] *Second All-Russia Congress of Soviets of Workers' and Soldiers' Deputies*, p. 74.

[3] V. I. Lenin, "The Constituent Assembly Elections and the Dictatorship of the Proletariat", *Collected Works*, Vol. 30, p. 265.

Lenin's decree on forming the Council of People's Commissars, the new government of Russia, which the congress adopted unanimously at the end of its second session on October 26. One can hardly overestimate the importance of replacing the chief body of the bourgeois-landlord state machinery with a workers' and peasants' government to administer the country and socialist construction. "Its significance is, first of all, that we shall have a Soviet government, our own organ of power, in which the bourgeoisie will have no share whatsoever."[1] The decree expressed Lenin's persistent search for new ways of organising state power, his endeavour to create a proletarian administrative apparatus which would successfully combine the principles of collectivism and single authority and have the closest ties with the mass organisations of the working people.

The Council of People's Commissars, which the decree charged with exercising state power under the control of the All-Russia Congress of Soviets and its Central Executive Committee, consisted of the chairmen of 13 commissions: the people's commissars of the interior, nationalities, agriculture, labour, military and naval affairs, trade and industry, education, finance, foreign affairs, justice, food, post and telegraph, and the railways.

Aware of the great diversity of Russia's socio-economic system and the preponderantly agricultural population, the Bolsheviks headed by Lenin accepted in principle, and even welcomed, the participation in the Soviet government, together with the working-class party, of representatives of other democratic parties which expressed the interests and enjoyed the support of various sections of working people, especially, of course, the working peasantry. The only condition for such co-operation was that these parties recognised the accomplished proletarian revolution and the socialist platform, as expressed in the decrees of the Second All-Russia Congress of Soviets. "It is not our fault that the Socialist-Revolutionaries and the Mensheviks have gone," Lenin told a conference of regimental delegates of the Petrograd garrison four days after the victorious October uprising. "They

---

[1] V. I. Lenin, "Meeting of the Petrograd Soviet of Workers' and Soldiers' Deputies, October 25 (November 7), 1917," *Collected Works*, Vol. 26, p. 239.

were invited to share political power, but they want to sit on the fence until the fight against Kerensky is over.

"We asked everyone to take part in the government. The Left Socialist-Revolutionaries said they wanted to support the Soviet Government's policy. They did not even dare voice disagreement with the new government's programme... Here everyone knows that the Socialist-Revolutionaries and the Mensheviks went [they left the Second Congress of Soviets—*M. I.*] because they were left in a minority. The men of the Petrograd garrison are aware of this. They know that we wanted a coalition Soviet government. We did not exclude anyone from the Soviet. If they do not want to work with us, so much the worse for them. The mass of soldiers and peasants will not follow the Mensheviks or the Socialist-Revolutionaries. I am sure that nine-tenths of any workers' or soldiers' meeting will be on our side."[1]

The RSDLP(B) Central Committee advocated reaching agreement with other parties on the composition of the government on the basis of the platform of the Second All-Russia Congress of Soviets and the decisions adopted by it, and held talks on October 26 with the Left Socialist-Revolutionaries on the inclusion of their leaders in the Council of People's Commissars. Lenin played a direct role in the talks. But in reply to the Bolsheviks' proposal the Left Socialist-Revolutionaries stubbornly insisted on the creation of a "homogeneous socialist government" representing all parties, including the Mensheviks and the Right Socialist-Revolutionaries, who had demonstratively withdrawn from the October 25 session of the congress in protest against the October armed uprising. They wanted, as Nadezhda Krupskaya aptly put it, "to harness to the Soviet cart a swan, a crab and a pike, to create a government that would be unable to come to an agreement, to move from the spot."[2]

As it was impossible to reach agreement with the Left Socialist-Revolutionaries, 14 representatives of Lenin's Bolshevik Party were nominated as socialist ministers.

---

[1] V. I. Lenin, "Conference of Regimental Delegates of the Petrograd Garrison. October 29 (November 11), 1917", *Collected Works,* Vol. 26, pp. 269-70.

[2] N. K. Krupskaya, *Reminiscences about Lenin,* 2nd ed., Politizdat, Moscow, 1968, p. 337 (in Russian).

On approving the composition of the first Soviet government, the congress elected Vladimir Lenin, the leader of the socialist revolution, Chairman of the Council of People's Commissars. The people entrusted the administration of the country to the Bolshevik Party. And, as developments confirmed, the Soviet government made up of representatives of Lenin's working-class party honoured the trust placed in it by the working people of Russia, consistently implementing "the programme, *approved by the whole* Second All-Russia Congress of Soviets, for gradual, but firm and undeviating steps towards socialism".[1]

The overwhelming majority of the members of the Leninist Council of People's Commissars, who themselves came from families of workers and peasants, the democratic intelligentsia, various sections of office employees and the military, genuinely represented the interests and aspirations of the working people. The first Soviet government led by Lenin consisted of Russians and Ukrainians, Byelorussians and Jews, Poles and Letts, Armenians and Georgians, and thus reflected the geography of Russia, from its most important industrial centres to the outlying ethnic regions. The Leninist Council of People's Commissars was an example of a genuine internationalist alliance of the best representatives of the working people of all nations and nationalities, irrespective of their size, in the struggle against exploitation and oppression.

The working people of Russia had every right to be proud of the composition of the Soviet government, which consisted of leaders, champions and organisers of the Bolshevik Party. The Party appointed as people's commissars and to other responsible posts in the Soviet state apparatus lawyers, doctors, journalists, military men, engineers, economists, chemists, mathematicians, biologists and statisticians, many of whom had studied abroad or had lived there as emigrés, who had a good command of foreign languages, and were splendid speakers and publicists. Judging by the number of books written by its members, the languages they speak, and their culture and education, said

---

[1] V. I. Lenin, "From the Central Committee of the Russian Social-Democratic Labour Party (Bolsheviks) to All Party Members and to All the Working Classes of Russia", *Collected Works*, Vol. 26, p. 307.

Colonel R. Robins, the leader of the US Red Cross mission in Russia in 1917, the first Council of People's Commissars is superior to any Cabinet of Ministers in the world.[1]

The creation of the worker-peasant Council of People's Commissars—a fundamentally new type of government both in its nature and purpose—was a major step on the way to establishing a proletarian state. The historic Congress of Soviets, as *Izvestia* of October 28, 1917 stressed in this connection, created "a new type of government, a genuine people's government that is linked with people's organisations and works together with them and through them, thereby establishing a government of the people by the people".

For the first time in the history of states a special organ was set up within the Council of People's Commissars to deal with the liberation of the oppressed nationalities and co-operation of the peoples—the People's Commissariat for Nationalities. It was headed by Joseph Stalin, a prominent leader of the Party. In its work the Commissariat relied on the national commissariats, local national departments of the provincial Soviets, and urban and district Soviets. This structure made it possible to take account of all the requirements of the working people of the ethnic regions.

The victory of the October armed uprising in Petrograd and the formation at the Second All-Russia Congress of Soviets of a new Bolshevik government of Russia gave rise to fierce reaction on the part of all the bourgeois and petty-bourgeois parties, which had virtually united under the Cadets in a single anti-Bolshevik and essentially anti-Soviet bloc.

While the fugitive "socialist" Prime Minister Kerensky first in Pskov, then in Gatchina and Krasnoye Selo was, with the tsarist General Krasnov, frenziedly preparing an anti-Soviet campaign against Petrograd, a Committee for the Salvation of the Fatherland and the Revolution was formed in the early hours of October 26 at a session of the Petrograd City Duma by the Cadets, Mensheviks, Right Socialist-Revolutionaries and other bourgeois and conciliatory parties and groups. As a centre of counter-revolutionary activity in Petrograd, the Salvation

---

[1] See *Novy Mir*, No. 5, 1967, p. 260.

Committee exhorted the citizens of the Russian Republic not to recognise Soviet power and announced that it would "take the initiative in restoring the Provisional Government". On October 27 the leaders of the Salvation Committee dispatched a delegation to Gatchina and reached agreement with Kerensky on joint actions; that same day they visited the British Embassy and assured Ambassador Buchanan and General Knox that " 'Kerensky was leading a whole army corps' and that the Bolsheviks would inevitably 'fall' within the next two days".[1]

The emergency mobilisation of all the revolutionary forces of the city under the direct guidance of the Chairman of the Council of People's Commissars ensured speedy and decisive success. The cadet officer revolt was defeated in Petrograd on October 29, and on the following day, October 30, contingents of the Petrograd Red Guards, soldiers and sailors dealt a telling blow at Krasnov's troops in the battles near the Pulkovo heights, throwing back the rebelling Cossack hundreds from the revolutionary capital. "Kerensky's troops have been routed!" said a special announcement of the Petrograd Revolutionary Military Committee published in *Pravda* on November 2. "Kerensky's entire staff, with General Krasnov and Voitinsky at the head, have been arrested. Kerensky has fled disguised in a sailor's uniform... Kerensky's venture has failed. The revolution has triumphed."

In addition to their first armed counter-revolutionary attack, the Menshevik and Socialist-Revolutionary bloc persisted in its "peaceful" attempts to remove the Bolsheviks headed by Lenin from government by forming a so-called homogeneous socialist government consisting of representatives of the "entire democracy". This proposal was advanced by the conciliatory Executive Committee of the All-Russia Railway Workers' Union (Vikzhel), disguised under the flag of neutrality and seeking to conciliate the "entire democracy". It presupposed the inclusion in a "homogeneous" government of all the parties represented in the Soviets, including the Mensheviks, Right Socialist-Revolutionaries and Popular Socialists, which had declined to take part in the

[1] V. S. Vasyukov, *Prior to the Intervention*, Politizdat, Moscow, 1968, p. 210 (in Russian).

work of the Second Congress of Soviets and declared the Bolsheviks "usurpers of power".

On October 29, at a critical moment of the counter-revolutionary forces' activity near Petrograd and in Moscow, when, as Lenin put it, the political question converged with the military, Vikzhel organised, in the former Ministry of Railways, a meeting of a commission charged with drafting an agreement between the parties and organisations. The then Left Socialist-Revolutionary B. F. Malkin, who took part in the "work" of the commission, wrote this about Vikzhel's unseemly role: "The cream of the unemployed ministers . . . all distinguished members of the compromise which had been overthrown by the October Revolution, were here in full force, foaming at the mouth, demanding in hatred the complete rout of the October uprising. From time to time the conciliatory leaders kept running to the telephone and telegraph in the next room, which the hospitable Vikzhel had willingly put at their disposal, to learn the latest news of the counter-revolution on the Gatchina front."[1]

It was during these days, when a fierce battle was being waged for the very existence of Soviet power, that a group of oppositionists (L. B. Kamenev, G. E. Zinoviev, V. P. Nogin, A. I. Rykov, V. P. Milyutin) yielded to the demand of the Menshevik and Socialist-Revolutionary bloc to set up "a homogeneous socialist government", and came out against the Leninist policy of the RSDLP(B) Central Committee and the Council of People's Commissars. The counter-revolutionaries were jubilant, and the bourgeois newspaper *Dyen* hurried to announce on November 7 the "failure" of the power of the Council of People's Commissars: "It is on the verge of collapse, and this is realised by Lenin's friends. Does Lenin himself understand this?"

Lenin's working-class party of Russia gave a rapid and firm reply. Already on November 7 *Pravda* printed an appeal written by Lenin to all Party members, to all the working classes of Russia. "There must be no government in Russia other than the *Soviet Government. . .,*" stressed the appeal. "The majority at the Second All-Russia Congress of Soviets belonged to the Bolshe-

---

[1] B. F. Malkin, "Lenin and Vikzhel", *Za industrializatsiyu,* No. 17, January 21, 1930, p. 4.

vik Party. Therefore the only Soviet Government is the one formed by that Party."[1] "The response from the whole country was like a blast of hot storm," wrote John Reed, "...*upon the Tsay-ee-kah* rolled in like breakers the fierce popular condemnation of the 'deserters'. For days Smolny was thronged with angry delegations and committees, from the front, from the Volga, from the Petrograd factories."[2]

The firm stand adopted by the RSDLP(B) Central Committee and the Council of People's Commissars under Lenin's guidance was vigorously supported by the local Party organisations, and also the Soviets and the revolutionary working people throughout the country, above all in Moscow and Petrograd. After the wave of mass rallies and meetings held at the Admiralteisky and Nevsky shipyards and the Nevsky mechanical works, the Obukhov, Izhorsky, Russko-Baltiisky, Kabelny, Optichesky, Geisler and many other plants and factories, firmly denounced the anti-party group. The oppositionists were also denounced at meetings of representatives of the troops of the Petrograd garrison, held on November 11 at the soldiers' club of the Preobrazhensky Regiment. The garrison meeting adopted a resolution which recommended: "first, express sharp criticism of the parties which under cover of slogans of accord are in fact seeking to foil the gains of the people during the days of the October Revolution; second, express full confidence in the Central Executive Committee and the Council of People's Commissars and promise them full support".[3]

The Council of People's Commissars and the RSDLP(B) Central Committee advanced tried and true Leninists to the government posts abandoned by the oppositionists. On November 8, on Lenin's proposal, Yakov Mikhailovich Sverdlov was elected Chairman of the Central Executive Committee of the Soviets in place of L. B. Kamenev, who was removed in accordance with the decision of the RSDLP(B) Central Committee. G. I. Petrov-

---

[1] V. I. Lenin, "From the Central Committee of the Russian Social-Democratic Labour Party (Bolsheviks) to All Party Members and to All the Working Classes of Russia", *Collected Works*, Vol. 26. p. 303.

[2] John Reed, *Ten Days That Shook the World,* The Modern Libraries, N.Y., 1935, pp. 274-75.

[3] *Pravda,* November 3 and 14, 1917.

sky, a prominent member of the Party and former member of the Fourth State Duma, was appointed People's Commissar of the Interior, and A. G. Shlikhter, a veteran Bolshevik who had worked in the Moscow Provincial Council, acting deputy People's Commissar for Agriculture. On the initiative and with the direct participation of Lenin, who had a perfect knowledge of the Party cadres, such tried revolutionaries and skilled organisers as V. R. Menzhinsky, N. I. Podvoisky, A. S. Bubnov, F. E. Dzerzhinsky, A. N. Vinokurov, A. M. Kollontai, P. I. Stučka, A. D. Tsyurupa, D. P. Bogolepov and many other prominent Party leaders were drawn into work in the Soviet government and the boards of the people's commissariats in the post-October days and in the subsequent period.

The counter-revolutionaries placed great hopes on sabotage by civil servants, the idea being to make it practically impossible for the victorious proletariat to assume state leadership of the country. "The inactivity of the administrative apparatus," the journal *Tribuna gosudarstvennych sluzhashchikh* (Rostrum of the Civil Servants) wrote at the time, "poses a greater danger to the domination of the Bolsheviks than the actions of the officer cadets and Kerensky. Kerensky can be arrested, the cadets can be shot with a gun, but the very best gun cannot replace a battered typewriter, nor the bravest sailor a modest clerk in any of the departments." The article not unjustifiably concluded: "Without the state mechanism, without the apparatus of power, the entire activity of the new government resembles a machine without a driving belt—it goes round and round, but produces nothing."[1]

Proletarian power faced undeniably formidable difficulties in the period immediately after the October revolution. A socialist state apparatus was being created for the first time in history. The representatives of the working class and revolutionary peasantry who had come to power had no experience of state administration. Of one thing there was no doubt: the old bureaucratic machinery had to be destroyed. But this did not imply rejection of all old specialists and employees. On the contrary, as Lenin

---

[1] *Tribuna gosudarstvennykh sluzhashchikh,* No. 19, 11-17 November, 1917.

had pointed out even before the victory of the socialist revolution, a new administrative apparatus could only be set up by making maximum use of all the old accounting and distribution bodies, their experts, communications network, information materials, and clerical techniques.

However, the People's Commissars and the Commissars of the Petrograd Revolutionary Military Committee who helped them found all the former ministries almost abandoned, with files tossed about or messed up, with no keys for the outside doors or the offices, locked desks, bookcases and safes. "You went up a staircase," recalled A. M. Kollontai, the first People's Commissar for Social Security, or, as it was then known, State Charity, "and you met a stream of people—clerks, typists, bookkeepers, heads of departments... They were in a hurry and did not even look at us. While we were mounting the stairs, they were coming down. The sabotage of the civil servants had started. Only a few persons remained. They declared their readiness to work with us, with the Bolsheviks. We went into the offices of the minister and other offices. Empty. Abandoned typewriters, papers thrown about. The in and out registers had been cleared away. Locked up. But there were no keys. Nor were there keys for the safe.

"Who had them? How could we work without money? The state charity was an organisation that could not stop working: it was concerned with children's shelters, the war-maimed, orthopaedic workshops, hospitals, sanatoria, and the leper colonies, children's homes, girls' institutions, and homes for the blind... There was an awful lot of work to be done. There were incessant demands from every quarter imaginable... But there were no keys."[1]

With some variation, the same held true for the other ministries. "Already from the first days of the 'triumph' of the victors, the civil servants have refused to work in all institutions, in all ministries. The entire government and administrative mechanism has ground to a halt," the Menshevik *Iskra* rejoiced on November 5. "And immediately all the 'decrees' of the new power that

---

[1] A. M. Kollontai, *Recollections About Ilyich,* Politizdat, Moscow, 1959, pp. 5-6 (in Russian).

were counted upon to make an impact have been left hanging in the air."

The Party of Lenin, the organiser and leader of the October Revolution, was, after the Great October victory, also the chief organiser of socialist state development in Russia. It was under the leadership of the Bolshevik Party, its Central Committee, the Soviet government and Lenin that the acute problem of staff for the new state apparatus was successfully resolved. The main source in selecting and promoting appropriate candidates to leading posts and in general for work in the Soviets, in military, economic and other departments and institutions was the Bolshevik Party itself. The nomination of Bolsheviks to responsible posts in the new state apparatus was an inalienable right and the direct responsibility of the Bolshevik Party, which had assumed leadership of the country. "So long as the ruling Party governs, so long as this Party has to decide all questions concerned with various appointments, you will not allow important state appointments to be made by anyone but the ruling party."[1]

Moreover, as the Bolshevik Party concentrated on taking charge of the construction of a new social system, the approach to the responsibilities of all workers, of any Party member had to undergo a change. "Every Party Committee now has to look from a new angle upon every propagandist, who used to be regarded merely as a man belonging to a definite circle, a definite organisation. Each of them belongs to a ruling party which directs the whole state... He is a representative of a fighting class and of a party which runs, and must run, an enormous machine of state."[2] Thus, when it came to power, Lenin's working-class party of Russia and its Central Committee had the additional organisational and important political function of correctly and expediently using Party cadres, selecting and allocating them in proper fashion.

---

[1] V. I. Lenin, "The Eighth All-Russia Congress of Soviets, December 22-29, 1920", Collected Works, Vol. 42, Progress Publishers, Moscow, 1971, p. 252.

[2] V. I. Lenin, "Speech Delivered at an All-Russia Conference of Political Education Workers of Gubernia and Uyezd Education Departments, November 3, 1920", Collected Works, Vol. 31, Progress Publishers, Moscow, 1974, p. 369.

In the post-October months, when everything was new, when everything was being done for the first time ever, the selection and education of employees for the Soviet state institutions was a major concern of the Party and the Council of People's Commissars. The commissariats and the institutions under their jurisdiction all needed competent, skilled, experienced people. But where to find them? The old experts were in no hurry to offer their services to Soviet power. Some adopted a wait-and-see attitude, others resorted to sabotage. "It was a desperate situation," recalled G. P. Oppokov (A. Lomov), a notable leader of the Bolshevik Party and the Soviet state. "There were among us many splendid, highly-skilled workers, many loyal revolutionaries who had crossed Russia in all directions, in foot irons from Petersburg, Warsaw, Moscow—the whole road to calvary up to Yakutia and Verkhoyansk... But we had no idea how to run a state, no experience in the technicalities of banking, nor the work of ministries... Very few wanted to become People's Commissars ... fearing they could not cope with the job. Lenin energetically searched for candidates for People's Commissars and for other responsible posts. After which the Executive Committee immediately arranged the appointment. There were no disagreements."[1]

And yet the Bolshevik Party and its Central Committee with Lenin at its head coped successfully with the formidable task of setting up the Soviet state apparatus. This became possible largely because even under the tsar, when the Party was underground, it had been able to educate cadres of reliable, experienced proletarian revolutionaries and organisers who were loyal to the working-class cause. It was this advanced contingent of the Party, made up of professional revolutionaries and others who had joined the Party long before the October Revolution and who had passed through the hard theoretical and practical school of illegal revolutionary work, which led the construction of a new type of state, a socialist state. "... we had such a vanguard of organisers because they had passed through a severe school of life when they had to work in underground organisa-

---

[1] G. I. Lomov, "Days of Storm and Onslaught", *Proletarskaya revolyutsia,* No. 10, 1927, pp. 171-72.

tions".[1] Guided by the principle of assessing staff in accordance with their political and practical qualities, a principle tested by underground work, the Bolshevik Party assigned most of its finest workers to responsible posts in the people's commissariats and other Soviet institutions. This is noted in the report of the Secretariat of the RSDLP(B) Central Committee for the period from the Sixth Congress (August 1917) to February 1918. "The best Party forces were dispatched to work in government institutions."[2]

Lenin's activity, his instructions and demands were decisive in organising the work of the Soviet government and all the people's commissariats which were set up in place of the former ministries abolished by the revolution. "Ilyich was at the centre of all this work," Nadezhda Krupskaya recalled, "he organised it. It was more than just intensive work, it was work that demanded all his strength... So not surprisingly, at night, after coming behind the partition of the room where I lived with him in the Smolny, he couldn't fall asleep, would get up again and phone somebody, give some urgent instructions, and, finally falling asleep, would continue talking about the work in his dreams."[3]

The Party and Lenin assigned to state posts people who combined boundless loyalty to the cause of the proletarian revolution with organisational talents, people with courage and initiative, who were not afraid of responsibility, and were capable of organising the work of large collectives. There were instances when, on hearing of a probable appointment, rank-and-file Party members and even notable professional revolutionaries would shrink from accepting high posts, referring to lack of experience and knowledge, and would ask to be allowed to continue working in the lower echelons. In such cases Lenin was adamant.

"I also have no experience," he usually replied. "You must

[1] V. I. Lenin, "Speech at a Meeting in Memory of Y. M. Sverdlov, March 16, 1920. Brief Newspaper Report", *Collected Works*, Vol. 30, p. 33.

[2] *The Extraordinary Seventh Congress of the RCP(B)*, Politizdat, Moscow, 1962, p. 239 (in Russian).

[3] N. K. Krupskaya, *Reminiscences about Lenin*, pp. 354-55.

learn. It is just a prejudice that a state can be administered only by the rich or by civil servants coming from rich families."[1]

The materials of the first census of Soviet office employees in Moscow, held in August-September 1918, shows that the greatest number of Communists were engaged in the All-Russia Extraordinary Commission, 52.2 per cent (408 persons), and in the People's Commissariat for Foreign Affairs, 46.8 per cent (134 persons). These facts confirm Lenin's widely known description of the People's Commissariat for Foreign Affairs (it may refer also to the All-Russia Extraordinary Commission) as a special institution in the sense that in it "all sections with any authority are composed of Communists"[2] The numbers of Communists in the People's Commissariat for Nationalities, the Administrative Department of the Council of People's Commissars, the All-Russia Central Executive Committee, the People's Commissariat for Justice and others were also quite high.

It is interesting and indicative to look at the data for the People's Commissariat for Nationalities, an unprecedented body which was specially created by proletarian power to implement a fundamentally new type of nationalities policy, a policy of equality and friendship of peoples. Altogether, inclusive of both full and candidate members and members of the national sections of the RCP(B) and representatives of other communist organisations, there were 85 Bolsheviks, or 38.3 per cent of the overall staff, in the People's Commissariat for Nationalities in mid-1918.[3] The board of the Commissariat was comprised almost totally of well-known leaders of the Party and its national sections—Joseph Stalin (People's Commissar), F. A. Rozins, S. S. Pestkovsky, J. M. Leszczynski, S. M. Dimanstein, V. S. Mickevičius-Kapsukas, V. A. Avanesov, A. G. Chervyakov and others. Representatives of various national revolutionary organisations, such as M. Vakhitov, G. Ibragimov, and others, contri-

---

[1] *V. I. Lenin. Biography,* Politizdat, Moscow, 1970, p. 412 (in Russian).

[2] V. I. Lenin, "The Question of Nationalities or 'Autonomisation'", *Collected Works,* Vol. 36, Progress Publishers, Moscow, 1971, p. 609.

[3] See M. P. Iroshnikov, *Chairman of the Council of People's Commissars V. I. Ulyanov (Lenin). Essays on State Activity in 1917-1918,* Nauka Publishers, Leningrad, 1974, pp. 389 et. al.

buted by their participation to the organisation and successful work of the Commissariat.

Y. M. Sverdlov, Chairman of the All-Russia Central Executive Committee, emphasised at the Extraordinary Seventh Congress of the RCP(B) that the Bolshevik Party, in creating local bodies of the Soviet state system, "put its whole soul into the Soviets, it was through the Soviets and in the Soviets that it conducted its major work".[1] Suffice it to recall that by the end of 1918 in just 29 provinces of central Russia 724 out of the 874 members of the provincial executive committees were Communists; of the 4,046 members of the district executive committees, 2,625 were Communists.[2]

As a result of the vast and detailed work conducted by the Bolshevik Party, Communists, primarily tested professional revolutionaries who were personally known to the Party Central Committee and to Lenin, were appointed to key posts in the system administering the Soviet republic: the All-Russia Central Executive Committee, the Council of People's Commissars, the people's commissariats, and to the leadership of diverse institutions and departments, and local Soviets. To crucial sections of state and economic development the Party of Lenin appointed its finest representatives, who best combined high political qualities and efficiency, loyalty to the socialist revolution, organisational talent, professional experience and knowledge. Their boundless fidelity to the working-class cause, their cohesion, prestige and influence on the masses played a major role in strengthening and developing the socialist revolution.

For a Stronger Alliance of the Working Class and Peasantry

The ruling Bolshevik Party, which held leading positions in state development and administration, was at the same time willing to co-operate with representatives of the democratic parties

---

[1] Y. M. Sverdlov, *Selected Works*, Vol. 2, Politizdat, Moscow, 1959, p. 140 (in Russian).

[2] See *History of the Communist Party of the Soviet Union*, Vol. 3, II, Politizdat, Moscow, 1968, p. 54.

which supported Soviet power and its decrees. As noted earlier, the first Council of People's Commissars was comprised of members of one party, for the Left Socialist-Revolutionary Party[1] leaders rejected the Bolsheviks' proposal to take part in the first Soviet government. Winning the firm support of the working peasantry, and strengthening its alliance with the working class was a crucial factor in consolidating Soviet power and successfully continuing the construction of the new state. In a bid to achieve the unity of the country's working people under the leadership of the working class the Bolshevik Party had to wage stiff battles against the bourgeois and petty-bourgeois parties for winning the broad peasant masses over to its side. The highlights of this struggle were the Extraordinary and Second All-Russia congresses of Soviets of Peasants' Deputies held in Petrograd in late November and early December 1917, which were followed by the establishment of a single All-Russia Central Executive Committee (CEC) of the Soviets of Workers', Soldiers' and Peasants' Deputies.

On the question of power the majority at the Extraordinary Peasants' Congress advocated merging the Executive Committee of the Soviets of Peasants' Deputies on a parity basis with the All-Russia Central Executive Committee of Soviets of Workers' and Soldiers' Deputies. The congress voted also for co-operation of the Left Socialist-Revolutionaries with the Bolshevik Party in the Soviet government, even if the extreme right and left socialist groups declined to join it. The conclusion of an agreement on the organisation of power hinged on recognition of the decrees on land, on peace and control over production.[2]

The agreement reached on November 14 between the presidiums of the All-Russia CEC and the Extraordinary All-Russia Congress of Soviets of Peasants' Deputies was approved on the next day (November 15) both by the CEC and the delegates of the Extraordinary Congress who elected 108 of their representatives as CEC members in line with the agreement. Arriving on

---

[1] Left Socialist-Revolutionaries, a splinter group of the Socialist-Revolutionaries headed by M. Spiridonova who subscribed to the transfer of power to the Soviets and land to the peasants.

[2] See *Znamya Truda,* November 12, 14 and 21, 1917.

November 14 at the Extraordinary Peasants' Congress as head of the delegation of the All-Russia CEC, the workers' neighbourhoods and the Red Guards of Petrograd, Yakov Sverdlov addressed the participants, emphasising: "By uniting with the Soviets of Workers' and Soldiers' Deputies you have strengthened the entire cause of the revolution."[1]

After the merger of the All-Russia CEC with the Executive Committee elected by the Extraordinary All-Russia Peasants' Congress, the Left Socialist-Revolutionaries decided to take part in the work of the Council of People's Commissars. Initially, by a special resolution of the All-Russia CEC of November 17, the Left Socialist-Revolutionaries were put in charge of the People's Commissariat of Agriculture. On November 24 the CEC approved the Left Socialist-Revolutionary A. L. Kolegayev as the People's Commissar of Agriculture. Representatives of the Left Socialist-Revolutionaries were also appointed to all the boards of the other people's commissariats.

The Second All-Russia Congress of Soviets of Peasants' Deputies, held in Petrograd from November 26 to December 10, 1917, dealt a final blow at the Right Socialist-Revolutionaries' influence among the peasant masses. Denouncing the activity of the old Right Socialist-Revolutionary Executive Committee, which urged reaching agreement with the bourgeoisie and the landowners against the workers and peasants, the congress adopted a number of important resolutions meeting the interests of the socialist revolution, with special emphasis on the immediate establishment of workers' and peasants' power. Tremendous importance attached to the congress resolution denouncing any attempt by the Constituent Assembly to counterpose itself to Soviet power. "The Second All-Russia Congress of Soviets of Peasants' Deputies will consider any attempt by the Constituent Assembly to wage a struggle against the Soviets of Peasants', Workers' and Soldiers' Deputies, the organs of revolutionary power, as an encroachment on the gains of the revolution, and will vigorously counter any such attempt."[2] The Second All-Russia Con-

---

[1] *Struggle for the Establishment and Strengthening of Soviet Power. A Chronicle. October 25, 1917-January 10, 1918,* Nauka Publishers, Moscow, 1962, p. 194 (in Russian).

[2] *Golos trudovogo krestyanstva,* December 10, 1917.

gress of Soviets of Peasants' Deputies elected a new Executive Committee of the Soviets of Peasants' Deputies, and concluded its work with the adoption of the appeal "To the Labouring Peasantry", which was based on the draft written by Lenin.

The victory at the Second All-Russia Peasants' Congress of the Left Socialist-Revolutionaries, who entered into a bloc with the Bolsheviks, provided for the successful conclusion of the Left Socialist-Revolutionary Party Central Committee's talks with the Council of People's Commissars, as a result of which in the small hours of October 10 a final agreement was reached on the inclusion of seven Left Socialist-Revolutionaries in the Soviet government. A. L. Kolegayev remained the People's Commissar of Agriculture, I. Z. Steinberg was appointed People's Commissar for Justice, and P. P. Proshyan, People's Commissar for Post and Telegraph. Representatives of the Left Socialist-Revolutionaries also headed two new commissariats: for local self-government and for the property of the republic. The agreement was concluded on the basis of the Bolsheviks' socialist platform. The Left Socialist-Revolutionary leaders pledged themselves to follow the general policy of the Council of People's Commissars.[1]

It should be emphasised that the Bolsheviks adopted a positive attitude towards such a coalition government, as stated time and again by Lenin. And it is not through any fault of the Leninist Party that already in March 1918 the Left Socialist-Revolutionaries withdrew from the Council of People's Commissars on the pretext of their opposition to the Brest peace treaty. The appearance in the Soviet state of a one-party political system was due primarily to the stand of the petty-bourgeois parties which rejected co-operation with the Bolsheviks on the basis of the socialist programme of the Second All-Russia Congress of Soviets expressing the will of the revolutionary working people of Russia, and took the road of struggle against the power of the proletariat.[2]

It should be noted in this connection that a study of the

[1] See *Decrees of Soviet Power*, Vol. I, Politizdat, Moscow, 1957, pp. 200, 215 (in Russian).
[2] *History of the Communist Party of the Soviet Union*, Vol. 3, Book I, p. 438.

history of Soviet state development in 1917-1918 conclusively disproves the allegations of bourgeois ideologues, avowed anti-Sovieteers, reformists and revisionists of all hues that the Communist Party and Soviet power declined to employ members of other democratic and socialist parties. A survey of the findings of the first census of Soviet employees clearly shows that not only after the Left Socialist-Revolutionary leaders' withdrawal from the Council of People's Commissars, but even after the defeat of their adventuristic attempt to organise on July 6, 1918 an armed revolt against the Soviet government headed by Lenin, the new state apparatus set up by the Bolsheviks employed members of the party of the Left Socialist-Revolutionaries, and of many other non-communist parties (Right and Centrist Socialist-Revolutionaries, Mensheviks, Anarchists, Popular Socialists, Trudoviks, and others)[1].

New State Apparatus

An important source for the formation of the Soviet state apparatus were the workers and peasants, soldiers and sailors who fully supported Soviet power and worked actively for its establishment and consolidation. In the working class and the peasantry, Lenin pointed out, there is an untapped, rich wellspring of organisational talent, only we must help to reveal them. Lenin urged that we must patiently seek and discover competent organisers, people who combine loyalty to socialism with a clear mind and shrewd practical sense. "Such people," he went on, "after they have been tested a dozen times, by being transferred from the simplest to the more difficult tasks, should be promoted to the responsible posts of leaders of the people's labour, leaders of administration."[2] The Soviets, trade unions, factory committees, plants and factories, the Red Guards and the revolutionary contingents of the army and fleet were the primary source of

---

[1] See *Voprosy istorii KPSS,* No. 9, 1974, pp. 116-17, M. P. Iroshnikov, op. cit., pp. 396-99.

[2] V. I. Lenin. "The Immediate Tasks of the Soviet Government", *Collected Works,* Vol. 27, p. 263.

replenishment for the new state apparatus in the period of the triumphant march of the proletarian revolution in the country, and put their finest representatives at the disposal of the Council of People's Commissars, the people's commissariats, and the local organs of Soviet power. A resolution adopted by the Petrograd Soviet of Workers' and Soldiers' Deputies on November 17, 1917 urged: "1) To make an immediate and clean break with the rotten bourgeois prejudice that only bourgeois officials are able to administer the state. 2) To divide without delay the district and city Soviets into departments, each of which undertakes one or another sphere of local administration. 3) To enlist for each of these departments the most class-conscious and capable organisers from among comrades working at the factories and serving in the army, thereby dispatching forces to the aid of each People's Commissar."[1]

Among the first employees of the Soviet government apparatus were the tested Petrograd Red Guard workers led by metal-worker P. P. Polovinkin, who serviced the telephone exchange behind the partition in Lenin's study and simultaneously guarded the Chairman of the Council of People's Commissars. The Rozhdestvensky district Party committee assigned E. K. Koksharova to work in the secretariat of the Council of People's Commissars at the Smolny; Y. P. Sergeyeva, a factory worker, became a clerk at the Managing Department of the government; together with other revolutionary soldiers and sailors, S. Zheltyshev, a soldier of the Volyn Regiment machine-gun unit, and A. Zhuzhzhalov, a sailor from Destroyer No. 129 of the Baltic Fleet, were on duty at the Council of People's Commissars.

Representatives of the working people participated directly in the work of the Soviet people's commissariats. Among the first who came to set up the People's Commissariat for Foreign Affairs together with the Bolsheviks I. A. Zalkind and N. G. Markin in the abandoned building of the former Ministry of Foreign Affairs at 6 Palace Square were workers from Vasilyevsky Island, from the Siemens-Schuckert works (now Elektroapparat), revolutionary soldiers of the Pavlovsky Regiment and sailors of the Baltic Fleet. In organising the People's Commissariat for Labour,

---

[1] *Izvestia,* November 18, 1917.

an important role was played by the trade unions of the Petrograd workers, above all the metal and textile workers. In organising the activity of the People's Commissariat for Education, together with A. V. Lunacharsky and N. K. Krupskaya, an active part was played by a group of workers from the factories and enterprises of the Vyborg District with F. I. Kalinin, a Party member since 1903, at their head. Among the first employees of the People's Commissariat for Social Security were mechanics and workers from a Petrograd factory, as well as medical nurses and other paramedical personnel; employees at the People's Commissariat of the Interior included Putilov workers and students of the Petrograd University, the Electrical Engineering and other institutions of higher learning; at the People's Commissariat for Railways there was a group of non-Party printers from the printshop of the former ministry and Bolshevik workers from the Chief Repair Works of the Northwestern Railway.

Relying above all on the tested vanguard of the proletariat—Lenin's working-class party—on the revolutionary working people of Russia and their mass organisations, the Bolshevik Party and the first Soviet government, with Lenin at its head, also employed many old experts and office employees, members of the bourgeois intelligentsia who had been won over to the construction of the new society, in the formation of the proletarian state apparatus.

The problem of using bourgeois experts and intelligentsia in the interests of socialist development was elaborated by Lenin already prior to the October Revolution in his works *The State and Revolution, Can the Bolsheviks Retain State Power?*, and in April 1918 in the notable work *The Immediate Tasks of the Soviet Government* and other post-October works and speeches. We must, after removing the reprobates and hopeless "oppositionists", Lenin noted, put the old experts and employees to the service of the new state under the control and supervision of the Soviets. Lenin's premise was that socialism must be built on the cultural and economic foundation left by capitalism, and with the aid of those people the new system inherited from the old society: "It is not enough to crush capitalism. We must take the entire culture that captialism left behind and build socialism with it. We must take all its science, technology, knowledge and art. Without these we shall be unable to build communist society. But this science, technology and art are in the hands and in the heads of the experts."[1] Account was taken of the fact that the majority of the bourgeois employees found themselves in a proletarian or semi-proletarian situation. "The best organisers and the top experts can be utilised by the state either in the old way, in the bourgeois way (i.e., for high salaries), or in the new way, in the proletarian way (i.e., creating the conditions of national accounting and control from below, which would inevitably and of itself subordinate the experts and enlist them for our work)."[2]

As early as the beginning of 1918, as a result of the flexible and far-sighted policy of the RSDLP(B) Central Committee and the Council of People's Commissars led by Lenin, successfully combining revolutionary actions against the active saboteurs with broad explanatory work among the main mass of the bourgeois experts and intelligentsia, organised mass sabotage by the state officials and employees was crushed. A tremendous role in expanding the old intelligentsia's co-operation with the Soviet state was played by Lenin's well-known "Draft Plan of Scientific and Technical Work" and a number of important measures aimed at uniting the scientific and technical forces of the country for the successful solution of urgent economic tasks, and reconstruction of the economy in the interests of socialist development. The importance of the successes of Soviet power in involving the old experts and bourgeois intelligentsia is graphically borne out by the following figures: approximately a year later, on July 26, 1919, the Chief Bureau for the Registration and Distribution of Scientific and Technical Forces of the Supreme Economic Council registered 29,122 experts, and in 1920, 50,275 experts working at the enterprises and institutions of various departments and people's commissariats.[3]

---

[1] V. I. Lenin, "The Achievements and Difficulties of the Soviet Government", *Collected Works*, Vol. 29, p. 70.

[2] V. I. Lenin, "The Immediate Tasks of the Soviet Government", *Collected Works*, Vol. 27, p. 248.

[3] See S. A. Fedyukin, *Soviet Power and Bourgeois Experts*, Mysl Publishers, Moscow, 1965, p. 114; V. A. Ulyanovskaya, *Formation of the Scientific Intelligentsia in the USSR*, Politizdat, Moscow, 1966, pp. 64-65 (both in Russian).

Thus, in place of the old state machinery of exploitation and coercion, which was demolished by the socialist revolution in a very short historical period, a fundamentally new state apparatus—the apparatus of the dictatorship of the proletariat—was built. Already at the first "purely political", as Lenin put it, main stage of the proletarian revolution in Russia within a mere 10 weeks—from October 25, 1917 to January 5, 1918—the debacle of the Constituent Assembly—there was created "the Soviet *type* of state, which was a gigantic step in advance of 1793 and 1871".[1] "This is a historic victory," Lenin said on March 27, 1922 at the Eleventh Congress of the RCP(B). "The greatest invention in history has been made."[2]

The formation of the Soviet central state apparatus was concluded in the main by the beginning of July 1918, that is, by the opening of the Fifth All-Russia Congress of Soviets. Substantial successes were achieved in the building of a Soviet state system in the localities, too. Throughout Russia by mid-1918 there were some 12,000 Soviets.[3]

Triumphal Advance of Soviet Power

In the period from October 25, 1917 to February-March 1918 Soviet power was established almost throughout the vast country. It was, in Lenin's words, a "period of the victorious, triumphal advance of the dictatorship of the proletariat and Soviet power, when great masses of the working and exploited people of Russia were drawn to the side of Soviet power definitely and irrevocably".[4] This triumph stemmed from the correlation of class forces in Russia towards the end of 1917 and the beginning of 1918. The establishment of Soviet power was resisted by the overthrown exploiter classes—the big landed proprietors and

---

[1] V. I. Lenin, "New Times and Old Mistakes in a New Guise", *Collected Works*, Vol. 33, Progress Publishers, Moscow, 1966, p. 22.

[2] V. I. Lenin, "Eleventh Congress of the R.C.P.(B.)", *Collected Works*, Vol. 33, p. 301.

[3] See *The Soviets in the First Year of Proletarian Dictatorship*, Nauka Publishers, Moscow, 1967, p. 188 (in Russian).

[4] V. I. Lenin, "Report on Ratification of the Peace Treaty, March 14", *Collected Works*, Vol. 27, p. 175.

capitalists—as well as by the petty bourgeoisie and the conciliatory Menshevik and Socialist-Revolutionary parties siding with them. In favour of Soviet power were the overwhelming majority of the multi-million masses of working people who had become convinced by their own experience that it was the sole realistic way to the conclusion of peace, elimination of landed proprietorship, to the establishment of worker control over production and distribution, and elimination of national oppression.

Along with the revolutionary activity of the masses who rendered broad support to the new, Soviet government, another decisive factor in the rapid spread of Soviet power in the localities was the leadership of this process by the Leninist working-class party of Russia.

An exceptionally important role in the successful establishment of Soviet power in all parts of the country was also played by the colossal organisational and propaganda work of the new national centre of Soviet power—the All-Russia Central Executive Committee and the Council of People's Commissars—and other leading bodies of the triumphant proletarian revolution.

During the first days of the October armed uprising the Petrograd Revolutionary Military Committee (RMC) sent to the localities 520 commissars, 97 emissaries and 644 agitators. Altogether in the period of the triumphal advance of Soviet power the RMC, All-Russia CEC, Council of People's Commissars and People's Commissariat of the Interior dispatched to the different cities and regions several thousand representatives—members of the Bolshevik Party, workers, soldiers, sailors, the progressive intelligentsia—as well as the delegates of the Second and Third All-Russia Congresses of Soviets, with whose active participation Soviet power was established in the localities.

The united actions of the RCP(B) Central Committee and the Council of People's Commissars headed by Lenin were ensured not only by their common socialist programme and political course, but also by the fact that the Leninist Central Committee continuously examined and discussed all major domestic and foreign policy questions of proletarian power. Linked with the unity of the Party and state leadership was the following characteristic feature of the first Soviet decrees. They were not merely revolutionary laws and landmarks in socialist development. In the extremely complex conditions of the period under review the decrees of Soviet power served simultaneously as a major form of propaganda of the ideas of socialism, a powerful means of attracting the broad masses to the side of the working class and its Leninist Party. "The road to socialism has been opened by the workers' and peasants' revolution," *Pravda* reported on October 31, 1917. "Steps forward along this road are the revolutionary decrees of the Council of People's Commissars around which the workers and soldiers, all oppressed townspeople and the village poor should be united."

Expressing the policy of the Bolshevik Party and Soviet power, its first decrees were aimed at winning confidence and arousing "creative activity at the grass roots", which, as Lenin pointed out, constituted "the basic factor of the new public life".[1]

Shortly after the victory of the proletarian revolution in Petrograd, Soviet power was established also in Moscow, the old capital of the country. Already on October 25, on receiving the news of the armed uprising in Petrograd, a joint session of Deputies of the Moscow Soviets adopted a Bolshevik resolution on the creation of a Revolutionary Military Committee. Replying to the appeal of the RMC to support the heroic Petrograd proletariat the Moscow workers and revolutionary soldiers, aided by the Red Guards and worker contingents from Ivanovo-Voznesensk, Petrograd, Shuya, Tula, Vladimir and other cities, in fierce battles lasting from October 28 to November 2, routed the counter-revolutionary forces of officers, cadets and the bourgeois White Guards, who had organised armed actions. Announcing the victory of the proletarian revolution, the Moscow RMC on November 3, 1917 wrote: "After a five-day bloody battle the enemies of the people who raised an armed hand against the revolution, have been completely routed. They have surrendered and been disarmed. At the cost of the blood of courageous fighters—soldiers and workers—victory has been achieved. From now on people's power is being established in Moscow—the power of the Soviets of Workers' and Soldiers' Deputies."[2]

---

[1] V. I. Lenin, "Reply to a Question from the Left Socialist-Revolutionaries", *Collected Works*, Vol. 26, p. 288.

[2] *Triumphal Advance of Soviet Power*, Part 1, Nauka Publishers, Moscow, 1963, p. 298 (in Russian).

The victory of the proletarian revolution in both capitals was a crucial factor in the spread of Soviet power throughout Russia. Following Petrograd and Moscow, Soviet power was speedily established in the overwhelming majority of large cities and provincial centres, first of all in the Petrograd province and in the Central Industrial District, which were populated predominantly by Russians, including about 1,300,000 workers, that is, over half the country's industrial workers, and where the poor made up the majority of the rural population.

In many large industrial cities, above all Lugansk, Ivanovo-Voznesensk, Voronezh, Tver, Samara, Yaroslavl, Yekaterinburg, Ufa, Irkutsk, Rostov-on-the-Don, Vladivostok, Chelyabinsk, Perm, Tsaritsyn and others, where the Bolsheviks led the Soviets already before the victory of the Great October Revolution, the new power was established peacefully. At the same time in a number of other cities—Kiev, Kazan, Nizhni Novgorod, Astrakhan, Saratov, Kaluga, Tashkent and some others—the workers and peasants had to overcome the armed resistance of the counter-revolutionary forces in establishing Soviet power. The establishment of Soviet power in the provincial centres and large industrial towns facilitated its speedy spread to the territories of the districts, volosts and villages.

The establishment of Soviet power throughout the country can be clearly seen in the following data: from October 25 to November 20, 1917 the Soviets took power in 48 provincial and other large towns; from November 21, 1917 to January 18, 1918, in 31 provincial centres; from January 19 to February 11, 1918, in eleven, and from February 12 and later, in seven towns. Only in 17 out of the 97 large cities and provincial centres was Soviet power established through an armed struggle.[1]

Establishment of Soviet Power in the Non-Russian Regions

Central Russia and other regions with a predominantly Russian population became the mainstay of proletarian revolution. From there the revolution quickly spread to the non-Russian

---

[1] See I. I. Mintz, *History of the Great October Revolution*, Vol. 3, Nauka Publishers, Moscow, 1972, pp. 704-05 (in Russian).

regions of the country. Fulfilling their internationalist duty, the Russian proletariat under the leadership of the Leninist Party rendered military support and aid to the working people of the country's other nations in proclaiming and consolidating Soviet power. Everywhere—in the Ukraine and Northern Caucasus, in the Baltic region, Byelorussia, Central Asia and other ethnic regions the struggle for the triumph of Soviet power was an inalienable part of the general process of the Great October Socialist Revolution.

In Byelorussia Soviet power was consolidated more rapidly than in the other non-Russian regions (already by the end of October 1917), and shortly afterwards, in the Baltic area—in Estonia and Latvia. The success in Byelorussia was due primarily to the fact that the Bolsheviks, who enjoyed the firm support of the working people, stood at the head of the Soviets in the major cities (Minsk, Vitebsk, Gomel, Mogilev, Dvinsk and others).

An important factor too was the proximity of revolutionary Petrograd, and the Western and Northern fronts, where the Bolshevik organisations strongly influenced the soldiers' masses.

In Minsk power was taken over by the Soviet already on the 25th of October. Two days later, under the chairmanship of A. F. Myasnikov, a Bolshevik, the Revolutionary Military Committee was formed, which wielded power over the entire Northwestern Region and the Western Front. The decrees of the Second All-Russia Congress of Soviets were supported by the congresses of provincial Soviets of the region and the front. The Regional Soviet of the Northwestern Region and the Western Front was formed. The new revolutionary government set up by it in Byelorussia had to wage an intensive struggle in the Byelorussian Rada—an organ of the bourgeois nationalists who sought to join the Minsk, Vitebsk, Mogilev and part of the Vilno provinces to Poland. And when the bourgeois nationalists, unwilling to recognise the power of the working people, organised the so-called "All-Byelorussia Congress", the Council of People's Commissars of the region dissolved it and held provincial and district congresses of Soviets, which took action against this counter-revolutionary venture.

With the victory of the proletarian revolution in the centre

Soviet power began making headway in Latvia, Estonia and Lithuania. Towards the end of 1917 Estonia and the unoccupied part of Latvia were virtually a frontline area, where the bases of the Baltic Fleet and troops of the Northern Front were concentrated. This was particularly important for the successful development of the revolution here, for after the Baltic sailors, among whom Bolshevik influence had always been exceptionally strong, the Lettish rifle regiments of the 12th Army definitely went over to the side of the Leninist Party already in May 1917. On November 8-9, 1917 the Soviet of Workers', Soldiers' and Landless Peasants' Deputies of Latvia proclaimed the transition of all power in the region to the Soviets. And the Second Congress of Soviets of Latvia, held on December 16-18, approved the laws on the nationalisation of land and the introduction of an 8-hour working day, and elected the first Soviet government here—the Executive Committee of the Soviets of Latvia headed by the Bolshevik F. A. Rozins (Azis).[1]

In Estonia, the Soviets took over power even earlier, in fact, two days before the victory of the armed uprising in Petrograd. The working people of Estonia enthusiastically hailed the news about the victory of the proletarian revolution and the adoption of historic decrees by the Second Congress of Soviets. On October 27 the Bolshevik V. Kingissepp, a commissar of the RMC, took over from I. Poska, the provincial commissar of the overthrown Provisional Government. On November 12, on the decision of the Executive Committee of the Soviets of Estonia, the District Council, a centre of the nationalistic counter-revolution, and a week later the District Board ceased to exist. Shortly afterwards the other organs of bourgeois power were also abolished. In the localities—districts and district towns—Yuryev, Narva, Pärnu and others, all power also passed into the hands of the Soviets. The Bolsheviks V. Kingissepp, J. Anvelt, I Rabchinsky, I. O. Mägi, H. Pöögelmann, N. Janson and others, who headed the Executive Committee of the Soviets of Estonia, ensured the implementation of a number of important socio-economic mea-

---

[1] See G. P. Makarova, *Implementation of the Leninist Nationalities Policy in the First Years of Soviet Power. 1917-1920,* Nauka Publishers, Moscow, 1963, pp. 41, 43 (in Russian).

sures. They were due to be formalised by the Constituent Assembly of Estonia, the elections to which were organised by the local Bolshevik organisations. A draft Constitution of the Estonian Soviet Republic was drawn up.

However, in the period under review the initiated transformations were not destined to be completed. This was due to the fierce resistance of the national bourgeoisie and particularly the incursion of the Austro-German troops, which by the beginning of March 1918 occupied the whole territory of Estonia.

Hence, the difficulty in winning power for the Soviets in many ethnic regions was due, among other things, to the fact that the local apparatus of the overthrown Provisional Government and diverse bourgeois-nationalist organisations joined ranks against the working people led by the Bolsheviks. This circumstance determined, in particular, the especially persistent battles for the triumph of Soviet power in the Ukraine. As a result of three days of armed battles by the workers and soldiers of the Kiev garrison (October 29-31, 1917) against the Provisional Government, Soviet power was established in the city. However, the bourgeois Central Rada was able to rally around itself all the counter-revolutionary forces and, disarming the contingents of the Red Guard workers and soldiers, seized power in Kiev, and then in the provinces of Pravoberezhye and the south of the Ukraine.

On November 1 the Central Rada declared itself the "supreme territorial power in the Ukraine", and shortly afterwards (November 7), it announced the setting up of a bourgeois Ukrainian People's Republic and its secession from Soviet Russia. The Third Universal adopted by the Rada detailed its false promise to introduce an 8-hour working day, establish state control over industry and to turn the land over to the peasants after the definitive solution of this question by the Constituent Assembly. The bourgeois-nationalistic content of the Central Rada and its executive organ, the General Secretariat, was graphically displayed by its attitude to the Soviets and the Ukraine's secession from Russia.

The Central Rada, leaning on the local bourgeoisie and the kulaks, as well as the parties of the Ukrainian National-Mensheviks and National Socialist-Revolutionaries, and using the

Cossacks, cadet officers, and Haidamak detachments,[1] dispersed the Soviets and entered into a collusion with the counter-revolutionary headquarters in Mogilev and the so-called governments of the Don, Kuban, Northern Caucasus, Crimea and Moldavia. Taking the road of uniting the Kuban and the Ukraine in "one power", the Ukrainian bourgeois nationalists sought to set up a so-called homogeneous socialist government with Kiev as its centre. Simultaneously they disorganised the front and, stepping up aid to the counter-revolutionary forces of the Cossack Ataman Kaledin in the Don, launched fierce actions against Soviet power.

However, the October battles in Kiev irreversibly influenced the growth of the united actions of the Ukrainian and Russian workers and poor peasants, and the entire course of the struggle for the establishment of Soviet power in the Ukraine. As a result of the armed uprising Soviet power was proclaimed in Vinnitsa. On the Southwestern Front, and in units of the Romanian Front power also passed over to the Bolshevik-led revolutionary military committees, which recognised the power of the Council of People's Commissars in the whole country. The revolutionary soldiers of these fronts helped the workers and soldiers of the rear garrisons to establish Soviet power in Kamenets-Podolsk, Proskurov, Zhmerinka and a number of other towns of the Podolsk and Volyn provinces, in Kharkov Province, Yekaterinoslav, a number of towns of the Donets and Krivoi Rog coal basins. These victories clearly attested to the strengthening internationalist unity of the Bolshevik-led Russian and Ukrainian workers and peasants.

Enormous significance also attached to the vigorous measures taken by the Council of People's Commissars of the RSFSR to expose the perfidious policy of the Central Rada. The Leninist Council of People's Commissars demanded that the Rada put a stop to its struggle against the Ukrainian Soviets and its support of the Cossack counter-revolutionaries in the Don area. At the same time Soviet Russia rendered effective aid to the revolutionary working people of the Ukraine. The result of all

---

[1] The Haidamak troops were national formations of the counter-revolutionary nationalists.

this was that in November-December 1917 a new correlation of class forces took shape in the Ukraine, which substantially differed from the situation obtaining in October 1917.

In the new conditions, which favoured the rout of the counter-revolutionary forces of the Central Rada, the Ukrainian workers and revolutionary soldiers led by the Bolsheviks launched nation-wide struggle against it.

An important role in the successful conclusion of this struggle was played by the victory of the uprising in Kharkov, where power was taken over by the Revolutionary Committee led by the Bolshevik Artyom (F. A. Sergeyev). The First All-Ukraine Congress of Soviets held here on December 11-12, 1917 proclaimed the Ukraine a Soviet Republic, elected an All-Ukraine Central Executive Committee and formed the People's Secretariat (Artyom, E. B. Bosh, V. P. Zatonsky, N. A. Skrypnik and others) —the first Soviet government in the Ukraine. The congress adopted the resolution submitted by the Bolsheviks on the self-determination of the Ukraine, emphasising that the implementation of this right became possible only after the victory of the socialist revolution in Russia.

Proclaiming the federative link of the Ukrainian Republic with the Russian Republic, the congress extended the validity of the decrees of Soviet power to the territory of the Ukraine and declared that it would wage a vigorous struggle against the counter-revolutionary activity of the Central Rada. During December 1917 and January 1918 Soviet power was established throughout the Ukraine. On January 26, 1918, as a result of the successful uprising of the workers, supported by the Soviet troops, Kiev, the old capital, was liberated.

The formation of Soviet power in Moldavia was closely linked with the revolutionary process taking place throughout Russia. The struggle for the triumph of working people's power here, as in a number of other non-Russian regions, was complicated also by the socio-economic and political backwardness of the local multinational population, the insignificant numbers of the working class, the substantial influence wielded among the working people by the Menshevik, Socialist-Revolutionary and bourgeois-nationalistic parties and groups. The local counter-revolutionary forces grouping around the bourgeois-nationalistic Territorial Council Sfatul-Tseria had strong ties with and the support of the command of the Romanian Front headed by General Shcherbachev, the Socialist-Revolutionary and Menshevik Central Executive Committee of the Soviets of the Front, and the Ukrainian Central Rada. Successfully surmounting all these difficulties, the revolutionary workers and peasants, led by the Bolsheviks, established Soviet power in Kishinev, Bendery, Tiraspol, Ungeny and other cities and localities in Moldavia.

The triumph of working people's power in Kishinev on January 1 (14), 1918 was the date of the proclamation of Soviet power in Moldavia. However, the new power was able to consolidate itself only in the eastern part (Left Bank of the Dniester) of Moldavia. The Right Bank (between the Prut and Dniester), known as Bessarabia, was occupied in March 1918 by Romania, which brought in its troops in accordance with an agreement with the Sfatul-Tseria bourgeois nationalists and the governments of the Entente states.

After the rout early in 1918 of the counter-revolutionary sallies of the Cossack atamans, Dutov in the Southern Urals and Kaledin on the Don, Soviet power was established there. It was also consolidated in the Crimea, where, despite the resistance of the Tartar bourgeois nationalists the Taurida Soviet Socialist Republic was formed, and in the Caucasus.

The formation of proletarian power in the Northern Caucasus took place in extremely complex conditions. The counter-revolution was able to rely here on the wealthy Kuban and Terek Cossacks, who together with the Don, Orenburg and other Cossacks had been a privileged military estate under the former regime and had long been a reliable support of tsarism. The local Bolsheviks under the leadership of S. A. Buachidze, S. M. Kirov, I. D. Orakhelashvili and U. D. Buinaksky led the active struggle of the working masses for the victory of the revolution in fierce battles against the Cossack and White Guard troops who were aided by the foreign capitalists, and surmounted enormous difficulties stemming from the relatively small numbers of the working class and the existence of inter-national enmity between the numerous peoples of the region. At the Second Congress of the Terek Region, held in March 1918 in Pyatigorsk, the Terek People's Soviet Republic was proclaimed, which joined the RSFSR, and in April Soviet power emerged victorious in almost all of Daghestan.

As for Transcaucasia, Soviet power was first established in Baku, where already at the end of October 1917 all power in the city and the oil-industry region in the vicinity passed into the hands of the Soviet, which later elected the Council of People's Commissars (S.G. Shahumyan, M. A. Azizbekov, P. A. Japaridze, Y. D. Zevin, F. I. Makharadze, M. M. Tskhakaya and others), which has gone down in history under the name of the Baku Commune. On the rest of the territory of Transcaucasia, despite the selfless struggle of the Bolshevik-led revolutionary workers and soldiers, the bourgeois nationalistic parties—Azerbaijanian Musavatists, Armenian Dashnaks and Georgian Mensheviks—with substantial financial aid and military support of the imperialist powers formed a so-called Transcaucasian commissariat—a reactionary dictatorial regime, which did everything possible to prevent the victory of Soviet power, and to isolate Transcaucasia from the Soviet Republic.

The struggle for Soviet power in the regions of Central Asia and Kazakhstan was waged in equally harsh conditions. On October 31, 1917 as a result of four-day armed battles the railway workers' and soldiers' uprising overthrew the old power in Tashkent. The Third Territorial Congress of Soviets which met here in mid-November proclaimed Soviet power in the entire territory of Turkestan, and formed the Turkestan Council of People's Commissars under the chairmanship of F. I. Kolesov, a Bolshevik. A well-known figure in the Bolshevik Party, P. A. Kobozev, was appointed as special Commissar for the Affairs of Turkestan. However, the congress failed to resolve the question of national autonomy for Turkestan. Taking advantage of this, the bourgeois-nationalist groups with the support of the Russian counter-revolutionaries and foreign imperialist organisations organised a general Muslim Congress in the city of Kokand, where they set up their own government, styled "Kokand Autonomy". However, the Kokand separatists' attempts to overthrow Soviet power and to sever Turkestan from Soviet Russia, failed completely. Already in February 1918 the revolutionary contingents of the Red Guard workers, soldiers and dekhkans liquidated the "Kokand Autonomy". By March 1918 the main centre of the bourgeois-nationalist counter-revolution in Kazakhstan (Alash-Orda) was also eliminated.

Thus in the period from October 25, 1917 till the spring of 1918, within a few months, Soviet power was established on the enormous territory of the country, "not only ... in the large towns and factory areas, but also in the most remote corners of the country".[1] Explaining the causes of such a speedy success of the new proletarian power, Lenin said: "A wave of civil war swept over the whole of Russia, and everywhere we achieved victory with extraordinary ease precisely because the fruit had ripened, because the masses had already gone through the experience of collaboration with the bourgeoisie. Our slogan 'All Power to the Soviets', which the masses had tested in practice by long historical experience, had become part of their flesh and blood".[2] Thus, in the struggle for the triumph of the Great October Revolution and Soviet power firm foundations were laid for the unbreakable friendship of all the peoples of the Soviet state.

---

[1] V. I. Lenin, "Speech in the Moscow Soviet of Workers', Peasants' and Red Army Deputies, March 12, 1918. Verbatim Report", *Collected Works*, Vol. 27, p. 166.

[2] V. I. Lenin, "Extraordinary Seventh Congress of the R.C.P.(B.)", *Collected Works*, Vol. 27, p. 89.

Chapter II

FORMATION OF THE RSFSR, THE FIRST FEDERATIVE SOCIALIST STATE

As a result of the victory of the Great October Socialist Revolution a Soviet state was created in Russia. The establishment of proletarian power, a fundamentally new type of power by virtue of its class character and objectives, also signified a radical change in the nationalities policy of the new state. In place of the former Russian empire, that prison of the peoples, the construction was immediately launched, under the leadership of the Leninist Party, of a new, Soviet Russia, the first multinational socialist state in the history of the world.

First of all it was necessary to put into effect the chief provisions of the nationalities programme of the Bolsheviks: to ensure all the country's nations and nationalities full freedom and equality, support them in creating their national statehood, rally them into a single fraternal state union for struggle against the joint forces of internal counter-revolution and intenational imperialism, for the consolidation of Soviet power and the building of a socialist society.

The immediate conclusion of peace was an essential condition for the successful solution of all these tasks and simultaneously the first insistent demand of the war-weary working masses of all peoples of Russia.

The Struggle by the Soviets for Russia's Withdrawal from the Imperialist War

Following the adoption of the Decree on Peace by the Second All-Russia Congress of Soviets the Soviet government began persistently to implement the Leninist peace programme set forth in the text of the decree.

"On November 23rd I went to the Foreign Office," wrote the correspondent of the British *Manchester Guardian* in Russia, Morgan Philips Price.

"What a change the walls of the Russian Foreign Office had witnessed in these days! I remembered that two years previously, in the beautiful room overlooking the Winter Palace Square, with its French eighteenth-century chairs and tables and its portraits of the Romanoff Tsars and Tsaritzas on the wall, I had interviewed M. Sazonoff, when he was Nicolas II's Foreign Minister. We had spoken about possible reforms in Russia. Yes, the Minister had said, they were possible, even perhaps inevitable, provided that they remained within the bounds of Russia's traditions... As I looked at the chair where Sazonoff had sat, I wondered what he would say now. The Romanoffs were gone, Kerensky had gone, and what had become of the traditions?

"In the next room the Soviet Commissars were busy sorting over the documents and secret treaties, which Sazonoff and the Allied Ambassadors had drawn up and signed on behalf of their Governments...

"These, perhaps, were the 'ancient traditions' to which M. Sazonoff was referring! There could be no doubt that the Soviet Commissars were making short work of them by the simple medium of publicity.

"From the balcony of the Foreign Office a great red banner was flying in the winter wind. On it were inscribed the words, 'Long live peace'. The whole atmosphere of the place gave the impression that the Russian revolutionaries had seriously entered upon a struggle for peace."[1]

Indeed, the text of Lenin's Decree on Peace, apart from being

---

[1] Morgan Philips Price, *My Reminiscences of the Russian Revolution*, London, 1921, pp. 182-83.

published in newspapers, was repeatedly transmitted over the cruiser *Aurora*'s radio transmitter, the "New Holland" naval radio station, which was stationed in Petrograd, and by the Tsarskoye Selo radio, a powerful station of the time. The peasant messengers, emissaries from the factories and plants and particularly the soldiers' delegates took with them from the Smolny heavy packages of newspapers with the peace proposals of the Bolsheviks. Soviet power also organised the mass printing of leaflets with the text of the Decree on Peace not only in Russian, but in foreign languages as well, which were quickly distributed throughout Russia, and above all at the fronts, among the troops in the field. As the newspaper *Novaya Zhizn* reported on October 28, 1917, "Four million copies of the Decree on Peace have been distributed from planes on all fronts." The leaflets circled over the jagged lines of dugouts and trenches like white birds. The plane in the grey sky brought the joyful news to the frontline: Lenin demands peace! To all the belligerent nations and their governments revolutionary Petrograd had announced the proposal of the Workers' and Peasants' Government of Russia to start immediate talks for a just and democratic peace.

On November 5, *Pravda* reported, a delegation of some 300 Belgian workers, who were working at the Sestroretsk plant and at other plants in Petrograd, came to the Smolny. Lenin, Chairman of the Council of People's Commissars, received the delegation, who asked to convey to the working class of Russia that the "Belgian workers were wholeheartedly with them in the struggle for peace and socialism".[1]

The Soviet peace programme (a proposal for universal democratic peace, defence of countries and peoples fighting for their liberation, abolition of secret diplomacy and publication of secret treaties) aroused an immediate response abroad, too. Already on November 9 the United States government held a special session, which lasted a whole day. During those days alarming reports, dispatches and telegrams were sent from Petrograd to London and Paris.

George Buchanan, British Ambassador to Russia, dispatched

---

[1] *Vladimir Ilyich Lenin. Biographical Chronicle,* Vol. 5, Politizdat, Moscow, 1974, p. 35 (in Russian).

detailed information to the British government on the events in Petrograd and the first statements and actions of the Bolshevik government. Captain Jacques Sadoul, a member of the French military mission to Russia in 1917, wrote about this in his *Notes on the Bolshevik Revolution:*

"*Petrograd, November 9 (22), 1917*

"This morning the general picked me up in his car. They had searched for me all night. The Embassy had been struck by lightning in the form of a note of the Bolshevik government, which officially declared its formation and confirmed the proposal for an immediate armistice on all fronts made at the Congress of Soviets. . ."[1]

On November 8-10 Western political circles hardly believed in the longevity and soundness of the Bolshevik experiments and therefore were just as sceptical about Soviet intentions to publish the secret treaties. "That the real Russia will ever consent to make a separate peace, or can acquiesce in all the extravagances of the Soviet manifestos, is impossible to believe," the London *Times* wrote on November 9, 1917 (p. 7).

At 6 p.m. on November 8, 1917, in a mansion belonging to the British Embassy there gathered the alarmed diplomats of the Entente countries. US Ambassador Francis, British Ambassador Buchanan, French Ambassador Noulens and others, the chiefs and members of military missions, various advisers and journalists discussed the situation and adopted a decision: not to recognise Soviet power nor to enter into any relations with it. Accordingly, the Soviet Decree on Peace, the statement contained therein, and the declaration were perceived as a propaganda ploy that did not merit serious attention.

However, several days later, after the rout of the Kerensky-Krasnov revolt and after the victory of Soviet power in Moscow and many other cities, it became clear that the first forecasts and predictions of the Western diplomats were totally unfounded.

The Soviet Republic gained in strength and began putting into effect its foreign policy programme. On November 8, the

---

[1] Jacques Sadoul, *Notes sur la révolution bolchevique,* Sirène, Paris, 1920, p. 101.

People's Commissariat for Foreign Affairs dispatched official notes to the ambassadors and envoys of the USA, Britain, France, Italy, Serbia, and Belgium requesting them to consider the Decree on Peace as a proposal for an armistice on all fronts and the opening of peace negotiations. Two days later the Commissariat sent notes to the neutral countries (Switzerland, Norway, the Netherlands, Spain, Denmark, and Sweden), requesting them to convey the Soviet government's peace proposals to the governments and the public of the neutral countries.[1]

The envoys of Norway, Switzerland and Sweden, and later that of Denmark, confirming the receipt of the appeal, reported that they had taken "corresponding steps". Even more active and friendly was the response of the Spanish Ambassador who replied in a letter that he would immediately telegraph the contents of the note to Madrid in order to facilitate the conclusion of peace which all humanity was impatiently awaiting. However, the Spanish government, as it turned out, not only did not approve of the actions of its Ambassador, but, on the contrary, hastened to punish him for his acceptance of the Soviet government's appeal by recalling him from Russia.

The Soviet government's vigorous actions showed to the West that it was no joking matter and that the situation was even more serious than had been supposed. The turbulent November of 1917 passed in endless diplomatic meetings, conferences, negotiations. Politicians and diplomats held sessions in the spacious offices on Downing Street in London and the Quai d'Orsay in Paris, in the White House in Washington and on Wilhelmstrasse in Berlin. Also in Petrograd Buchanan and Francis discussed almost daily the question "what to do" about the Bolsheviks, and made long- and short-term forecasts.

Late at night on November 9 the ambassadors gathered in the premises of the British Embassy and reaffirmed their previous decision—under no circumstances to recognise the Soviet government nor to reply to its peace proposals. And in the meantime in accordance with instructions received from London, Washington and Paris the diplomats and military representatives

---

[1] See *Documents on the Foreign Policy of the USSR*, Vol. I, Politizdat, Moscow, 1957, pp. 17, 22-23 (in Russian).

of Britain, the USA and France established active contacts with the counter-revolutionaries, helping them to organise the anti-Soviet forces for the overthrow of Soviet power.

The chief of the US military mission, Mr. Kerth, established close contact with the acting commander-in-chief of the Russian army, General N. N. Dukhonin. General Lavergne of France also set off for Dukhonin's headquarters in Mogilev. The Entente representatives also headed towards the Don and Northern Caucasus, to Kaledin and other counter-revolutionary and bourgeois-nationalistic leaders. Their attention was drawn to the Ukrainian Rada and the Transcaucasian governments; they were plotting the seizure of the lands and riches of Siberia, and the North and South of Russia.

Meanwhile General Dukhonin notified the Allied diplomats in Petrograd that all contacts should be made through him alone. The Socialist-Revolutionary leaders Chaikovsky and Skobelev visited US Ambassador Francis, assuring him of their loyalty and requesting aid and support for Dukhonin. On his part, General Kerth of the USA handed Dukhonin an official US protest against any kind of peace negotiations. An analogous protest was sent to Dukhonin by the British and French representatives. It appears that the Entente diplomats followed precisely Dukhonin's request to have dealings only with him as the commander-in-chief of the Russian army.

The Entente countries' reckoning was simple: to hamper the opening of peace talks between the Soviets and the Austro-German bloc and in a short period to overthrow Soviet power.

All the enemies of the Soviet Republic flocked to Dukhonin in Mogilev—generals and officers, deposed ministers of the Provisional Government, leaders of the Socialist-Revolutionaries and the Mensheviks, etc. Here also were based numerous representatives of the Entente countries, the chiefs and members of military missions, correspondents, all manner of observers, etc. General Dukhonin's headquarters turned into an active and dangerous seat of counter-revolution, blocking the realisation of both the domestic and foreign policy plans of Soviet power.

In the circumstances, urgent measures were essential for the rout of the counter-revolutionary headquarters. In the early hours of November 9 the "New Holland" radio station transmitted on behalf of the Council of People's Commissars a special government order to General Dukhonin. "Now that Soviet power has been established in all the major parts of the country," it stated, "the Council of People's Commissars considers it necessary to make an immediate formal armistice proposal to all the belligerent countries, both allied and hostile."[1] Dukhonin was instructed immediately to propose an armistice to the Austro-German troops.

During talks with Dukhonin over the direct line that same night, Lenin demanded that he report on how the above instructions of the Council of People's Commissars were being fulfilled. Dukhonin replied that he did not recognise the Soviet government. In answer to this Lenin announced the removal of Dukhonin from the post of commander-in-chief. Former ensign N. V. Krylenko, a 32-year-old Bolshevik, was appointed in his place.

On the same day (November 9) the Council of People's Commissars sent, over the heads of the army and navy command, a direct wireless message to the soldiers and sailors, to all regimental, divisional, corps, army and other committees. "Soldiers, the cause of peace is in your hands!" read the message written by Lenin. "Do not allow the counter-revolutionary generals to frustrate the great cause of peace... Maintain the strictest revolutionary and military order.

"Let the regiments at the front immediately elect representatives to start formal negotiations for an armistice with the enemy. The Council of People's Commissars authorises you to do this... Soldiers, the cause of peace is in your hands! Maintain vigilance, restraint and energy, and the cause of peace will triumph!"[2] In his speech to a meeting of front representatives the new commander-in-chief, N. V. Krylenko, described the Soviet government's wireless message of November 9 to the Army and Navy

---

[1] *Documents on the Foreign Policy of the USSR,* Vol. I p. 17 (in Russian).

[2] V. I. Lenin, "Wireless Message to all Regimental, Divisional, Corps, Army and Other Committees, to All Soldiers of the Revolutionary Army and Sailors of the Revolutionary Navy", *Collected Works,* Vol. 26, p. 312.

on the question of peace, written by Lenin, as a "de factor cease-fire". At the time, the representatives of Britain, the USA and France were doing everything possible to save Dukhonin's head-quarters, establishing intensified official and unofficial contacts with him and his retinue.

But the appeal by the Council of People's Commissars and Lenin decisively influenced the course of events. On all fronts the revolutionary army committees launched negotiations with the Austro-German troops on concluding an armistice. These were the so-called soldiers' peaces. First "peaces" were signed on the scale of regiments and divisions, then corps and armies, and, finally, on the scale of the fronts. Already on November 14, 1917 the first soldiers' armistice treaty was signed between representatives of the soldiers of the Russian Grenadier corps, forming part of the Second Army of the Western Front, and the representatives of the German army confronting it. Soon nego-tiations on the conclusion of such "soldiers' peaces" were signed by the 19th Infantry Division, the 38th and 3rd corps of the Tenth Army, the 15th Army Corps of the Third Army, and other units. The entire Western Front signed a two-months armistice on November 21. This signified an important success for the Bolsheviks and Soviet power in the struggle for peace. In this connection a large demonstration of workers and soldiers was held in Minsk on November 25 under the slogans: "Down with the world blood bath!" "Long live the Third Internation-al!" "Long live the Council of People's Commissars!", "Long live Soviet power!"[1]

Shortly afterwards, on November 27, an armistice was con-cluded on the Northern Front, on December 1—on the South-western, on December 4, on the Romanian Front. It should be noted that in the struggle for the realisation of the Leninist Decree on Peace on the latter two fronts the soldiers' masses, headed by the Bolsheviks, had to overcome the stubborn resis-tance of both the top generals, Cadets, Mensheviks and Socialist-Revolutionaries, and the Ukrainian Central Rada and local

---

[1] See N. M. Yakupov, *Revolution and Peace (The Soldiers' Masses Against the Imperialist War. 1917-March 1918)*, Mysl Publishers, Moscow, 1980, pp. 157-59 et al.

bourgeois nationalists, who sought in every way to thwart the measures taken by the Council of People's Commissars to put a stop to the hostilities. The conditions of the soldiers' peaces were analogous, as a rule. They envisaged a stop to the hostilities and creation of a neutral zone between the troops, and defined the proper order of passing through this zone. The armistice treaties included also clauses forbidding the transfer of German troops from the East to the West. The heretofore unheard-of soldiers' peaces served as an important step on the way to an armistice and to peace. On November 24, 1917 *Pravda* wrote in this respect: "There is no more shooting between the Black and the Baltic seas... The soldiers will conclude peace even if the generals do not want to."

Later, N. I. Podvoisky, an outstanding leader of the Bolshevik Party and the Soviet state, who was the People's Commissar for War at the time, wrote in his memoirs: "The most striking in this experience of direct struggle by the masses for peace, unprecedented in the history of wars, was the fact that the talks yielded the required results... The important thing ... was to achieve an actual end to the hostilities on all fronts while the conditions for an armistice were being worked out in Brest, to where the Soviet delegation had already started out from Petrograd. And this calculation proved to be fully justified."[1]

Simultaneously with the conclusion of the soldiers' peaces the counter-revolutionary headquarters was successfully routed. During these November days N. V. Krylenko, with a detachment of Baltic sailors and soldiers from the Petrograd garrison, set out for the headquarters. From Petrograd the Bolshevik M. K. Ter-Arutyunyants was dispatched to the Revolutionary Military Committee of the Western Front. According to a special plan for seizing the headquarters, two detachments were sent there—the Northern under the command of R. I. Berzin and the Southern, led by E. I. Lysakov, member of the RMC of the Second Army.

So as not to permit Dukhonin to rely on the troops located in the vicinity of the headquarters, experienced propagandists and agitators, members of the Bolshevik military organisations who

---

[1] *Istorichesky arkhiv,* No. 5, 1957, p. 150.

were well known in the army, were sent to these detachments. An active stance was adopted by the Bolsheviks in Mogilev itself. On November 18 they set up a Revolutionary Military Committee, which took power into its own hands. On the following day the Petrograd detachment headed by N. V. Krylenko entered the city. The counter-revolutionary headquarters was eliminated, and Dukhonin was shot dead by the soldiers and sailors.

At the time of the rout of the headquarters the Soviet Republic was notified by the government and military command of Germany and its allies of their consent to conduct armistice negotiations. On November 20 a Soviet delegation arrived in Brest-Litovsk, where the headquarters of the German Eastern Front was situated. Together with diplomats, delegates from all strata of the working people of Russia—the worker N. A. Obukhov, the peasant R. N. Stashkov, the sailor F. V. Olich and the soldier N. K. Belyakov—arrived in Brest.

The talks were held in a complex situation. The German delegation was unwilling at first to accept the Soviet conditions, but eventually, on December 3(15) an armistice treaty was signed between Soviet Russia on the one hand, and Germany, Austria-Hungary, Bulgaria, and Turkey, on the other.

In accordance with the treaty, an armistice was established for 28 days at first, with a subsequent prolongation of the term unless one of the sides rejected it by giving a seven-day advance warning. A particularly disputed issue during the talks was the question of transferring German troops from the Eastern to the Western front. The Soviet delegation was vigorously opposed to such transfers, insisting on the inclusion of a corresponding clause in the treaty. The government of the Soviet Republic sought to prevent the strengthening of German positions in the West, to ensure a real armistice for the fraternising soldiers, and not merely to prepare their transfer to the Western Front.

Despite the strenuous opposition of the German delegates the Soviet representatives achieved the inclusion in the treaty of the following clause: "Further, the contracting parties obligate themselves not to undertake any transfers of troops until January 14, 1918 (January 1, 1918, Russian Time), on the front between the Black Sea and the Baltic Sea, unless such transfers had already been begun at the moment of the signing of the armistice."[1]

Thus along the entire front from the Black to the Baltic seas the guns and machine-guns became silent. Millions of soldiers of the Russian army were able to return home and to take part in the coming transformations of the country.

The conclusion of the armistice on the Russo-German front met with a broad response throughout the world. The example of Russia was extremely infectious and attractive. That is why at the end of 1917 and beginning of 1918 anti-war moods and actions were greatly enhanced in the majority of the European countries. A wave of strike actions and demonstrations spread through Germany, France, Britain and Austria-Hungary.

While concluding the armistice with the German-Austrian bloc, the Soviet government late in November 1917 continued its attempts to involve the Entente countries in the talks. On November 28 the Council of People's Commissars appealed anew to the governments and peoples of all belligerent states. But once again the governments of Britain, France and the USA remained silent. They held numerous consultations, elaborating a common policy towards the Bolshevik regime, which was gaining in strength day by day. In the first two weeks after the Bolsheviks' coming to power the diplomatic representatives of the Entente countries adhered in the main to wait-and-see positions. But around the 20th of November there began to take shape the contours of the future policy, which was destined to become the course of the Western powers over a number of years.

On November 24, US Secretary of State L. Lansing dispatched a letter to America's allies proposing the convening of a special conference to discuss the situation in Russia. By then the Dukhonin venture had failed and the positions of Soviet power had obviously grown stronger.

The representatives of Britain and France, Colonel House, an emissary of the US President, and several former diplomats of the Provisional Government (who, having been deposed by So-

---

[1] John W. Wheeler-Bennett, *Brest-Litovsk, The Forgotten Peace, March 1918*, MacMillan and Co., London, 1939, p. 379.

viet power, represented nobody) met in Paris. The participants in the Paris meeting confirmed their intention not to recognise Soviet power and to ignore its peace proposals.

There followed also new statements by the foreign ministers of the Entente countries on the non-recognition of Soviet power. Minister Balfour of Britain stated that the British government had no intention of recognising Lenin's government, but would support the Cossacks, Ukrainian nationalists and other forces which stood in opposition to Lenin and his programme of negotiating with Germany. Pichon, head of the diplomatic department of France, made it amply clear in the Chamber of Deputies that France would be in contact with all the sober-minded elements in Russia, with those who retained a feeling of independence and loyalty, an instinct for the need for order and freedom. US State Secretary R. Lansing also urged support for any movement directed against the Bolsheviks.[1]

On December 22-23 the representatives of the Entente countries gathered in Paris for a new conference. Assistant Secretary of State for Foreign Affairs Lord R. Cecil and Secretary for War Lord A. Milner arrived from London. The USA was again represented by Colonel House. The role of hospitable hosts was played by the Prime Minister, "iron tiger" Georges Clemenceau, and Foreign Minister Pichon. By the opening of the conference the allied diplomatic departments disposed of broad information on the situation in Russia. They had already decided to render financial aid to the counter-revolutionary and nationalistic forces. Talks on granting hundreds of thousands of dollars to General Kaledin were reaching conclusion. Substantial sums were allocated to the Ukrainian Rada and the Transcaucasian anti-Bolshevik forces.

The Paris conference formalised the planned measures and distributed duties among the allies. They were preparing for an organised and prolonged struggle against Soviet power envisaging the use, in particular, of separatist strivings of the bourgeois nationalists of a number of non-Russian regions of the country.

---

[1] See M. P. Iroshnikov, A. O. Chubaryan, *The Secret Is Disclosed. On the Publication of the Secret Treaties of the Tsarist and Provisional Governments,* Politizdat, Moscow, 1970, pp. 42-43 (in Russian).

On the first day of the conference's work its participants adopted a special memorandum stating the need to render aid to all forces fighting against the Bolsheviks in the Caucasus, Siberia, Finland, the Ukraine, and the Don. The next day the British and French representatives signed a special agreement on the division of spheres of influence in Russia. The British undertook to oversee the development of events in the Caucasus, in Armenia, Georgia, and the Don region; the French, in Bessarabia, the Crimea, and the Ukraine. Parallel with the Paris conference, the USA, Britain and France reached an agreement to the effect that the Russian Far East and Siberia came within the sphere of influence of the USA and Japan.

Thus, at the end of December 1917 the Entente countries and the USA determined their political course with respect to the Soviet Republic. They resolved not to recognise Soviet power, to reject the Soviet peace programme, and to begin active preparations to unite all the anti-Bolshevik and nationalistic forces.

In the circumstances, the interests of the revolution insistently demanded the speedy realisation of other fundamental provisions of the Soviet peace programme, including the publication of the secret treaties concluded by the tsarist and Provisional governments. It was essential to expose the real aims of the policy of the domestic bourgeoisie and international imperialism—seizure of foreign territories and amassing new profits—before all the working people of Russia and of foreign countries. This also played a crucial role in exposing the mercenary class content of the separatist plans of the bourgeois nationalists of various hues, in consolidating the new state union of the peoples of Russia, and strengthening their friendship in the joint struggle for the definitive triumph of the Great October Revolution and implementation of socialist transformations throughout the country.

After the takeover of the former Foreign Ministry on November 4, Red Guard workers from the Siemens-Schuckert company's military and naval equipment plant situated on Vasilyevsky Island, and Baltic sailors were put on guard duty in the premises, and soldiers from the revolutionary Pavlovsky regiment guarded the entrance of the special "armoured rooms" where in several huge fire-proof safes special folders were kept with copies of dispatches, reports and secret treaties.

On November 7 the Petrograd newspaper *Dyen* printed an interview of its correspondent with a well-known Bolshevik I. A. Zalkind, whom the Council of People's Commissars appointed representative of the People's Commissariat for Foreign Affairs. A professional revolutionary and biologist with a knowledge of several foreign languages, the man now entrusted with ensuring the fulfilment of the pledges given to the country's working people by the Bolshevik Party and Soviet power, said that now that the Bolsheviks had taken over the Ministry, he had in his hands the keys from all the secret treaties Russia had concluded with the imperialist governments. We had been handed also all the keys from the filing cabinets containing the codes, he said, and hence from now on Russia's foreign policy would be a foreign policy of the people.

Intensive work on the selection, translation and decoding of the secret papers began as soon as direct access to the filing cabinets and safes of the Foreign Ministry's diplomatic archives was made possible and a behind-the-scenes view was obtained of the launching of the First World War. The entire work was carried out under the direct guidance and with the active participation of I. A. Zalkind, his close assistant N. G. Markin, who was one of the Bolshevik leaders of the Baltic sailors, and assistant-professor E. D. Polivanov, a noted linguist who was enlisted as an expert. They were aided by experienced cipher clerks sent on the instructions of the Naval Revolutionary Committee from the Chief Naval Headquarters, and the coding department was headed by V. P. Leman, an expert in military codes.

Charged with the task of finding something to print the next day in the newsapers. E. D. Polivanov entered the "secret room". "There was," he relates in his memoirs, "a huge built-in filing cabinet with a sturdy lock on six thick steel bars, which moved simultaneously simply by turning the key. It was intended for storing especially important and secret papers. All alone in the room, I opened the filing cabinet and first it seemed hopeless quickly to find the necessary papers: in front of me on several shelves stood rows of huge cardboard folders; some of them had labels listing the contents, but they gave no hint of containing any secret treaties. However, as though by intuition I took the first folder on the left from the top shelf, and in a minute realised that I held in my hands just what was needed, and that it would suffice for at least the first days of publication.

"They were not the texts of the treaties themselves," E. D. Polivanov continued, "they were something even more essential to us at the moment: here was a resumé of all the treaties and obligations that had been concluded between Russia and its allies in the period 1914-1917.

"The thing is that when Tereshchenko had taken over the Foreign Ministry he apparently had been totally unacquainted with the Ministry's previous work; the content of the secret treaties themselves could not have been familiar to him prior to his appointment. And the folder I had chosen, it turned out, contained a concise but quite detailed outline of our relations with the allies, an outline including a number of direct quotations from the treaties, references to their most important points, and some agreements were even given in full. The resumé was compiled directly for the personal use of the Minister (Tereshchenko) and in addition to a straightforward summary of documentary material it also contained commentaries on it. For instance, regarding the promises given Romania for its action, a cynical note had been added to the effect that these promises were clearly exaggerated and neither the Russian government nor the allies intended to honour them. In short, it was just what we needed.

"It was decided that I would select whatever could be dispatched to the newspapers right away, and once again I found myself in the 'secret room' which I had not left until 2 a.m. A telephone call was put through to the Smolny for a typist, a Party member, to whom I dictated, translating document after document straight from the French original until the early hours of the morning. The next day the newspapers were sold out immediately. It was the day the printing of the secret treaties was begun, and the sensational publication continued for several weeks, met every day with unabated interest and tension and the avid curiosity of the masses who were revolted on learning of the dear price the peoples of Russia had paid for the tsar's secret diplomacy."[1]

---

[1] *Archeographic Yearbook for 1963*, Nauka Publishers, Moscow, 1964, pp. 201-02 (in Russian).

On November 10, 1917 *Pravda, Izvestia, Gazeta Vremennogo Rabochego i Krestyanskogo Pravitelstva,*[1] and *Rabochy i Soldat* printed the first lot of secret materials from the former Foreign Ministry's archives. *Pravda* wrote the same day: "Now the Russian revolution is tearing apart and laying bare the secrets of capitalist diplomacy... The soldiers of Russia, Britain and France will learn what they shed their blood for." Among the secret papers first published that day were a 1916 agreement between Great Britain, France and Russia concerning Constantinople and the Straits, and several secret telegrams addressed to the diplomatic representatives of Russia in Paris, London, Rome, Washington, Tokyo, and Stockholm.

The People's Commissariat for Foreign Affairs did not restrict itself to the publication of the secret diplomatic materials in Soviet periodicals. Already the following month (December 1917) a booklet was issued in a simple blue-grey paper cover, bearing the title *Compilation of Secret Papers from the Archives of the Former Ministry of Foreign Affairs.* N. G. Markin was the chief editor of all seven instalments of the *Compilation,* the last of which was put out in February 1918. Every single copy of the *Compilation*'s two editions was sold out immediately

The main feature of the *Compilation* was its extraordinary topicality and its political incisiveness. Each of the seven instalments helped to expose the annexationist foreign policies of the imperialist states and to strengthen the prestige of the Soviet Republic' on the international arena, and helped Soviet power to win the trust and solid support of the multinational working people of Russia and the world over. Symbolically, the first instalment of the *Compilation* was put out under the slogan: "Long live the brotherthool of all peoples! Down with the alliances of imperialist capitalists and the bourgeoisie. Long live the alliance of the labouring people of the whole world!" The foreword to the first instalment of the papers noted: "The aim of this *Compilation* is to acquaint the broad masses with the content of the papers that had been stored in the armoured rooms and fire-proof safes of the former Ministry of Foreign Affairs—one of the bailiwicks of the bourgeoisie of all countries... Let

---

[1] Organ of the Council of People's Commissars of Soviet Russia.

the working people of the world know how the diplomats sold their lives behind their backs; annexed lands; brazenly oppressed small nations.

"How they oppressed and suppressed them politically and economically; concluded infamous treaties.

"Let everyone know how the imperialists seized entire regions with the stroke of a pen, watering the fields with human blood.

"Each disclosed paper is a sharp weapon against the bourgeoisie."[1]

The published papers on the secret diplomacy of tsarism and the imperialist bourgeoisie of various states became known to the broad masses of working people of Russia and throughout the world. From these papers the peoples of Russia, and then also all the belligerent and neutral states learned the appalling truth about the behind-the-scenes wrangling and dirty deals of the imperialist bourgeoisie and its political henchmen, which resulted in the outbreak of the First World War.

The publications of the secret treaties was of enormous importance in strengthening the positions of the Bolsheviks and the Leninist Council of People's Commissars, and not only in Russia's central regions, but also among the inhabitants of its outlying ethnic areas. This made it possible speedily to implement another important item of the Bolshevik programme, demonstrating once again the trustworthiness of its pledges. By publishing the secret treaties and exposing their predatory, oppressive content, Soviet power displayed its fundamental break with the policy of the tsarist and Provisional governments. The abolition of secret diplomacy not only was a major foreign policy action of the Council of People's Commissars, but formed part of the fundamentally new type of nationalities policy conducted by the Soviet government, with Lenin at its head, following the triumph of the October Revolution.

Delivering the political report of the Central Committee to the Seventh RCP(B) Congress on March 7, 1918, Lenin emphasised that the triumphal advance of Soviet power through-

---

[1] *Compilation of Secret Papers from the Archives of the Former Ministry of Foreign Affairs*, No. 1, 2nd ed., December 1917, p. 1 (in Russian).

out the country following the victory of the October armed uprising in Petrograd was largely made possible by the fact that the proletarian revolution took place in Russia at an exceptionally favourable moment, "when neither of the two gigantic groups of plunderers was in a position immediately either to hurl itself at the other, or to unite with the other against us".[1]

Launching a vigorous struggle for the achievement of a universal, democratic and just peace, the Soviet government successfully used the imperialist contradictions between the two belligerent coalitions, that is, the Entente states and the Quadripartite Austro-German Alliance.

Encountering the manifest refusal of the "allied" powers (Britain, France, the USA, Italy, etc.) to take part in the peace talks repeatedly proposed by Soviet power "to all the belligerent peoples and their governments", the Council of People's Commissars, with the active support of the revolutionary masses of soldiers, succeeded in achieving a temporary ceasefire already in mid-November 1917, and then, at the beginning of December, also the signing of an armistice agreement with Germany and its allies. However, as it became ever clearer that the governments of the Entente countries would not take part in the Brest-Litovsk peace conference, the position of the German militarists also changed, and, in the form of an ultimatum, they proposed extortionate conditions for peace at the beginning of January 1918. Thus there emerged a direct threat of armed intervention by Kaiser Germany.

The principled line of struggle for the withdrawal of Soviet Russia from the imperialist war and the conclusion of the Brest peace, elaborated and implemented under the leadership of Lenin, clearly showed how, in complex conditions, the Communist Party and Soviet government, adhering to genuine Marxist positions, subordinated at a critical moment the solution of the nationalities question to the primary issue of consolidating the victory of the proletarian revolution and strengthening the Soviet state. The minutes of the sessions of the Party Central Committee and other Party documents, and numerous materials writ-

---

[1] V. I. Lenin, "Extraordinary Seventh Congress of the R.C.P.(B.)", *Collected Works*, Vol. 27, p. 93.

ten by Lenin testify to the sharp struggle which Lenin and his followers had to wage simultaneously on two fronts. In the Central Committee a struggle was waged against the pseudo-revolutionary tactics of the group of "Left Communists",[1] who demanded the continuation of the war at any cost "in the interests of world revolution", and the adventuristic position of L. D. Trotsky, who advanced a "cunning" formula: neither a war, nor an extortionate peace.

Lenin's approach was that after the victory of the October Revolution the decisive factor in solving national and international questions was the absolute need to preserve and consolidate the first proletarian power. It was extremely important, Lenin held, to ensure the strengthening of the Soviet Republic in every possible way as the sole existing basis of the world proletarian revolution, as the basis for the further successful development of the entire world revolutionary and national liberation process. That is why in the "Afterword to the Theses on the Question of the Immediate Conclusion of a Separate and Annexationist Peace", in a speech at the session of the Party Central Committee on February 18, 1918, and in other articles and speeches of this period, Lenin persistently demonstrated the need to accept the extortionate peace conditions in order to save the proletarian revolution that had triumphed in Russia. "Our socialist republic," he noted, "has done all it could, and continues to do all it can to give effect to the right to self-determination of Finland, the Ukraine, etc. But if ... the existence of the socialist republic is being imperilled at the present moment on account of the violation of the right to self-determination of several nations (Poland, Lifland, Courland, etc.),"[2] he stressed, "...the preservation of the republic that has already begun the socialist revolution is most important to us and to the *international socialist movement*".[3]

---

[1] An opposition among the Bolsheviks who opposed Lenin's theory of the socialist revolution.

[2] V. I. Lenin, "On the History of the Question of the Unfortunate Peace", *Collected Works*, Vol. 26, p. 449.

[3] V. I. Lenin, "Afterword to the Theses on the Question of the Immediate Conclusion of a Separate and Annexationist Peace", *Collected Works*, Vol. 26, p. 452.

In a truly dramatic struggle lasting almost two months the Bolshevik Party rejected the adventuristic policy of the "Left Communists" and Trotsky. Lenin substantiated and proved without a shadow of doubt the correctness of his line to achieve an immediate peace, uphold unity within the Party and the Central Committee, and ensure the young, as yet vulnerable proletarian state the vitally necessary peaceful respite. As borne out by later events, Lenin's course for the conclusion of the Brest peace was an example of a scientifically grounded and at the same time principled, genuinely Marxist approach to a correct correlation of the national and international in the development of the revolutionary process. At the cost of heavy losses the first proletarian state and the working people of Soviet Russia honourably discharged their internationalist duty to the international working-class and national liberation movements.[1]

Socialist and Democratic Transformations

The principled approach by the proletarian power to the practical solution of complex and responsible problems of the nationalities policy in the conditions of Russia was of tremendous international significance not only for the destinies of socialism in the Soviet Republic, but for the world revolutionary liberation movement as a whole.

The new Soviet government headed by Lenin convincingly showed from the outset to the peoples of the country and the whole world that its nationalities policy was the very opposite of the policy of oppression of the peoples and fanning of international hostility conducted by tsarism and the bourgeois-landlord governments. "There is not, and cannot be, another government," said Lenin, "which would recognise as clearly as we do and declare so distinctly to one and all that the attitude of old Russia (tsarist Russia, Russia of the war parties) to the nationalities populating Russia was criminal, that this attitude was im-

---

[1] See S. S. Gililov, *V. I. Lenin, the Organiser of the Soviet Multinational State*, Politizdat, Moscow, 1972, pp. 52-53 (in Russian).

permissible, that it aroused the rightful and indignant protest and discontent of the oppressed nationalities. There is not, and cannot be, another government which would so openly admit this, which would conduct this anti-chauvinist propaganda, a propaganda that recognises the guilt of old Russia, tsarist Russia, Kerensky Russia—a government which would conduct propaganda against the forcible incorporation of other nationalities into Russia. This is not mere words—this is an obvious political fact, absolutely indisputable and plain for all to see."[1]

The historic Second All-Russia Congress of Soviets began immediately putting into effect the Bolshevik programme on the nationalities question, which was aimed at eliminating the consequences of the bourgeois-landlord domination, at establishing peace and friendship between the peoples. The first decrees of Soviet power served as the practical expression of this programme of the Bolsheviks in the proletarian revolution. Expressing the policy of the Leninist working-class party, the first Soviet decrees were directed at the destruction of the bourgeois-landlord system and at the legislative formulation and development of new social relations. They were a powerful tool in the hands of Soviet power with the aid of which it implemented, as we already know, the dismantling of the old state machinery, waged a struggle against counter-revolution, created a new administrative apparatus, eliminated all forms of social and national oppression, and carried out socialist changes.

These were fundamentally new laws by their class essence, laws which were no longer a tool of oppression and suppression of the working people and the exploited masses but a major means for suppressing the exploiters and achieving the social emancipation and national liberation of the working people of the whole of multinational Russia. Embodying the basic requirements of the working masses, and being the result of their revolutionary creativity, the first decrees became an incontrovertible proof of the fact that Soviet power took its policy from the soldiers at the front, the peasants in the countryside, the workers in the city. As Lenin emphasised in this connection in the early post-

---

[1] V. I. Lenin, "Ninth All-Russia Congress of Soviets", *Collected Works*, Vol. 33, pp. 148-49.

The cruiser *Aurora* (1917)

Къ Гражданамъ Россіи.

Временное Правительство низложено. Государственная власть перешла въ руки органа Петроградскаго Совѣта Рабочихъ и Солдатскихъ Депутатовъ Военно-Революціоннаго Комитета, стоящаго во главѣ Петроградскаго пролетаріата и гарнизона.

Дѣло, за которое боролся народъ: немедленное предложеніе демократическаго мира, отмѣна помѣщичьей собственности на землю, рабочій контроль надъ производствомъ, созданіе Совѣтскаго Правительства — это дѣло обезпечено.

ДА ЗДРАВСТВУЕТЪ РЕВОЛЮЦІЯ РАБОЧИХЪ, СОЛДАТЪ И КРЕСТЬЯНЪ!

Военно-Революціонный Комитетъ
при Петроградскомъ Совѣтѣ
Рабочихъ и Солдатскихъ Депутатовъ.

25 октября 1917 г. 10 ч. утра.

"To the Citizens of Russia!". The 1917 Appeal of the Revolutionary Military Committee

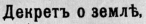

The Decree on Land

The Decree on Peace

Declaration of Rights of the Peoples of Russia

A peasant revolutionary detachment (1917)

Peasant youth going to defend Petrograd (1919)

Demonstration of workers and Red Guards (Chita, 1917)

Red Guards and soldiers in Petrograd (1917)

Proclamation of Soviet power in Tashkent (1917)

Y. M. Sverdlov

N. A. Semashko

P. A. Japaridze

S. G. Shahumyan

G. V. Chicherin

J. J. Anvelt

G. K. Orjonikidze

V. M. Primakov

A. M. Kollontai

N. G. Chervyakov

A. V. Lunacharsky

A. V. Belshev

M. V. Frunze

E. Yaroslavsky

V. S. Mickevičius-Kapsukas

A. F. Sergeyev (Artyom)

N. I. Podvoisky

S. M. Kirov

F. E. Dzerzhinsky

V. A. Antonov-Ovseyenko

P. E. Dybenko

M. S. Uritsky

N. V. Krylenko

A. S. Bubnov

ДЕКЛАРАЦИЯ
ОБ ОБРАЗОВАНИИ СОЮЗА СОВЕТСКИХ СОЦИАЛИСТИЧЕСКИХ РЕСПУБЛИК.

Со времени образования советских республик государства мира раскололись на два лагеря: лагерь капитализма и лагерь социализма.

Там, в лагере капитализма—национальная вражда и неравенство, колониальное рабство и шовинизм, национальное угнетение и погромы, империалистические зверства и войны.

Здесь, в лагере социализма—взаимное доверие и мир, национальная свобода и равенство, мирное сожительство и братское сотрудничество народов.

Попытки капиталистического мира на протяжении десятков лет разрешить вопрос о национальностях путем совмещения свободного развития народов с системой эксплоатации человека человеком оказались бесплодными. Наоборот, клубок национальных противоречий все более запутывается, угрожая самому существованию капитализма. Буржуазия оказалась бессильной наладить сотрудничество народов.

Только в лагере советов, только в условиях диктатуры пролетариата, сплотившей вокруг себя большинство населения, оказалось возможным уничтожить в корне национальный гнет, создать обстановку взаимного доверия и заложить основы братского сотрудничества народов.

Только благодаря этим обстоятельствам удалось советским республикам отбить нападения империалистов всего мира, внутренних и внешних; только благодаря этим обстоятельствам удалось им успешно ликвидировать гражданскую войну, обеспечить свое существование и приступить к мирному хозяйственному строительству.

Но годы войны не прошли бесследно. Разоренные поля, остановившиеся заводы, разрушенные производительные силы и истощенные хозяйственные ресурсы, оставшиеся в наследство от войны, делают недостаточными отдельные усилия отдельных республик по хозяйственному строительству. Восстановление народного хозяйства оказалось невозможным при раздельном существовании республик.

С другой стороны, неустойчивость международного положения и опасность новых нападений делают неизбежным создание единого фронта советских республик перед лицом капиталистического окружения.

Наконец, само строение Советской власти, интернациональной по своей классовой природе, толкает трудящиеся массы советских республик на путь объединения в одну социалистическую семью.

Все эти обстоятельства повелительно требуют объединения советских республик в одно союзное государство, способное обеспечить и внешнюю безопасность, и внутреннее хозяйственное преуспеяние, и свободу национального развития народов.

Воля народов советских республик, собравшихся недавно на съезды своих советов и единодушно принявших решение об образовании „Союза Советских Социалистических Республик", служит надежной порукой в том, что Союз этот является добровольным объединением равноправных народов, что за каждой республикой обеспечено право свободного выхода из Союза, что доступ в Союз открыт всем социалистическим советским республикам, как существующим, так и имеющим возникнуть в будущем, что новое союзное государство явится достойным увенчанием заложенных еще в октябре 1917 г. основ мирного сожительства и братского сотрудничества народов, что оно послужит верным оплотом против мирового капитализма и новым решительным шагом по пути объединения трудящихся всех стран в Мировую Социалистическую Советскую Республику.

Заявляя обо всем этом перед всем миром и торжественно провозглашая незыблемость основ Советской власти, нашедших свое выражение в конституциях уполномочивших нас социалистических советских республик, мы, делегаты этих республик, на основании данных нам полномочий, постановляем подписать договор об образовании „Союза Советских Социалистических Республик".

ДОГОВОР
ОБ ОБРАЗОВАНИИ СОЮЗА СОВЕТСКИХ СОЦИАЛИСТИЧЕСКИХ РЕСПУБЛИК.

Российская Социалистическая Федеративная Советская Республика (РСФСР), Украинская Социалистическая Советская Республика (УССР), Белорусская Социалистическая Советская Республика (БССР) и Закавказская Социалистическая Федеративная Советская Республика (ЗСФСР—Грузия, Азербейджан и Армения)—заключают настоящий союзный договор об объединении в одно союзное государство—„Союз Советских Социалистических Республик"—на нижеследующих основаниях.

1. Ведению Союза Советских Социалистических Республик в лице его верховных органов подлежат:

а) представительство Союза в международных сношениях;

б) изменение внешних границ Союза;

в) заключение договоров о приеме в состав Союза новых республик;

г) объявление войны и заключение мира;

д) заключение внешних государственных займов;

е) ратификация международных договоров;

ж) установление систем внешней и внутренней торговли;

з) установление основ и общего плана всего народного хозяйства Союза, а также заключение концессионных договоров;

КОНСТИТУЦИЯ

РОССИЙСКОЙ СОЦИАЛИСТИЧЕСКОЙ ФЕДЕРАТИВНОЙ СОВЕТСКОЙ РЕСПУБЛИКИ

1 9 1 8

The 1918 Constitution of the RSFSR

At a communist *subbotnik* in the town of Zhlobin (1920)

At a communist *subbotnik* in the town of Vitebsk (1920)

A. M. Kollontai among women from the East (1920)

The First Congress of Soviets of the Kirghiz Autonomous Republic (October 1920)

October days, "the new regime is setting up milestones in the development of new forms of life by issuing laws to meet the aspirations and hopes of the broad masses".[1]

The very first programme document of the Second Congress of Soviets—the appeal "To Workers, Soldiers and Peasants!", adopted on October 25, 1917, pointed out that Soviet power "will ensure all nations inhabiting Russia a genuine right to self-determination".[2] Let us recall also that another important congress document—Lenin's Decree on Peace—clearly defined the essence of annexation of nations and formulated conditions for the solution by any nation, without any compulsion whatsoever, of the question of the form of its state existence. By approving this fundamental decree, Soviet power flatly rejected the policy of annexations, that is, of forcible retention within the federal framework of peoples who had fallen victim to aggression and incorporation.

While solving the chief task of the socialist revolution—the establishment and consolidation of proletarian power—the Communist Party and Soviet government at the same time consistently and speedily solved a number of general democratic tasks: elimination of the remnants of feudalism, social estates, national inequality, and of life styles harking back to serfdom; abolition of the inequality of women; separation of the church from the state and the school from the church. Already on November 12, 1917 a decree was issued on the abolition of social estates and civil ranks as well as the privileges and restrictions, organisations and institutions based on social estates. All names designating social estates (nobility, merchants, petty bourgeoisie, peasants) and titles (princes, counts, etc.) that had existed in Russia, were also abolished. For the entire population the decree established a single form of address—citizen of the Russian Republic. This, in particular, opened the way to creating a unified new school for all citizens.

The publication in December 1917 of the decrees of the All-Russia Central Executive Committe and the Council of Peo-

<hr>

[1] V. I. Lenin, "Reply to a Question from the Left Socialist-Revolutionaries", *Collected Works,* Vol. 26, p. 287.
[2] *Decrees of Soviet Power,* Vol. I, p. 8.

ple's Commissars "On common-law marriage, children and the introduction of acts of civil registration" and "On the dissolution of marriage" abrogated the old tsarist legislation on marriage and the family, which formalised the inequality of women. "No other state and no other legislation," Lenin rightfully emphasised, has ever done for women a half of what Soviet power did in the first months of its existence."[1]

Following the nationalisation of landlord, church and monasterial lands, the abolition of all and every kind of national or religious privileges or restrictions, establishment of the legal common-law (Soviet) marriage, on December 11, 1917 the Council of People's Commissars adopted a decree on transferring the affairs of education from the religious departments into the jurisdiction of the People's Commissariat for Education. Shortly afterwards, by a special resolution of the People's Commissariat for Education teaching of religion in all schools was abolished altogether, as was the post of teacher of religion. All these acts of Soviet power laid the groundwork for the publication of the historic decree "On the freedom of conscience, and on church and religious societies", which was carefully edited by Lenin and adopted by the Council of People's Commissars on January 20, 1918. Abolishing all the privileges of the church, the decree separated it from the state and the school; at the same time the decree established the full freedom of conscience and religious belief. The text of the decree noted that "every citizen may profess any religion or not profess any religion". It further explained that "the free discharge of religious ceremonies is ensured insofar as they do not violate public order and do not encroach on the rights of citizens of the Soviet Republic".[2]

"What were the chief manifestations, survivals, remnants of serfdom in Russia up to 1917? The monarchy, the system of social estates, landed proprietorship and land tenure, the status of women, religion and national oppression," Lenin wrote subse-

---

[1] V. I. Lenin, "The Tasks of the Working Women's Movement in the Soviet Republic. Speech Delivered at the Fourth Moscow City Conference of Non-Party Working Women, September 23, 1919", *Collected Works*, Vol. 30, p. 43.

[2] *Decrees of Soviet Power*, Vol. I, p. 373.

quently and added with pride: "We cleansed out all that monarchist muck as nobody had ever done before."[1]

The Emancipation of the Peoples

The fundamental provisions of the Leninist programme of the Bolsheviks on the nationalities question were embodied in the Declaration of Rights of the Peoples of Russia, issued by the Soviet government on November 3, 1917 over the signatures of Lenin and the People's Commissar for Nationalities, Joseph Stalin.

This historic document confirmed legislatively the right of all peoples of the country to free development and full equality in all spheres of socio-political and socio-economic life. The Declaration stressed that there was not and could not be anything in common between the policy of the new, proletarian power and the policy of the old, bourgeois-landlord governments. The Soviet government based its activity in the sphere of national relations on complete mutual trust between all the peoples. The former policy of enmity between nations and setting one nation against another was replaced by an open and honest policy leading to full trust between the peoples of Russia. "Only as a result of such trust," the Declaration noted, "can a sincere and solid alliance of the peoples of Russia take shape. Only as a result of such an alliance can the workers and peasants of the peoples of Russia be welded into one revolutionary force capable of withstanding any encroachments on the part of the imperialist-annexationist bourgeoisie."[2]

Confirming the right of nations to free self-determination proclaimed already in the Decree on Peace, the Declaration formulated and drafted into law the main principles of the nationalities policy of the Soviet state, which determined the new relations between nations: 1) equality and sovereignty of the peoples of Russia; 2) the right of the peoples of Russia to free self-

---

[1] V. I. Lenin "Fourth Anniversary of the October Revolution", *Collected Works*, Vol. 33, p. 52.

[2] *Decrees of Soviet Power*, Vol. I, p. 40.

determination, up to and including secession and the formation of an independent state; 3) abolition of all manner of national and national-religious privileges and restrictions; 4) free development of the national minorities and ethnic groups inhabiting Russia.[1]

A characteristic and indicative feature of this fundamental act was that, while calling for a voluntary and sincere alliance of the peoples of Russia, based on mutual respect and trust, the Declaration at the same time offered no direct recommendations regarding the concrete state form of such an alliance. Thus Soviet power once again demonstrated its respect for the sovereign rights of all nations of the country, both big and small, who were granted freedom of expression on this important question.

Shortly after the publication of the Declaration of Rights of the Peoples of Russia, on November 20, 1917 the Council of People's Commissars adopted an "Address to all the Working Muslims of Russia and the East". It proclaimed the freedom and inviolability of national and cultural institutions, customs and beliefs of the Muslims, and guaranteed the unhampered and free organisation of their national life. Soviet power, the Address noted, fully abrogates all the secret treaties of tsarism, which were confirmed by the Provisional Government, concerning the seizure of Constantinople and the partitioning of Persia and Turkey. The peoples of the East were urged to rise up in struggle against imperialism and to become the genuine masters of their destinies.[2]

An important feature of the nationalities policy of Soviet power was also the fact that it not only declared the emancipation of the oppressed peoples and the complete abolition of national inequality, but demonstrated by deed to the whole world its resolve firmly and consistently to implement the Leninist principles of genuine self-determination, equality and friendship of the peoples. Following the Declaration of Rights of the Peoples of Russia, the Council of People's Commissars and the All-Russia Central Executive Committee of Soviets adopted a series of new decrees and resolutions that were designed to implement the

---

[1] See *Decrees of Soviet Power,* Vol. I, p. 114.
[2] See ibid.

stated principles and sealed the equality and free development of the numerous nationalities and peoples of Russia in practical terms.

In the first few months following the October Revolution, in accordance with the Soviet power's decrees, the national and religious relics taken away from them by tsarism were returned to the former oppressed peoples: to the Ukrainians—their banners, guns and Hetman's mace confiscated by Empress Catherine II; to the Muslims inhabiting Russia, the "Sacred Koran of Oman", as well as the Sumbeki tower in Kazan. The Council of People's Commissars granted independence to the Bukhara Emirate and the Khiva Khanate, which were protectorates of Russia; Bukhara and Khiva were exempted from any obligations that had been imposed on them in the past by the tsarist government.[1] Soviet power was also the first to recognise Poland's right to self-determination and independent existence, and returned to the Polish people unique artistic articles which had been taken out of Poland on the order of the tsarist government.[2]

In accordance with the proclaimed right of nations to self-determination, the Soviet government recognised the state independence of the People's Ukrainian Republic on December 4, 1917. "Everything concerning the national rights and national independence of the Ukrainian people," the Manifesto to the Ukrainian people said in part, "is recognised by us, the Council of People's Commissars, immediately and without any restrictions or conditions."[3] On December 18, in reply to an address of the government of Finland, the Council of People's Commissars adopted a decree on the state sovereignty of Finland, that is, its complete state independence. As distinct from the Provisional Government, the Council of People's Commissars, with Lenin at its head, immediately, openly and sincerely, without any diplomatic reservations gave the Finnish people that which had been proclaimed in the first decrees of Soviet power.[4]

Consistently implementing the Leninist nationalities policy,

---

[1] See *The USSR—a Great Community of Fraternal Nations,* p. 48.
[2] See *Decrees of Soviet Power,* Vol. I, pp. 343-44.
[3] Ibid., p. 178.
[4] Ibid., p. 250.

Soviet power shortly reaffirmed before the whole world its stand on the "real self-determination of Poland, Lithuania, and Courland". "We will never recognise as just," the resolution of the All-Russia Central Executive Committee of the Soviets stated on December 19, 1917, "the imposition of someone else's will on any nation."[1] A few days later, on December 29, 1917, yet another decree was approved, which announced that the Workers' and Peasants' Government supported the right of the Armenians of "Turkish Armenia" occupied by tsarist Russia to free self-determination, including full independence.[2]

All these steps of the newly born Soviet state dealt a telling blow at the propaganda and activity of the bourgeois-nationalistic counter-revolutionary organisations and groups that were active in a number of non-Russian regions. They clearly showed that by opposing the attempts of the imperialist powers to seize the outlying ethnic districts of the country, Soviet power respected the self-determination of nations and sincerely sought peaceful, good-neighbourly relations with the newly emerged state entities which had earlier formed part of the Russian Empire. The Council of People's Commissars led by Lenin incontrovertibly demonstrated for all to see the full conformity of word and deed of the workers' and peasants' power.

The People's Commissariat for Nationalities as an Organ for Rallying the Peoples

The People's Commissariat for Nationalities had an important role to play in the practical implementation of the nationalities policy of the Leninist Party. This was a fundamentally new state organ, unheard-of in exploitative societies, at the head of which the Bolshevik Party appointed Joseph Stalin (Jugashvili), one of its prominent leaders.

With the aid of the Commissariat's employees—professional Bolshevik revolutionaries S. S. Pestkovsky (first secretary, later member of the collegium of the Commissariat) and F. M. Se-

---

[1] *Decrees of Soviet Power,* Vol. I, pp. 258-59.
[2] Ibid., pp. 298-99.

nyuta (first head of the managing department of the Commissariat), whose services were enlisted in organising the apparatus of the Commissariat—immediately following the triumph of the October armed uprising work was begun to create in the People's Commissariat for Nationalities individual national commissariats from representatives of the national political parties which adhered to the Soviet platform.

Already in November the first of these was set up—the Commissariat for Polish Affairs headed by J. Leszczynski and his deputies K. Cychowski and S. Bobinski, who were in charge of the affairs of Polish citizens living on the territory of Soviet Russia. After the Commissariat for Polish Affairs had been set up, other national commissariats were organised under the auspices of the People's Commissariat for Nationalities: at the end of November 1917—for Lithuanian affairs, in the first half of 1918—for Muslim, Byelorussian, Jewish, and Armenian affairs. From April to June 1918 the Estonian, Chuvash, Kirghiz, Ukrainian, and Czechoslovak departments were set up. By the autumn of 1918, 18 national commissariats and departments had been created.[1] Appointed as heads of these commissariats were tested revolutionaries and notable national functionaries who were well known to the masses of the national minorities of Russia and enjoyed great prestige among them. Many of them, first of all the heads of the national commissariats of the western regions, were active workers in the corresponding national sections of the Bolshevik Party.

With the participation of leading representatives of a number of national commissariats—K. Cychowski and Bortnowski (Polish affairs), Z. Aleks-Angarietis and V. Mickevičius-Kapsukas (for Lithuanian affairs), M. Vakhitov and Sh. Manatov (Muslim), D. Zhilunovich, V. Skorynko and A. Chervyakov (Byelorussian), S. Dimanstein (Jewish) and V. Avanesov (Armenian)—on February 2, 1918 the collegium, the central organ of the People's Commissariat for Nationalities, was formed to exercise direct supervision over the development of national relations.

In all its activity in the localities the Commissariat relied on a wide network of local national departments at provincial, dis-

---

[1] See G. P. Makarova, *Implementation of the Leninist Nationalities Policy in the First Years of Soviet Power*, p. 75.

trict and city Soviets. This expedited implementation of the measures of the central power, made it possible to take due account of the specifics of the ethnic regions, and promoted their economic and cultural development. Particular note should be made of the extensive and varied agitation and propaganda work conducted by the Commissariat among the country's multinational population. It should be recalled that already during the first year of its activity the Commissariat put out newspapers in more than 20 languages of the peoples inhabiting Russia.

The central and local organs of the Commissariat were truly authoritative representatives of the peoples of Russia in the Soviet government. Together with the local Bolshevik organisations and Soviets they conducted vast and diverse educational, propaganda, organisational and political work, and selected and trained cadres for the realisation of the Leninist nationalities policy. All this opened the way for the drawing together of the peoples, for building friendly relations between them. "To the old world, the world of national oppression, national bickering, and national isolation," Lenin noted, "the workers counterpose a new world, a world of the unity of the working people of all nations, a world in which there is no place for any privileges or for the slightest degree of oppression of man by man."[1]

Meeting the vital interests of the working masses, the Leninist policy of abolishing national and social oppression and implementation of the right of nations to self-determination not only ensured the triumphal advance of Soviet power through the whole of multinational Russia, but was a major factor in effecting a crucial change in the relations between its peoples. "The establishment of the Soviet system in Russia and the proclamation of the right of nations to state secession," as was justly noted in the decisions of the Tenth Party Congress, "brought about a complete change in the relations between the working masses of the nationalities inhabiting Russia, dealt a blow at the old national enmity, cut the ground from under national oppression, and won for the Russian workers the trust of their brothers of other nationalities not only in Russia, but in Europe and Asia

---

[1] V. I. Lenin, "The Working Class and the National Question", *Collected Works,* Vol. 19, p. 92.

as well, enhancing this trust to the point of enthusiasm, to the readiness to fight for the common cause."[1]

New State Forms of Peoples' Unification

The triumph of the October Revolution and the affirmation of Soviet power in the entire country created the political foundation and real conditions for the transformation of the revolutionary alliance of the peoples that took shape during the struggle against the exploiters and oppressors into a voluntary state federation of free nationalities.

Having carried out the task of abolishing the prison of the peoples, as pre-revolutionary Russia was known, it was essential to begin solving a no less complex and responsible task—the practical creation of an unprecedented state federation of the peoples of the Soviet Socialist Republic. But as Lenin repeatedly pointed out, "such a union cannot be effected at one stroke; we have to work towards it with the greatest patience and circumspection, so as not to spoil matters and not to arouse distrust, and so that the distrust inherited from centuries of landowner and capitalist oppression, centuries of private property and the enmity caused by its divisions and redivisions may have a chance to wear off".[2] The consistent pursuance of a genuinely internationalist Leninist nationalities policy helped Soviet power to win the sincere trust of the working masses of the peoples of Russia and ensure their invariable support in the construction of the first ever multinational socialist type of state.

From the first day of the existence of Soviet power the question of new state forms of unification of the country's peoples was at the centre of attention of the Central Committee of the Bolshevik Party and the Council of People's Commissars. A major contribution to the elaboration of concrete ways of solving

---

[1] *The CPSU in Resolutions...*, Vol. 2, Politizdat, Moscow, 1970, p. 249.

[2] V. I. Lenin, "Letter to the Workers and Peasants of the Ukraine Apropos of the Victories Over Denikin", *Collected Works*, Vol. 30, p. 293.

the nationalities question in the country was Lenin's idea of creating a Soviet federal socialist state.

Along with Soviet national autonomy as a possible form of a national-state system, proposed even prior to the October Revolution, Lenin formulated the main principles of a Soviet federation, showed how it differed from a bourgeois federation, and substantiated the need for uniting the independent Soviet peoples in a single union state. As we already noted, initially (October 1917—mid-1918) the process of abolishing national oppression and of liberation of the peoples, the majority of which had acquired their national statehood for the first time, developed at a fast rate. At the same time, clearly discernible in this double-pronged process was another side—an obvious attraction to an alliance with Soviet Russia, and a striving to establish federal ties between the Soviet republics. On the basis of an analysis of existing conditions and the first experience of revolutionary practice in national-state development, Lenin arrived at the conclusion that a federal system based on the equality, friendship and mutual aid of its peoples was an essential condition for a multinational Soviet state.

Under Lenin's leadership in the course of the socialist revolution concrete forms of federal ties between Soviet Russia and other independent Soviet republics were being established. For the first time, on Lenin's initiative, the federal principle formed the basis of a state union of two sovereign Soviet republics—Russia and the Ukraine. The Manifesto to the Ukrainian People with an Ultimatum to the Ukrainian Rada dated December 3, 1917, which was written by Lenin, officially recognised the independence of the Ukraine and its right to "enter into a treaty with the Russian Republic on federal or similar relations between them".[1] The Russian Federative Republic is directly mentioned for the first time also at the beginning of December 1917 in the Statute on the Land Committees, which bears Lenin's signature.

The federal form of union between Soviet Russia and the Ukrainian Soviet Republic was put into effect immediately: co-

---

[1] V. I. Lenin, "Manifesto to the Ukrainian People with an Ultimatum to the Ukrainian Rada", *Collected Works*, Vol. 26, p. 361.

operation between them developed intensively in the military, economic and political spheres. The diplomats of both republics jointly took part in talks with Germany and its allies on the conclusion of the Brest peace. On the proposal of the Chairman of the Council of People's Commissars of the Russian Federation a representative of the Ukrainian Republic together with the people's commissars of Soviet Russia signed the more important decrees of Soviet power.[1]

The logical outcome of the first steps of revolutionary national-state development, which began in the country in the period of the triumphal advance of Soviet power, was the creation of the RSFSR (Russian Socialist Federative Soviet Republic). The proclamation of the first Soviet federal state took place at the Third All-Russia Congress of Soviets, held in January 1918.

The Convocation and Dissolution of the Constituent Assembly

An important result of the political stage of the Russian revolution was the creation of a Soviet type of state of the dictatorship of the proletariat, which was "a gigantic step in advance"[2] after the 1793 French Revolution and the Paris Commune.

This was a genuinely democratic state of the working people as embodied in the Soviets of Workers', Soldiers' and Peasants' Deputies. The Soviets provided a maximum of democracy for the working people as opposed to bourgeois democracy with its parliamentary republic and real freedoms for the propertied classes alone.

The Soviets, being fundamentally new organs of state power, provided an opportunity "to combine the advantages of the parliamentary system with those of immediate and direct democracy, i.e., to vest in the people's elected representatives both

---

[1] See V. M. Shapko, *Half-Century of the Union*, Politizdat, Moscow, 1972, p. 27 (in Russian).

[2] V. I. Lenin, "New Times and Old Mistakes in a New Guise", *Collected Works*, Vol. 33, p. 22.

legislative *and executive* functions".[1] As mentioned above, the Bolsheviks fought for the triumph of the socialist revolution under the Leninist slogan "All Power to the Soviets", which was profoundly, and comprehensively substantiated in Lenin's April Theses and in the decisions of the Seventh (April) Conference and the Sixth Congress of the Party.

The petty-bourgeois Menshevik and Socialist-Revolutionary parties saw the Soviets as temporary organs, which were to be replaced by a permanent power embodied in "a sovereign master of Russia"—the Constituent Assembly. The latter was to arrange everything: give land to the peasants, reconcile the workers and the capitalists, resolve the question of war and peace.

Although the idea was still popular among the petty-bourgeois peasant masses and a part of the workers, the Provisional Government was in no hurry to convene the Constituent Assembly: the initial dates for its election and convocation were set for September 17 and 30; in August new dates were set—November 12 and 28.

After the victory of the armed uprising in Petrograd and the transition of all power to the Soviets, the Soviet government on October 27, 1917 adopted a resolution on holding the Constituent Assembly elections on schedule—in November 1917.[2]

This decision was due to the fact that the petty-bourgeois masses of the country were unable immediately to rid themselves of parliamentary illusions, and would have misunderstood a failure to convene the Constituent Assembly.

The defeat of the first counter-revolutionary attempts to overthrow Soviet power in the period from October 25, 1917 to February 24, 1918 showed that the Soviets enjoyed the support of the broad masses of workers, soldiers and peasants.

The counter-revolution raised the slogan "All Power to the Constituent Assembly!". In Petrograd and in some other cities the Socialist-Revolutionaries and Mensheviks organised on November 28, 1917 anti-Soviet manifestations timed to coincide with the opening of the Constituent Assembly. However, the elec-

---

[1] V. I. Lenin, "Can the Bolsheviks Retain State Power?", *Collected Works*, Vol. 26, pp. 103-04.

[2] See *Decrees of Soviet Power*, Vol. I, pp. 25-26.

tions in all the districts had not been concluded by November 28, so the opening of the Constituent Assembly was postponed to January 5, 1918.

The civil war launched by the counter-revolutionaries excluded the possibility of solving the question of the future state system "in a parliamentary way" through a combination of the Soviet Republic and the Constituent Assembly, which the Bolsheviks considered acceptable in October 1917.[1]

The Provisional Bureau of the Bolshevik group in the Constituent Assembly—L. Kamenev, A. Rykov, Y. Larin and others—adopted a right-opportunistic line with relation to it, considering the convening of this parliament "the conclusion of the revolution". That is why the RSDLP(B) Central Committee dismissed the group's bureau; on December 12 the group discussed Lenin's "Theses on the Constituent Assembly" and approved them.[2]

The main idea of Lenin's Theses consisted in that the class and party composition of the Constituent Assembly reflected the old correlation of forces that had taken shape at the pre-October stage of the revolution; the triumph of the October Revolution and the first transformations in the country created a new correlation of class forces.

Hence subordination of the new power to the Constituent Assembly would have run counter to the interests of the victorious revolution. The Bolsheviks polled 25 per cent of the votes at the elections to the Constituent Assembly, in which the counter-revolutionary parties—Cadets, Mensheviks and Socialist-Revolutionaries—comprised the majority.

Such a composition predetermined the destiny of the Constituent Assembly, which was incapable of consolidating the revolution. The slogan "All Power to the Constituent Assembly!" ran counter to the gains of the socialist revolution and was used by the counter-revolution to wage a struggle against Soviet power.

In his "Theses on the Constituent Assembly", Lenin wrote:

---

[1] See V. I. Lenin, "Revision of the Party Programme", *Collected Works*, Vol. 26, p. 172.

[2] See *Minutes of the Proceedings of the RSDLP(B) Central Committee*, Politizdat, Moscow, 1958, p. 160 (in Russian).

"The course of events and the development of the class struggle in the revolution have resulted in the slogan 'All Power to the Constituent Assembly!' ... *becoming in fact* the slogan of the Cadets and the Kaledinites and of their helpers."[1]

Lenin attached great importance to explaining among the broad strata of working people the line of the Party with respect to the Constituent Assembly. The Moscow Bolsheviks faced important tasks: here the counter-revolutionary forces attempted to use the Constituent Assembly in their fight against Soviet power, creating for the purpose the Moscow Alliance for Defence of the Constituent Assembly.

In elaborating their tactics in relation to the Constituent Assembly the Moscow Bolsheviks were guided by Lenin's ideas. Already by the end of November 1917 Lenin in a conversation with O. A. Pyatnitsky, a member of the Moscow Party Committee, acquainted him with the tactics of the RSDLP(B) Central Committee with respect to the Constituent Assembly.[2] On returning to Moscow, Pyatnitsky set forth Lenin's stand on the question at a session of the Moscow Party Committee.

The resolution of the Moscow District Committee of the Party on the report by I. F. Armand, which was adopted by the city Party conference, stated that if the Constituent Assembly, owing to the predominance there of Cadet and Socialist-Revolutionary elements, became the tool of reaction, and attempted to nullify the gains of the October Revolution and to destroy Soviet power, the Moscow Committee would support the most vigorous measures in the struggle against the Assembly, including its dissolution.

On December 7-9, 1917 the Third Moscow Regional Conference of the RSDLP(B) clearly stated its attitude towards the Constituent Assembly. G. I. Lomov, who reported on the current events, stated: "It is essential to dispel all the illusions still existing in the masses, who naively believe that the Constituent Assembly ... will immediately bring about order and remove all ills. Nothing but physical force can change the character of the

[1] V. I. Lenin, "Theses on the Constituent Assembly", *Collected Works*, Vol. 26 pp. 381-82.

[2] See *Vladimir Ilyich Lenin. A Biographical Chronicle*, Vol. 5, p. 99.

Constituent Assembly. A colossal battle will have to be waged against the Constituent Assembly, for the counter-revolutionary forces are already using it for their own aims."[1]

However, replying to a question on the dissolution of the Constituent Assembly, Lomov said: "It should not be dissolved, because it itself will help to disperse constitutional illusions."[2] This mirrored the "rightist" sentiments regarding the fate of the Constituent Assembly; a similar point of view was expressed by some speakers from provincial organisations.[3] Others adhered to the "left" position of unconditional dissolution and even refusal to convene the Assembly.[4]

In a resolution on current events the conference noted that only representation of the masses in the Soviets organised according to class principles could ensure the development and strengthening of the socialist revolution. The Constituent Assembly was incapable of solving the tasks of the revolution. "The proletarian Party, in upholding the Soviet Republic, must relentlessly disperse all illusions linked with the Constituent Assembly and other parliamentary forms."[5]

The Bolsheviks of Moscow launched agitation work to explain to the working people the Party's tactics in relation to the Constituent Assembly. They urged the workers, peasants and soldiers to strengthen the Soviets, the plenipotentiary organs of the workers' and peasants' power.

Elections to the Constituent Assembly were held in Moscow from December 2 to 4, 1917. The Cadets, Mensheviks and Right Socialist-Revolutionaries demanded the immediate transfer of all power to the Constituent Assembly, and although they conducted frenzied agitation against the Bolsheviks, the latter polled 50.1 per cent of the votes, the Cadets, 35.9 per cent, and the Socialist-Revolutionaries, 8.5 per cent. The overall share of all the other parties amounted to 5.5 per cent.[6] In the Moscow

[1] *Proletarskaya revolyutsia*, No. 10(105), 1930, p. 121.
[2] Ibid., p. 123.
[3] Ibid., p. 124.
[4] Ibid., pp. 126, 127.
[5] *Proletarskaya revolyutsia*, No. 11 (106), 1930, p. 155.
[6] See E. N. Gorodetsky, *The Birth of the Soviet State*, Nauka Publishers, Moscow, 1957, p. 438 (in Russian).

Province the Bolsheviks received 56 per cent, and the Socialist-Revolutionaries, 25 per cent of the votes. However, as noted earlier, on a nationwide scale the bourgeois and petty-bourgeois parties held the majority of the seats in the Constituent Assembly. This was due to the fact that the lists of voters had been compiled prior to the October Revolution when the idea of convening the Constituent Assembly was popular among the population, who harboured constitutional illusions.

After publication of the election results the struggle gained in intensity: the bourgeois press attacked Soviet power and the Bolshevik Party; the leaders of the bourgeois and petty-bourgeois parties planned an anti-Soviet demonstration in Moscow on December 3, 1917 under the slogan: "All power to the Constituent Assembly!".

On the appeal of the Moscow Party Committee the working people of the capital remained at their work places that day: taking part in the demonstration were only representatives of the bourgeoisie, officers and military cadets, officials, Black Hundreds and other supporters of the old regime. Red Guards and revolutionary soldiers patrolled the city; urgent measures were taken to strengthen revolutionary order.

On December 6, the Presidium of the Moscow Soviet adopted, on the report of Party Central Committee member A. S. Bubnov, a resolution on the introduction of martial law in Moscow and its environs; it was decided to shut down all the bourgeois newspapers. These measures of the Moscow Soviet were opposed by the Mensheviks, alleging that the measures undermined Soviet power; hence the Menshevik faction protested against the introduction of martial law.

The counter-revolution was preparing for the anti-Soviet demonstration it had scheduled for January 5, 1918, the day of the opening of the Constituent Assembly, having decided to begin an armed uprising against Soviet power on that day.

On discussing the obtaining situation, the Moscow Committee decided to bar all demonstrations, calling on the workers and soldiers to repulse the counter-revolutionary forces. On January 4, the Presidium of the Moscow Soviet and the Moscow Party Committee urged all workers, soldiers and peasants not to participate in the demonstration: "The banner under which the pro-

ponents of the demonstration are operating is merely a cover. . .
Hidden behind it are all the exploiters, capitalists, bankers, landlords. . . That is where our enemies are, the enemies of the Soviets
of Workers', Soldiers' and Peasants' Deputies."[1]

On the decision of the Moscow Soviet demonstrations were
forbidden, and in Moscow and the province the Red Guards and
the units of revolutionary soldiers were put on the alert. The
security of the Party district committees and Soviet institutions
was strengthened, a strict surveillance was established over the
activity of the petty-bourgeois elements. Despite the bourgeoisie's proposal to consider January 5 a non-working day, the working people of Moscow went to work in an organised manner.

On the same day the Constituent Assembly opened in Petro-
grad and refused to recognise the Declaration of Rights of the
Working and Exploited People, and any decrees of Soviet power.
The Constituent Assembly was dissolved by a decree of the All-
Russia Central Executive Committee on January 6.[2] The Third
All-Russia Congress of Soviets, held from January 10 to 18, 1918,
approved the Declaration of Rights of the Working and Exploit-
ed People, formalising thereby the creation of the Soviet system.
It adopted a decree on the removal from Soviet legislation of
any reference to the Constituent Assembly.

Third All-Russia Congress of Soviets and Its Resolutions

On a frosty January evening people kept coming to the Taurida Palace from all parts of Petrograd, from the working-class
quarters, from the stations, from the city's environs. They all
hurried here for the opening of the Third All-Russia Congress
of Soviets of Workers' and Soldiers' Deputies. Two days later,
the delegates of the Third All-Russia Congress of Soviets of Peasants' Deputies also came from the Smolny to the Taurida Palace.
A joint session of the workers', peasants' and soldiers' delegates,

---

[1] *Leaflets of the Moscow Organisation of Bolsheviks. 1914-1925*,
Politizdat, Moscow, 1954, pp. 152-53.

[2] See *Decrees of Soviet Power*, Vol. I, pp. 335-36.

which opened here at 9 p. m. on January 13, 1918 under the chairmanship of Yakov Sverdlov, in a ceremonial atmosphere formalised the merger of all the Soviets throughout the country. The working class and working peasantry, all the peoples of Russia demonstrated their growing unity in the struggle to consolidate the gains of the October Revolution, for a new and bright world of socialism.

In the same hall where several days earlier the sole session of the Constituent Assembly (which existed only 12 hours and 40 minutes) was held, there now gathered the genuine representatives of the people—emissaries of the broad masses of working people of Russia. The black frock-coats were replaced by workers' jackets and peasants' home-spun blouses, soldiers' field shirts and sailors' duck jumpers. The upper tier and the boxes were filled with representatives of the press, delegations from the factories and plants, revolutionary units of the Petrograd garrison and the warships of the Baltic Fleet.

Unlike the Constituent Assembly, the Third Congress of Soviets of Workers', Soldiers' and Peasants' Deputies fully corresponded to what Lenin called a real, and not a fabricated "national constituent assembly". As early as 1905, Lenin wrote the following: "It is an assembly which, in the first place, really expresses the will of the people ... in the second place, *really has the power and authority* to 'inaugurate' a political order which will ensure the sovereignty of the people."[1] Needless to say, the congress represented the overwhelming majority of the working population of the country united in the Soviets and, consequently, expressed the real will of all the labouring people of Russia. Enjoying the solid support of the Soviets—organs of the victorious proletarian revolution—the congress had the real power definitively to consolidate the new state system which met the genuine interests of the people. That is why the Third All-Russia Congress of Soviets of Workers', Soldiers' and Peasants' Deputies was truly the supreme organ representing the people, and became the real national constituent assembly convened, under the lea-

---

[1] V. I. Lenin, "The Democratic Tasks of the Revolutionary Proletariat", *Collected Works*, Vol. 8, Progress Publishers, Moscow, 1977, p. 515.

dership of the Leninist working-class party, by the working people of Russia who had triumphed in the socialist revolution.

Represented at the Third Congress of Soviets were broad masses of working people: delegates were sent here from 710 provincial, district and other local Soviets, 245 soldiers' committees of the different armies, corps, divisions and regiments. Many delegates were dispatched to the congress by other mass organisations of the working people. Together with the Russian workers, soldiers and peasants, present at the congress were numerous representatives of working people of the various national minorities of Russia. Delegates were sent by the working people of the Ukraine, Byelorussia, the Baltic region, Central Asia, North Caucasus, Transcaucasia and the Far East. A total of 233 delegates including 141 Bolsheviks arrived from the outlying ethnic regions.[1] Altogether taking part in the work of the Third All-Russia Congress of Soviets were some 1,600 delegates with the right to vote, which was double the number of Constituent Assembly members. The composition of the congress delegates graphically illustrated the growing influence of the Bolshevik Party among the broad masses of working people of all nations and nationalities. The representatives of the Bolsheviks and Left Socialist-Revolutionaries, who formed a bloc, won an overwhelming majority at the congress. The Bolsheviks alone comprised more than 60 per cent of the overall number of delegates to the Soviets of Workers' and Soldiers' Deputies and 40 per cent of the delegates to the Soviets of Peasants' Deputies.[2]

In the resolutions and instructions received from the localities and the numerous messages of greetings and telegrams addressed to the Third All-Russia Congress of Soviets, the working people of multinational Russia expressed their approval of the activity of the first Soviet government with Lenin at its head, and their willingness to support in every possible way the

---

[1] See E. N. Gorodetsky, op. cit., p. 487.

[2] See E. G. Gimpelson, "Some New Data on the Composition of the Third All-Russia Congress of Soviets of Workers', Soldiers' and Peasants' Deputies", *Voprosy istorii*, No. 9, 1960, pp. 215-16; D. A. Chugayev, *The Communist Party Is the Organiser of the Union of Soviet Socialist Republics*, pp. 129-30.

workers' and peasants' power in the struggle against the counter-revolution and nationalistic separatism, and in building socialism. For instance, the Sevastopol Soviet of servicemen's, workers' and peasants' deputies instructed its delegates to the congress to uphold the unconditional recognition of the power of the Council of People's Commissars and all the decrees issued by it. The instructions of the Tula Provincial Soviet and the Fifth Provincial Congress of Peasants' Deputies stated: "1) Recognition of the Soviet power of the workers' and peasants' People's Commissars and every possible support for them; 2) the Constituent Assembly is recognised only on the condition that it recognises Soviet power and supports the decrees of the People's Commissars." "We greet the power of the Soviets of Workers', Soldiers' and Peasants' Deputies both in the centre and in the localities, headed by the Council of People's Commissars, which we will support by every possible means in the struggle against the bourgeoisie of all countries and for peace, bread, freedom and socialism," stated the first item in the resolution adopted in January by the congress of representatives of the Sixth Army Corps (Southwestern Front).

Just two more examples. The Congress of Soviets of Workers' and Soldiers' Deputies of the Akmolinsk Region (Kazakhstan) declared in its resolution of January 8 that it "will support by every means and all forces at its disposal the Council of People's Commissars and the All-Russia Congress of Soviets in their resolute struggle for Soviet power".[1] "We recognise the Russian Federative Republic of Soviets," said the instruction of the Soviet of Workers' and Soldiers' Deputies of the town of Lebedyan, Kharkov province, "and hence recognise both in Russian and in the Ukraine only the power of the Soviets of Workers and Peasants."[2] As John Reed aptly noted, "the masses of the people accepted the dissolution with perfect calm,—even forgot it entirely, and turned their attention to the Third Convention of All-Russia Soviets, which assembled in the seats of the Constituent Assembly five days later, and declared Russia forever the property of the toiling masses, a republic of Soviets, the

---

[1] *Krasny arkhiv*, No. 9 (85), 1937, p. 23.
[2] *Triumphal Advance of Soviet Power*, Part 2, pp. 348-49.

116

invincible sword of the social revolution... So ended the last act of the battle between the Russian bourgeoisie and proletariat, between the Soviets and the Constituent, between parliamentary democracy and—something new."[1]

The Third All-Russia Congress of Soviets opened to the ceremonial sounds of the international anthem of the proletarian revolution, The Internationale; then, as a symbolic tribute to the heroism of the revolutionaries of the past, the orchestra played the Marseillaise. Then Chairman of the All-Russia Central Executive Committee of Soviets Yakov Sverdlov spoke from the rostrum: "We are to pass extremely responsible and important resolutions here. We must juxtapose the act of dissolution of the Constituent Assembly to the convening of the Third All-Russia Congress of Soviets—the supreme organ which alone correctly reflects the interests of the workers and peasants... We must decide here definitively whether this power will be linked in some way with the bourgeois system, or a dictatorship of the workers and peasants will be established conclusively and irrevocably."[2]

Then the Congress of Soviets was greeted with exceptional warmth by representatives of the workers' and social-democratic parties of Switzerland, Sweden, Norway, the United States of America, Great Britain, and Romania: Comrades Fritz Platten, Adam Egede Nissen, Albert R. Williams, John Reed and others. The emissaries of the foreign proletariat, who had surmounted numerous obstacles on their way to Petrograd, the capital of revolutionary Russia, in their speeches told the congress delegates about the sincere support of the working people of their countries for the great proletarian revolution begun by the Russian workers and peasants, about the powerful international solidarity movement with Soviet Russia that had been launched throughout Europe.

"I greet you on behalf of the Social-Democrats of Sweden and Norway," Adam Egede Nissen said to the congress delegates. "I want to convey to you that on this day all my comrades are with you in their hearts, with your unprecedented meeting of genuine democracy." "The oppressed classes of Europe," said

---

[1] *The Revolutionary Age*, November 30, 1918, p. 6.
[2] Y. M. Sverdlov, *Selected Works*, Vol. 2, p. 100.

Fritz Platten, speaking on behalf of the Social-Democratic Workers' Party of Switzerland, "are following with admiartion the movement in Russia, which so far is the sole country in the world with a genuinely revolutionary parliament—the Soviets of Workers', Soldiers' and Peasants' Deputies—where the cause of the socialist revolution has been set on a firm basis." The congress greeted with loud applause the inspired speech by John Reed, the remarkable American writer who witnessed and took part in the events of the October Revolution on the side of the uprisen people. Before returning home, to the country which is the heartland of capitalism, John Reed said that the awareness that the victory of the proletariat in one of the more powerful countries was not a dream, but reality, was a source of deep satisfaction, and promised the congress delegates that he would tell the American proletariat what was happening in revolutionary Russia. In a telegram in reply to the foreign proletarian organisations of Europe and America the Third All-Russia Congress of Soviets expressed its warm gratitude for their continuous aid to the Russian proletariat in its struggle for socialism, and urged them in future, too, actively to support the newly-begun socialist revolution in Russia.[1]

After the foreign guests had spoken, Mikhail Kalinin, the mayor of the capital, greeted the congress on behalf of the working people of Petrograd, and sailor A. G. Zheleznyakov, on behalf of the revolutionary units of the army and fleet. On behalf of the Ukrainian Soviets the congress was greeted by the representative of the All-Ukraine Central Executive Committee V. P. Zatonsky, and on behalf of the Social-Democrats of Poland, Latvia and Lithuania—by Comrades J. Leszscynski, F. Rozins and S. Turlo.

The highlight of the work of the Third All-Russia Congress of Soviets was the report on the activity of the Council of People's Commissars made by Lenin on January 11. Only two-and-a-half months earlier he had appeared on the rostrum of the Second Congress of Soviets as the leader of the victorious armed

---

[1] See *Third All-Russia Congress of Soviets of Workers', Soldiers' and Peasants' Deputies*, Priboi Publishers, Petrograd, 1918, pp. 6-7, 11-14 (in Russian).

uprising. Now, at the Third Congress of Soviets, the leader of the proletarian revolution appeared for the first time before the supreme organ of Soviet power as the head of the first Workers' and Peasants' Government. The first proletarian government reported on its work during the two months and 15 days in which it had administered the huge country. This period surpassed by only five days the first experiment in proletarian dictatorship undertaken in 1871 by the heroic Paris Communards.

Beginning with a comparison of the Soviet Republic and the Paris Commune, Lenin pointed out first of all the exceptional importance of the fact that the uprisen workers, soldiers and peasants of Russia set up their own proletarian power led by the Soviet government, which in extremely complex conditions was capable of uniting the working class and the working peasantry and all the peoples of the country into a single powerful revolutionary force—a crucial factor for the government's authority. "They had no apparatus," Lenin said of the heroes of the Paris Commune, "the country did not understand them; we were immediately able to rely on Soviet power, and that is why we never doubted that Soviet power enjoys the sympathy and the warmest and most devoted support of the overwhelming majority of the people, and that therefore Soviet power is invincible."[1]

The alliance of the working class and working peasantry, which had gained in strength in the course of the revolution, Lenin continued, will in future too be the inviolable foundation of Soviet power.

Having defined the causes of the victory of the socialist revolution in Russia, the leader of the Bolshevik Party and Soviet government gave the delegates a detailed account of the enormous work done by the workers' and peasants' power in building the economic and political basis of the new social system in the first months of its existence. "We have initiated many measures undermining the capitalists' rule," he noted in this connection. "We know that our power had to unite the activities of all our institutions by a single principle, and this prin-

[1] V. I. Lenin, "Third All-Russia Congress of Soviets of Workers', Soldiers' and Peasants' Deputies", *Collected Works*, Vol. 26, p. 456.

ciple we express in the words: 'Russia is declared to be a socialist Republic of Soviets'."[1]

The Chairman of the Council of People's Commissars focussed attention on the characterisation of the main steps of Soviet power on the way to eliminating the old exploitative state machinery and creating a new Soviet administrative apparatus. There has not been a single revolution in which the working masses have not sought to set up a new state power, Lenin said. "Unfortunately, they only began to do this, but were unable to finish, they were unable to create the new type of state power. We have created it—we have established a socialist Republic of Soviets."[2]

Thus spoke the head of the first Soviet government. And everybody who was in the hall at that moment—delegates and guests, workers and peasants, sailors and soldiers—all who represented at the congress the numerous nations and nationalities of the first country to have taken the road of socialist transformations, knew that this was so.

Then Lenin went on to refute the allegations of the bourgeoisie and conciliators who accused the Bolsheviks of "dictatorial behaviour" and "cruelty". Concealed behind the slogans of the Mensheviks, Cadets and Socialist-Revolutionaries and the bourgeois nationalists, the head of the first Soviet government explained, are attempts at defending overt and covert counter-revolutionaries, who with the support of domestic and international bourgeoisie are resorting to every means—from counter-revolutionary sabotage to the organisation of open anti-Soviet revolts—and are seeking by diverse forms to achieve one thing—the restoration of the old landlord-bourgeois order. Sharply criticising the bourgeois and conciliatroy parties, and individual oppositionists among the Bolsheviks, who asserted that the victory of socialist revolution was impossible in one country alone, Lenin noted with pride that history had assigned the working people of Russia "the honour of being the vanguard of the international socialist revolution".

---

[1] V. I. Lenin, "Third All-Russia Congress of Soviets of Workers,' Soldiers' and Peasants' Deputies", *Collected Works*, Vol. 26, p. 465.

[2] Ibid., p. 464.

"Our socialist Republic of Soviets will stand secure, as a torch of international socialism and as an example to all the working people. Over there—conflict, war, bloodshed, the sacrifice of millions of people, capitalist exploitation; here—a genuine policy of peace and a socialist Republic of Soviets."[1]

Declaration of Rights of the Working and Exploited People

Just as closely as it had followed the report of the head of the first Soviet government, the congress listened to the text of the Declaration of Rights of the Working and Exploited People, which was read out by Yakov Sverdlov, Chairman of the All-Russia Central Executive Committee. The fundamental principles contained in the Declaration which was written by Lenin and which Sverdlov defined as one of the most important documents in world history, summing up "the position of man in socialist society", was greeted with loud applause by the packed hall.

The Leninist Declaration of Rights of the Working and Exploited People gave a precise formulation of two major principles expressing the class essence and political form of a fundamentally new, workers' and peasants' power set up by the revolutionary creativity of the masses: the sovereignty of the Soviets, and a federal state system of the dictatorship of the proletariat. "1) Russia is hereby proclamed a Republic of Soviets of Workers,' Soldiers' and Peasants' Deputies,"—proclaimed the Declaration. "All power, centrally and locally, is vested in these Soviets. 2) The Russian Soviet Republic is established on the principle of a free union of free nations, as a federation of Soviet national republics."[2] Unanimously approving these important provisions of the Declaration, the congress demonstrated the firm resolve of millions upon millions of workers, peasants and

---

[1] V. I. Lenin, "Third All-Russia Congress of Soviets of Workers', Soldiers' and Peasants' Deputies", *Collected Works*, Vol. 26, p. 472.

[2] V. I. Lenin, "Declaration of Rights of the Working and Exploited People", *Collected Works*, Vol. 26, p. 423.

soldiers of multinational Russia to continue the struggle to consolidate the victory of the Great October Revolution and fully implement socialist ideals as a close-knit family led by the Leninist working-class party. Thereby Soviet power, which triumphantly advanced throughout the colossal territory of the country in the period between the Second and Third All-Russia Congresses of Soviets, acquired its definitive legislative form. The world's first workers' and peasants' state, which emerged in Russia, was given the name Russian Soviet Federative Socialist Republic.

The Leninist Declaration of Rights of the Working and Exploited People proclamed the fundamental historic task of Soviet power—elimination of all exploitation, relentless suppression of the exploiters, socialist organisation of society, and elimination of the division of society into classes. Along with the adoption of a programme of socialist construction, the Declaration also recorded all the major Soviet decrees forming the basis for the further development of the new social system: decrees abolishing private landownership and declaring land the property of the whole people, decrees on worker control, the Supreme Economic Council, nationalisation of the banks, introduction of universal labour conscription, etc.

Formulated in the text of the Declaration were important principles of the international and domestic policy of the Soviet state. Confirming the fundamental importance of the Leninist Decree on Peace for the foreign policy and diplomacy of the workers' and peasants' state, the Declaration approved the Soviet government's vigorous renunciation of the imperialist policy of national and colonial oppression of the less developed nations and welcomed the government's first steps in conducting a genuinely peaceful and friendly policy towards all the peoples.

The Declaration of Rights of the Working and Exploited People, which was approved by the overwhelming majority of the congress delegates, summed up the revolutionary experience of socialist transformations effected during the first months of Soviet power. The legislative endorsement of the Declaration by the congress finalised the victory of the October Revolution and the gains of the workers and peasants of Russia in all spheres of political and economic life. Simultaneously, the Declaration summed up the first results in building a dictatorship of the proletariat, and sealed the creation of the Soviet state system. The Declaration became the first fundamental law of the victorious proletarian state, the main constitutional act proclaiming the fundamental principles of the domestic and foreign policy of the world's first workers' and peasants' state.

The resolution approving the Declaration of Rights of the Working and Exploited People adopted by the Third All-Russia Congress of Soviets stated: "The congress sees the Declaration of Rights of the Working and Exploited Peoples, adopted by the Central Executive Committee, as an expression of the genuine will of the working classes of Russia. Each line of this Declaration has been dictated by the working classes themselves, and all conscious workers, peasants and soldiers will fight to the last drop of their blood for the demands expressed in this programme of the Soviets."[1] To increase the circulation of the Declaration, the congress resolved to put up the text at all plants, factories, in the villages, and to have it read out in all the units of the army and fleet.

Historical Significance of the Third All-Russia Congress of Soviets

The national question was the focus of attention of the Third All-Russia Congress of Soviets. It adopted a special resolution on the report by Joseph Stalin, People's Commissar for Nationalities, on the basic principles of Soviet federation. It stressed that the Russian Republic was established on the basis of a voluntary alliance of the peoples of Russia as a federation of Soviet republics. Proclamed as the supreme organ of power of the federation was the All-Russia Congress of Soviets, which elected the All-Russia Central Executive Committee and the government of the federation—the Council of People's Commissars. The fed-

---

[1] *Decrees of Soviet Power*, Vol. I, p. 340.

eration members—Soviet republics and individual regions—were granted the right to resolve the question of participation in the federal government and the federal Soviet institutions.

Delivering a message on behalf of the Central Executive Committee of the Ukrainian Soviets, V. P. Zatonsky, a member of the Soviet government of the republic, had every reason to state that this congress was the supreme organ not only of Great Russia, but also of the entire territory of Russia.[1]

On the same day (January 15, 1918), the congress adopted a resolution fully approving the nationalities policy of the Council of People's Commissars, "aimed at carrying out the principle of self-determination of nations, interpreted in the spirit of the self-determination of the labouring masses of all nationalities of Russia".[2] Simultaneously the congress approved the decrees of the Council of People's Commissars and the All-Russia Central Executive Committee on Finland and Armenia, expressing the conviction that further steps of Soviet power in this direction "will help to transform the former Russian empire, which had resorted to oppression and violence to retain its domination over individual peoples, into a fraternal alliance of Soviet republics of Russia voluntarily united on federative principles".[3]

These resolutions of the Third All-Russia Congress of Soviets summed up the chief results of the initial stage of Soviet national-state development and determined the advance of the first socialist state on the basis of a Soviet federation. That is why on January 18, in his summing-up speech before the closing of the congress, Lenin confidently stated: "We do not rule by dividing, as ancient Rome's harsh maxim required, but by uniting all the working people with the unbreakable bonds of living interests and a sense of class. This our union, our new state is sounder than power based on violence which keeps artificial state entities hammered together with lies and bayonets in the way the imperialists want them ... and I am profoundly convinced that more and more diverse federations of free nations will group themselves around revolutionary Russia. This federation is invinc-

---

[1] See A. V. Likholat, *The Community of the Peoples of the USSR in the Struggle to Build Socialism. 1917-1937*, p. 25.

[2] *Decrees of Soviet Power*, Vol. I, p. 351,

[3] Ibid.

ible and will grow quite freely, without the help of lies or bayonets."[1]

After the proclamation of the RSFSR a complex process of uniting the peoples of the country into a single multinational state developed in two main directions—through the formation of a Soviet federation based on national-territorial autonomy (Turkestan, Tatar-Bashkir Republic, Daghestan, etc.), and through the creation of a federation based on agreements with independent Soviet republics (the Ukraine, Azerbaijan and others). As an example of the latter kind of relations we can cite the substantial strengthening of the federative alliance between the Ukraine and Soviet Russia, which was approved in the second half of January 1918 at the All-Ukraine Peasants' Conference.

On the other hand, as early as December 12, 1917, on the instructions of the Soviet government the People's Commissariat for Nationalities stated that the Council of People's Commissars was "prepared to recognise the federative system of political life in our country, if this is the wish of the working population of the different regions of Russia".[2] But in practical terms the intensive building of the Russian Federation was launched immediately after the Third All-Russia Congress of Soviets, when the first autonomous republics were organised within the RSFSR.

It should be recalled that the Terek Autonomous Republic, one of the first to be formed (February 1918), declared the inviolability of its ties with Soviet Russia. At the same time, the Kubano-Chernomorskaya, Don and Taurida Autonomous republics were formed within the RSFSR. In March 1918 a draft statute on creating the Tatar-Bashkir Autonomous Soviet Republic was elaborated and published. In April 1918 the Turkestan Republic was proclaimed on the principles of Soviet national autonomy.

The Statute on the Turkestan Soviet Socialist Republic, approved by the Fifth Congress of Soviets of the Turkestan Terri-

---

[1] V. I. Lenin, "Summing-Up Speech at the Congress, January 18 (31)", *Collected Works*, Vol. 26, pp. 480-81.
[2] Quoted in A. I. Lepyoshkin, *Soviet Federalism*, Gospolitizdat, Moscow, 1977, p. 73 (in Russian).

tory, stated that the Republic, "being administered autonomously, recognises and coordinates its actions with the central government of the Russian Soviet Federation".[1] In a telegram to the Fifth Congress of Soviets of Turkestan dated April 22, 1918, Lenin and Stalin wrote: "You may rest assured, comrades, that the Council of People's Commissars will support the autonomy of your territory on Soviet principles. We welcome your initiatives and are deeply convinced that you will cover the entire territory with a network of Soviets, and that you will act in full contact with the existing Soviets."[2]

In a rough outline of the draft programme of the Party, which was distributed among the delegates of the Extraordinary Seventh Congress of the RCP(B) early in March 1918, Lenin, who closely followed the progress of national-state construction, arrived at an important conclusion on the need for the "consolidation and further development of the Federative Republic of Soviets as an immeasurably higher and more progressive form of democracy than bourgeois parliamentarism".[3]

In substantiating this conclusion, Lenin carefully analysed the question, mindful of the fundamental changes that had occurred in the life of the country after the victory of the October Revolution, and noted that the key principle of Soviet development—democratic centralism—far from excluding autonomy, deems it necessary. Nor does federation run counter to it, Lenin stressed, if it is conducted within reasonable economic limits, if it is based on marked national distinctions that necessitate a certain measure of state isolation. The process of creating and developing the RSFSR clearly showed that the Soviet federation fully ensures both genuine freedom and equality of the peoples, successful solution of the tasks of socialist development, and consolidation of the defence capacity of the young proletarian state. It is precisely this that Lenin had in mind when in the original version of the article "The Immediate Tasks of the Soviet Government"

---

[1] *Formation and Development of the Union of Soviet Socialist Republics (in documents)*, Nauka Publishers, Moscow, 1973, p. 86 (in Russian).

[2] *Decrees of Soviet Power*, Vol. III, Politizdat, Moscow, 1959, p. 162.

[3] V. I. Lenin, "Extraordinary Seventh Congress of the R.C.P.(B.)", *Collected Works*, Vol. 27, p. 153.

he wrote: "The example of the Russian Soviet Republic shows us particularly clearly that federation, which we are introducing and will introduce, is now the surest step towards the most lasting union of the various nationalities of Russia into a single democratic centralised Soviet state."[1]

The Leninist principles of the construction and administering of the Soviet multinational state, and the experience of national-state development accumulated in the first post-October months, formed the basis of the first Constitution of the RSFSR.

On March 30, 1918, on Lenin's proposal, the Plenary Meeting of the RCP(B) Central Committee recommended that the All-Russia Central Executive Committee form a constitutional commission to prepare a draft Fundamental Law to be submitted for the approval of the Fifth All-Russia Congress of Soviets. The Constitutional Commission, of which Yakov Sverdlov was appointed chairman, and V. A. Avanesov, secretary, worked from April 5 to July 5. The entire work of the commission was conducted under the guidance and with the direct participation of Lenin. In particular, Lenin wrote the text of Clause 20, Section Two of the Constitution dealing with the recognition of the full civil and political equality of Russian citizens and foreign workers occupied in productive labour on the territory of the republic.[2]

Having discussed the question of the Constitution on June 26 and 28, the RCP(B) Central Committee formed a special commission under Lenin's chairmanship. The Central Committee's commission determined the direction of work of the commission of the All-Russia Central Executive Committee on concluding the preparatory work on the draft and introduced important changes and additions to it.[3] Thus, on Lenin's proposal Article 22 stated: "The Russian Socialist Federative Soviet Republic, recognising the equal rights of citizens irrespective of race or na-

---

[1] V. I. Lenin, "Original Version of the Article 'The Immediate Tasks of the Soviet Government', Verbatim Report, Chapter X", *Collected Works*, Vol. 27, p. 207.

[2] See *Lenin Miscellany XXXIV*, Gospolitizdat, Moscow, 1942, p. 57 (in Russian).

[3] See *The Soviets in the First Years of the Dictatorship of the Proletariat*, p. 316.

tionality, declares the establishment or granting of any privileges or advantages on this basis, as well as any kind of oppression of the national minorities or restriction of their equality, to be contrary to the Fundamental Law of the Republic."[1]

On July 10, 1918 the Fifth All-Russia Congress of Soviets adopted the Constitution of the RSFSR—the first Soviet Constitution, which included the unaltered text of the Declaration of Rights of the Working and Exploited People, written by Lenin. The Constitution legislatively formalised the great gains of the October Socialist Revolution: Soviet power as a state form of dictatorship of the proletariat, the abolition of private capitalist and landlord propery, the equality of all peoples inhabiting Russia. It ensured the masses of working people participation in running the state, in all the affairs of constructing a socialist society. Defining the significance of the Fundamental Law of the RSFSR, *Pravda* wrote in an editorial on July 12, 1918: "This Constitution, which starts with the Declaration of Rights of the Working and Exploited People, will become the gospel for the proletariat of all countries."

The 1918 Constitution of the RSFSR mirrored the victory of the new Soviet socialist democracy—democracy for the masses of working people, for the overwhelming majority of the peoples. Another feature of Soviet democracy, recorded in the first Fundamental Law of the Soviet Republic, was its consistent internationalism, ensuring the right of all nations and nationalities to self-determination, recognition of the equality of all citizens irrespective of race or nationalty.

At the same time the 1918 RSFSR Constitution legislatively recorded such a cardinally important principle of Soviet socialist federation as the voluntary nature of the state unification of peoples and the national-territorial character of their state entities— autonomous republics and regions. In creating the autonomous formations account had to be taken not only of the national composition of the population, but also of economic ties, geographical location, and life styles. The RSFSR comprised 16 autonomous republics, five autonomous regions and 10 national districts

---

[1] Quoted in S. S. Gililov, op. cit. p. 49.

which received their statehood for the first time under Soviet power.[1]

Lenin saw the creation by the Soviet peoples of their own states and the formation of an alliance in the form of a Soviet federation as a key achievement of the Great October Revolution. "We have granted *all* the non-Russian nationalities *their own* republics or autonomous regions."[2] Thus the first republic of the dictatorship of the proletariat—Soviet Russia—uniting on the principles of political and administrative Soviet autonomy many peoples of the former tsarist empire, became the first Soviet multinational state, which successfully resolved, by forming a federative system, the extremely complex problem of combining international and national interests.

Characterising the significance of the first Fundamental Law of the victorious proletarian state, Lenin said: "The Soviet Constitution ... is, as we know, not the invention of a commission, nor the creation of lawyers, nor is it copied from other constitutions. The world has never known such a constitution as ours. It embodies the workers' experience of struggle and organisation against the exploiters both at home and abroad."[3]

The Leninist principles of a socialist social and state system, first formalised in the 1918 RSFSR Constitution, were further developed in subsequent Soviet Constitutions, each of which marked an ascending development level of the Soviet socialist state, a new stage in the expansion and deepening of socialist democracy, in strengthening the friendship and co-operation of the peoples of the Land of Soviets.

---

[1] See *Pravda*, December 22, 1972.
[2] V. I. Lenin, "Fourth Anniversary of the October Revolution", *Collected Works*, Vol. 33, p. 53.
[3] V. I. Lenin, "Extraordinary Sixth All-Russia Congress of Soviets of Workers', Peasants', Cossacks' and Red Army Deputies", *Collected Works*, Vol. 28, Progress Publishers, Moscow, 1965, pp. 145-46.

Chapter III

THE FIRST SOCIO-ECONOMIC TRANSFORMATIONS. SETTING UP THE ECONOMIC BASIS OF CO-OPERATION BETWEEN THE FREED PEOPLES

Urgent Economic Transformations

In the epoch of imperialism, the world capitalist system was generally ripe for socialist revolution. However, the question of where the revolution might begin depended on concrete historical conditions.

During the First World War, socialist revolution was on the agenda in a number of European countries.

The "Resolution On the Current Situation", evolved by Lenin for the Seventh (April) All-Russia Conference of Bolsheviks, read: "The objective conditions for a socialist revolution, which undoubtedly existed even before the war in the more developed and advanced countries, have been ripening with tremendous rapidity as a result of the war."[1]

The victory of the 1917 February bourgeois-democratic revolution in Russia confirmed the foresight of the socialists of the whole world, who declared in the Basle Manifesto of 1912 that "precisely in connection with the imperialist war ... a *proletarian revolution* was inevitable". The Russian revolution was only the "first stage of the first of the proletarian revolutions".[2]

Since Russia was one of the most backward European countries and since, moreover, the large peasant section of the population was predominant the proletariat could not "aim at immediately putting into effect socialist changes".[3]

---

[1] V. I. Lenin, "The Seventh (April) All-Russia Conference of the R.S.D.L.P.(B.)", *Collected Works*, Vol. 24, p. 309.

[2] Ibid., p. 310.

[3] Ibid., p. 311.

However, it could realise a number of steps towards socialism such as nationalisation of the land, the establishment of state control over the banks, insurance institutions, and large trusts and syndicates, introduction of workers' control over production and distribution, as well as the transition to general labour conscription.

It was recorded in the resolution of the Seventh (April) Conference that "Economically, these measures are timely; technically, they can be carried out immediately; politically they are *likely* to receive the support of the overwhelming majority of the peasants, who have everything to gain by these reforms."[1]

The latter was significant for millions of peasants not only in central Russia but also in its numerous outlying ethnic regions.

The six months of bourgeois-landowner economic policy conducted by the Provisional Government confirmed that the analysis of this policy given at the Seventh (April) All-Russia Conference of Bolsheviks was correct. The fact that the bourgeoisie and its Socialist-Revolutionary and Menshevik allies sabotaged all democratic measures of struggle against economic dislocation placed Russia on the brink of economic disaster, which could be prevented only by the victory of a new, socialist revolution.

The Sixth Congress of the Bolshevik Party (July-August 1917) worked out an economic platform, based on an analysis of the changed historical situation and the new correlation of political forces in the country. As distinct from the programme of measures for the change over to socialism worked out by the Party in April 1917 and calculated for peaceful transition from a bourgeois-democratic revolution to a socialist one, the economic platform of the Party on the eve of the October Revolution was aimed at socialist revolution and the takeover of power by the proletariat in an alliance with the poorest peasantry in an armed uprising.

Revolutionary transformations demanded, first of all, nationalisation and centralisation of banks, and nationalisation of a number of branches of industry: oil, coal, sugar, metallurgy, and transportation.

The congress regarded the following measures directed at

---

[1] Ibid.

normalisation of the economy as most important: the organisation of proper exchange between town and country through such
mass organisations as co-operatives and food committees; cessation of further issue of paper money, refusal to pay state (external and internal) debts, but with due observance for the interests of small depositors; reform of the tax system; shifting industry over to peacetime production and redistribution of the
work force; the introduction of general labour conscription.

The establishment of effective workers' control over production
played a special role in the realisation of measures to regulate
the economy. Its organs were to include representatives of the
Soviets of Workers' Deputies, trade unions, and factory and plant
committees, drawing "technically and scientifically minded personnel into them."[1]

The congress regarded developing and encouraging the initiative of workers' organisations and generalisation of practical
experience on a national scale as one of the main conditions for
enhancing workers' control "through gradual introduction of
measures directed at the complete regulation of production".[2]

Lenin comprehensively analysed the material prerequisites
for the transition to socialism created by capitalism at the state-
monopoly stage. However, this transition would be possible only
if the reactionary-bureaucratic state were replaced by Soviet
power, which was capable of subordinating state capitalism to
the interests of the people, because "socialism is merely state-
capitalist monopoly *which is made to serve the interests of the
whole people* and has to that extent *ceased* to be capitalist monopoly".[3]

The proletariat's implementation of its leadership of all working people in their struggle for liberation from capitalist and
feudal exploitation and the establishment of its dictatorship was
the most important condition for the revolutionary replacement
of capitalism by socialism.

The dictatorship of the proletariat was necessary, above all,

---

[1] *The CPSU in Resolutions...*, Vol. 1, p. 490.
[2] Ibid.
[3] V. I. Lenin, "The Impending Catastrophe and How to Combat
It", *Collected Works*, Vol. 25, p. 362.

to suppress the resistance of the exploiters, as well as "to *lead* the enormous mass of the population—the peasants, the petty bourgeoisie, and semi-proletarians—in the work of organising a socialist economy".[1]

The most important condition for the proletariat to carry out its historical mission was that it had a new type of Marxist party "capable of assuming power and *leading the whole people* to socialism, of directing and organising the new system, of being the teacher, the guide, the leader of all the working and exploited people in organising their social life without the bourgeoisie and against the bourgeoisie".[2]

As was stated above, favourable objective and subjective prerequisites for the proletariat to seize power with the aim of transition to a new socialist mode of production had shaped up by the autumn of 1917.

Lenin's teaching on state-monopoly capitalism as a full-scale *material* preparation for socialism, as its threshold and a step to it lit the road to victory for the Russian proletariat and for the establishment of its power "for the swiftest and most radical transition to a superior mode of production".[3]

The Economic Basis of Peoples' Friendship

The working class, led by the Bolshevik Party, having won and consolidated its political power, began to set up the necessary prerequisites for victory in the decisive sphere of the struggle for socialism—the economic field. The implementation of this task was crucial for the strengthening of the community of nations and the building of a new society. A firm economic basis had to be set up so that the peoples could merge together, so that political equality could become not just a formality but a real factor for all the country's peoples. The Party reasoned that if under capitalism economically weak and culturally underde-

---

[1] V. I. Lenin, "The State and Revolution", *Collected Works*, Vol. 25, p. 409.

[2] Ibid.

[3] V. I. Lenin, "The Impending Catastrophe and How to Combat It", *Collected Works*, Vol. 25, p. 368.

veloped nations sought separation since they were oppressed by stronger and more developed nations, under socialism they should develop a natural desire to unite with other nations, including the ones that formerly ruled them. This ensures them all-round assistance while preserving their free national development.

The Russian working class was the first to eliminate capitalist rule and to begin setting up the economic foundations of socialism, overcoming enormous difficulties and acquiring the first practical experience ever in this historic undertaking. The scientifically substantiated programme of economic transformations directed at winning command for the proletariat in the national economy, at creating a socialist sector in economy, was evolved in Lenin's works and in the decisions of the Party on the eve of the October Revolution. After the victory of the socialist Revolution, the Party set about its practical realisation, relying on the creative initiative of the working masses.

Workers' Control

Workers' control over production and distribution, and setting up the organs of production management, as well as the nationalisation of banks, factories and plants were the most important undertakings of the Soviet state aimed at the radical reorganisation of the economic foundations of society and the replacement of private ownership of the means of production by public ownership. In his letter to *Pravda* of November 18, 1917, Lenin determined the sequence in which these undertakings should be conducted as follows: "...workers' control over the factories, to be followed by their expropriation, the nationalisation of the banks, and the creation of a Supreme Economic Council for the regulation of the entire economic life of the country".[1]

The tasks of workers' control were determined in the Draft Regulations on Workers' Control, worked out by Lenin in the

---

[1] V. I. Lenin, "Alliance Between the Workers and the Working and Exploited Peasants. A Letter to Pravda", *Collected Works*, Vol. 26, p. 334.

first days of the socialist revolution. The draft Regulations served as the basis of the resolution of the All-Russia Central Executive Committee adopted on November 14, 1917. In accordance with this decree, organs of workers' control were elected by the workers and office employees of an enterprise. This control could be implemented by the factory and plant committees, councils of elders, control commissions, and so on. The decree granted them broad rights and absolute initiative.

Workers' control envolved production, distribution of food-stuffs, as well as the financial activity of the enterprises.

The introduction of workers' control was a resolute invasion of the proletariat into capitalist private property: all the capitalists' activity was placed under direct control of the workers. Naturally, the introduction of workers' control sparked off violent resistance among the bourgeoisie. But the working class relentlessly broke down this resistance, put down counter-revolutionary revolts, and spread workers' control to all the branches of industry, the banking system, and commerce.

By the beginning of 1918, organs of workers' control already existed at most large and average-sized enterprises in Russia, the Ukraine and other national regions.

The workers of Petrograd and Moscow served as an example in the realisation of this control and rendered much assistance to the workers in the areas inhabited by non-Russians. The Fifth Conference of the Petrograd factory trade union committees held in November 1917 appointed a commission of 45 workers to visit Donbas mines and plants and conduct extensive propaganda work, mobilising the efforts of local workers to set up workers' control and organise production.

In the period from December 1917 to March 1918 workers' control spread to nearly all the branches of industry, railway and marine transport in the Ukraine. At the close of 1917—the beginning of 1918 workers' control was introduced at a number of factories and plants in Estonia. Organs of workers' control conducted an extensive campaign to adjust production, raise labour efficiency, and strengthen discipline, financing and supplying enterprises with raw and other materials, etc.

At the close of 1917, following the example of the Russian workers, the workers of Baku began to take control of the oil fields and industrial enterprises, making sure that all the oil extracted and all manufactured goods went to the state.

In December 1917, workers' control was established at many enterprises in Tashkent and other cities of Turkestan. In March 1918, in response to sabotage by the owners, who disrupted the work of the mines, the bodies of the workers' control of the mines of the Kizil Kiya joint-stock company took the management of the mines into their own hands. By the spring of 1918, workers' control was introduced at dozens of industrial enterprises in Samarkand, Bukhara, Khodzhent, Dzhizak, Kokand, and other cities. Workers of the indigenous nationalities participated in the work of the organs of workers' control alongside Russian workers. They fought for their class interests and learned to manage production.

Workers' control made it possible to break down sabotage by the capitalists, prevent disorganisation in industry and transport, and preserve the equipment of industrial enterprises from destruction and plunder. This process of bringing the working people closer to management in industry brought forth thousands of talented production organisers who successfully mastered the fundamentals of economics.

Lenin characterised workers' control as the working class's first step in the transition from capitalism to socialism. It played an enormous role in adjusting and regulating the country's economic life in the first months after the victory of the socialist revolution, and in training the workers for independent production management after the nationalisation of industry. Lenin wrote in April 1918 that until workers' control took a firm foothold, "it will be impossible to pass from the first step (from workers' control) to the second step towards socialism, i.e., to pass on to workers' regulation of production".[1]

New Organs of Management

In order to eliminate disorganisation and dissociation in the activity of the enterprises and to organise the centralised management of industry, at the beginning of December 1917 the All-

---

[1] V. I. Lenin, "The Immediate Tasks of the Soviet Government", *Collected Works*, Vol. 27, p. 255.

Russia Central Executive Committee and the Council of People's Commissars adopted a decision to set up the Supreme Economic Council (SEC), the task of which was to organise and plan the country's national economy, unify the activity of the central and local economic institutions, people's commissariats, organs of workers' control and so on. The SEC rendered extensive help to ethnic regions in organising the work of industry and other branches of the national economy.

Regional economic councils of the Northern, Central Industrial, Urals, Southern (with its centre in Kharkov), Volga Area, and Western-Siberian districts, and the Western Region were set up in accordance with the Regulations on the local economic councils adopted on December 23, 1917. Province and district economic councils were also set up in the first half of 1918. They were entrusted with the tasks of organising and regulating the economic life of the regions in accordance with state and local interests. Local economic councils coordinated all their activities with the Supreme Economic Council.

Nationalisation

In the very first months of the Soviet power, planned nationalisation of banks and major enterprises in the main branches of industry began simultaneously with the introduction of workers' control and setting up of economic councils. By its decree of December 14, 1917, the Soviet government announced a state monopoly on all financial and banking affairs. At the same time, all private banks were united into one State Bank. A decree was adopted annuling all state loans concluded by the tsarist and Provisional governments. Thus, the country shed the shackles of foreign capital. The nationalisation of the banks gave the workers' and peasants' government a mighty lever to influence all the branches of the national economy. The Soviet state turned the banks into a tool of socialist construction. "The source of distribution of capitalist riches was undermined. After that it was an easy step to annul state loans and shed financial yoke."[1]

[1] Central Party Archives of the Institute of Marxism-Leninism under the CC CPSU.

Based on the experience accumulated by the proletariat in the organs of workers' control, the Soviet state set about the planned gradual nationalisation of the basic means of production in the centre as well as in the outlying areas. In November 1917, the Council of People's Commissars discussed measures on the nationalisation of the Donbas coal industry. A decision was adopted "to telegraph a proposal to the Soviet of Deputies of the Donetsk Region and set up a corresponding local commission, to make the engineers work, etc."[1]

On the petition of the workers' organisations, big metallurgical, engineering, oil, coal enterprises and other important branches of industry were nationalised pending the decisions of the Supreme Economic Council and of its local organs.

The successful nationalisation of industry in the Donetsk-Krivoi Rog basin began after the defeat of the Kaledin troops. Practically all major enterprises of the coal and metallurgical industry and the railways were nationalised by the spring of 1918. Half of all the enterprises were managed by the workers.

The enterprises of the Khiva Joint-Stock Company, Semirechye Railway, enterprises of the cotton, oil manufacture, and coal and oil industries were nationalised in Turkestan in January-March 1918.[2]

The oil industry of Azerbaijan was made state property in June 1918 by the decree of the Baku Council of People's Commissars. Despite fierce resistance from the oil field owners and their agents, the oil industry was nationalised thanks to the energetic activity of the Baku Bolsheviks. The workers vigilantly guarded the oil fields and refineries and worked heroically to boost oil output and send the oil to the cities of Soviet Russia.

The decrees on the nationalisation of major industries were adopted in 1917-1918 by the workers' and peasants' governments of Byelorussia, Lithuania, Latvia, and Estonia.

The economic ties between Soviet Russia and the republics expanded and strengthened in the process of realising these rad-

---

[1] Central Party Archives of the Institute of Marxism-Leninism under the CC CPSU.

[2] *History of the Uzbek SSR*, Fan Publishers, Tashkent, Vol. III, pp. 131-32 (in Russian).

ical transformations. Thus, for instance, a single financial system was introduced in the Soviet Russia and the Ukraine in December 1917. The government of Soviet Russia undertook to finance the national economy of the Soviet Ukraine. Over 1,000 million roubles were transferred from the end of 1917 to the first half of 1918 alone by order of the Council of People's Commissars of the Russian Federation to the Kharkov office of the State Bank.[1]

The economic ties of Soviet Russia with the republics were effected through the economic councils.

The first transformations in the economic field conducted by the Communist Party and the Soviet government before March 1918 were in character, as Lenin put it, like a "Red Guard attack" on capital. This attack was completely successful—big bourgeoisie was deprived of the main means of production, while the most important industrial enterprises, banks, transportation, and the means of communication became the property of the Soviet state.

A new economic system, based on socialisation of the means of production, was set up for the first time in history. The nationalised industry, banks and transport became the foundation of the socialist structure in the country's national economy.

Transformations in the Countryside

Simultaneously with the first socialist transformations in industry there were big changes in agriculture.

The Great October Socialist Revolution realised the unresolved tasks of the bourgeois-democratic revolution. It eliminated the remnants of serfdom and freed the peasants from the landowners' yoke.

All lands of the crown, the landlords, the monasteries and church were confiscated by the Decree on Land of the Second All-Russia Congress of Soviets, and all the land in the country was nationalised.

---

[1] See I. A. Gladkov, *Essays on Soviet Economy, 1917-1920*, Gospolitizdat, Moscow, 1956, p. 240 (in Russian).

The peasants in the centre and outlying areas immediately set about realising the Decree on Land, thus creating the prerequisite for a gradual transition of the millions of working peasants to the socialist path.

Lenin pointed out that the elimination of private ownership of land in Russia "created an agrarian system which is the *most flexible* from the point of view of the transition to socialism".[1]

The realisation of the Soviet legislation on land met with fierce resistance from the overthrown classes and kulaks. It was connected with the deepening of the socialist revolution and the strengthening of the dictatorship of the proletariat in the village. Workers' food detachments* sent to the villages and Poor Peasants' Committees* set up in the summer of 1918 played an enormous role in this process. The latter united only the poor and drew the middle peasantry to their side. They existed from the summer of 1918 to the end of the year and were merged with local Soviets by decision of the Sixth Congress of Soviets.

Lenin pointed out that the greatest land reform—abolition of private ownership of land and liquidation of landed estates—would have remained on paper if the working class had not awakened village proletariat and organised village poor and the working peasantry to struggle against the kulaks (or rich peasants exploiting the poor).

Thousands of advanced workers from Petrograd, Moscow and other large industrial cities rendered assistance to the poor villagers of the Russian provinces and ethnic regions in suppressing the resistance of the kulaks and in supplying bread to the famine-stricken urban population. The workers' food detachments went to the village with the slogan: "The struggle for bread is the struggle for socialism." They rallied the poor villagers, shared their experience in struggle with them, and facilitated the strengthening of Soviet power in the village.

---

[1] V. I. Lenin, "The Proletarian Revolution and the Renegate Kautsky", *Collected Works*, Vol. 28, p. 314.

* *Food detatchments*—detachments organised in the summer of 1918 from among the workers to procure bread for the cities. *Poor Peasants' Committees* were set up by decree of the Council of People's Commissars of June 11, 1918 to effect socialist transformations in the village.

The setting up of the first collective communes and artels, state equipment rental stations and the first Soviet state farms was an inalienable part of the agrarian transformations sparked off by the Great October Socialist Revolution.

The first socialist transformations in agriculture were of great significance in consolidating the union of the working class and the peasantry and strengthening confidence of the millions of people living in the outlying ethnic areas in the Russian proletariat.

In the summer of 1918, the political differentiation in the villages both in the Russian provinces and in the ethnic regions had intensified. The socialist revolution in the countryside had entered a new, higher phase of development.

Towards New Culture and Science

In realising these major socialist transformations, the Party attached great significance to the creation of a new, socialist culture. The October Socialist Revolution swept aside all obstacles which the bourgeois system had placed in the way of allowing the masses access to the benefits of human culture. The liquidation of estates, the inequality of women, separation of church from the state and the schools from the church was of great significance in this respect.

The cultural revolution was one of the most important prerequisites for the triumph of the new, socialist system.

". . .without universal literacy, without a proper degree of efficiency, without training the population sufficiently to acquire the habit of book-reading, and without the material basis for this . . .—without this we shall not achieve our object".[1]

Lenin pointed out that the transition to socialism requires "a veritable revolution—the entire people must go through a period of cultural development".[2] He emphasised that we would never build socialism as long as our people were illiterate. The building of socialism required that the broadest organisational, polit-

---

[1] V. I. Lenin, "On Co-operaion", *Collected Works*, Vol. 33, p. 470.
[2] Ibid.

ical and educational work be conducted to raise the cultural level of the people and to qualitatively enrich their inner lives.

From the very first days of the revolution, the Soviet government set about organising the education of the working people and bringing the achievements of culture within their reach to realise the sweeping programme of cultural revolution.

Even before the revolution Lenin's works and the Party's programme mapped out the basic tasks of the cultural transformation: granting the working people the right to comprehensive cultural development, the right to education in their native language, free and compulsory general and polytechnical education for all children, making all the treasures of human culture the property of the masses, etc.

Speaking on the creation of a new culture under the dictatorship of the proletariat, national in form and socialist in content, Lenin stressed that the progressive heritage of the past—the cultural values, created by humankind in the preceding period— would serve as the initial phase of its development.

The fact that the Soviet country was poor and backward and that the cultural level, especially of non-Russian peoples, was low, made the carrying out the cultural revolution in the country all the more difficult. Thus, among the peoples of Central Asia and Kazakhstan, only 0.5 to 2 per cent were literate (Tajiks— 0.5, Kazakhs—2, Kirghiz—0.6, Turkmen—0.7, Uzbeks—1.6); among the Azerbaijanians and Armenians, 10 per cent were literate. And even in the Ukraine over 75 per cent of the population was illiterate.[1] Forty-eight nationalities in our country had no written language of their own.

"This cultural revolution ... presents immense difficulties of a purely cultural (for we are illiterate) and material character (for to be cultured we must achieve a certain development of the material means of production, must have a certain material base)."[2]

The Party regarded the complicated and diversified tasks of the cultural revolution as not isolated but as an inseparable part of Lenin's plan for socialist construction, which encompassed all

---

[1] See M. P. Kim, *Forty Years of Soviet Culture*, Politizdat, Moscow, 1957, p. 26 (in Russian).

[2] V. I. Lenin, "On Co-operation", *Collected Works*, Vol. 33, p. 475.

spheres of social relations and the retailoring of peoples' world view on the basis of the Marxist-Leninist theory.

The entire system of public education was restructured in the first months of Soviet power. According to the Provisions "On a Unified School System", approved by the All-Russia Central Executive Committee in October 1918, a single school system was introduced in place of the numerous and varied types of schools, which granted children of working people of all nationalities an opportunity to master not only the fundamentals of knowledge but all levels of learning at secondary schools and institutes of higher education. Workers' Faculties were set up in the centre and in the capitals of the Union republics to enable the children of workers and peasants to enroll in higher education courses more easily.

The Soviet press was dedicated to the tasks of political enlightenment and ideological education of the masses—the number of newspapers and magazines published in the languages of the peoples of the country was increased in the Union republics and autonomous regions. Radical restructuring began of the publishing industry with the aim of enlightening popular masses.

The role and the significance of science in the life of society changed under Soviet power. Science became a mighty force in the hands of the working people to help them restructure society along socialist lines.

As a result of the policy the Party and the Soviet government pursued with regard to the bourgeois intelligentsia, by March 1918, the bulk of the old intelligentsia began to side with Soviet power. In January 1918, the Commissariat for Education began talks with the Academy of Sciences about its participation in the solution of the most important state tasks of reorganising and rehabilitating the country's industry. Lenin, in his "Draft Plan of Scientific and Technical Work" (April 1918) suggested that the Academy of Sciences be given an assignment by the Supreme Economic Council "to set up a number of expert commissions for the speediest possible compilation of a plan for the reorganisation of industry and the economic progress of Russia".[1]

---

[1] V. I. Lenin, "Draft Plan of Scientific and Technical Work", *Collected Works*, Vol. 27, p. 320.

At its session of April 12, 1918 the Council of People's Commissars chaired by Lenin adopted the proposal of the Academy of Sciences to make a study of the country's natural resources. The Council of People's Commissars resolved: "to accept this proposal, to recognise in principle the necessity of financing corresponding works of the Academy of Sciences and point out to it that the task of resolving the problems of the proper locating of industry in the country and the most rational use of economic forces is most important and urgent."[1]

Lenin's instructions and the undertakings of the Soviet government were instrumental in enhancing the role of science in the solution of the most important tasks of socialist construction, in creating a new, socialist culture and strengthening the inner unity of the country's peoples.

The Party organised and inspired the working masses of the multinational country to join in the struggle for the establishment and consolidation of Soviet power. It also worked for the creation of the foundations of the socialist sector in the economy and for the development of the cultural and educational level of the people. It constantly kept in mind the organisation of co-operation between the peoples of the Soviet country, offering the fraternal assistance of the Russian proletariat and the entire Russian people to the working people of the Union republics.

The Non-Capitalist Road of Development

Ridiculing the dogmatism of the Mensheviks who asserted that it was impossible to build socialism in Russia due to its cultural backwardness, Lenin found a creative solution to the question of the possibility of attaining a definite level of cultural development on the basis of the new Soviet system and workers' and peasants' power.

"If a definite level of culture is required for the building of socialism," Lenin wrote, "(although nobody can say just what that definite 'level of culture' is, for it differs in every West-European country), why cannot we begin by first achieving the prereq-

---

[1] *Decrees of Soviet Power*, Vol. II, p. 94.

uisites for that definite level of culture in a revolutionary way, and, *then*, with the aid of the workers' and peasants' government and the Soviet system, proceed to overtake the other nations?"[1]

If we regard Lenin's proposition as applicable to the creation of objective economic prerequisites for socialist construction it must be said that they had clearly been prepared by the previous capitalist development on a nationwide scale.

On the whole the objective prerequisites for the transition from capitalism to socialism were already present in the country. The peoples of Russia who had not passed through the capitalist stage of the development in the previous epoch were given the opportunity to by-pass this stage.

With the law-governed development of world history, certain periods of development displaying "peculiarities in either the form or the sequence of this development"[2] are not precluded, but, on the contrary, are presumed.

There were a number of such peculiarities in Russia which found their expression in particular in the transition of many peoples to socialism by-passing capitalism.

The analysis of the social and economic transformations in Russia during the first years of the revolution allowed Lenin to substantiate the possibility of a non-capitalist road of development on the basis of the Soviet system.

The Tenth Congress of the Russian Communist Party (Bolsheviks) in its resolution on the national question noted that nearly 30 million people, mainly the Turkic population of Turkestan and Azerbaijan, the Northern Caucasus and other regions, had not passed through the capitalist stage of development by the October revolution of 1917.[3]

After the revolution, they got the opportunity, relying on the assistance of the triumphant proletariat and the Soviets of Peasants' Deputies, to take the non-capitalist path of development.

Lenin in his report to the committee on the national and colonial questions at the Second Congress of the Communist Inter-

---

[1] V. I. Lenin, "Our Revolution", *Collected Works*, Vol. 33, pp. 478-79.

[2] Ibid., p. 477.

[3] See *The CPSU in Resolutions. . .*, Vol. 2, p. 252.

national said: "Are we to consider as correct the assertion that the capitalist stage of economic development is inevitable for backward nations now on the road to emancipation and among whom a certain advance towards progress is to be seen since the war? We replied in the negative."[1] Lenin thought that the main conditions for the realisation of this opportunity were revolutionary propaganda of the victorious proletariat among these backward nations, as well as the assistance rendered them by the Soviet government with all the means at the disposal of the new power—economic, political and cultural.

The social and economic transformations in Russia both in the centre and the outlying regions facilitated the appearance of new production relations between nations and nationalities, placing them in an equal position as to the ownership on the implements and means of production.

However, many nations in Russia which at the time of the 1917 October Revolution had not passed the capitalist stage or formed into nations, had to resolve national questions under the dictatorship of the proletariat and join in the process of the internationalisation of societal life. This could be attained only on the basis of a close economic alliance and mutual assistance between the nations and of economic assistance rendered by the more developed nations to backward peoples.

Political assistance to backward nations was expressed in the training of personnel to work in the Soviets, institutions and departments, as well as in the creation of Soviets of the working people.

Cultural assistance included aid in the struggle against the clergy and other reactionary feudal elements influential in the backward areas, as well as the struggle against pan-Islamism and other trends "which strive to combine the liberation movement against European and American imperialism with an attempt to strengthen the positions of the khans, landowners, mullahs, etc."[2]

---

[1] V. I. Lenin, "The Second Congress of the Communist International", *Collected Works*, Vol. 31, p. 244.
[2] V. I. Lenin, "Preliminary Draft Theses on National and Colonial Questions", *Collected Works*, Vol. 31, p. 149.

The policy of the union of the working class with the revolutionary peasantry of Eastern outlying regions was an earnest of the success of this assistance.

The victory of the Great October Socialist Revolution and its triumphal march across the country testified to the maturity of the prerequisites for it. The revolution was effected under the sign of the actualisation of proletarian internationalism.

The realisation of the first revolutionary transformations in the social system, economy and culture under the guidance of the Communist Party and Lenin laid the groundwork for the establishment of friendship among the peoples of the Soviet state.

The first decrees of the Great October Revolution, Declaration of Rights of the Peoples of Russia and other legislative acts of Soviet power, recorded the full equality and free development of all peoples and nationalities, their right to self-determination and creation of their own national statehood. This helped draw the peoples of Russia closer together, strengthen their friendship and rally them to build a new socialist society.

Lenin attached great importance to the experience of socialist construction, acquired in the first period of the existence of a new socialist society. "This experience will never be forgotten... It has gone down in history as socialism's gain, and on it the future world revolution will erect its socialist edifice."[1]

The first socialist transformations in society, the economy and culture had a huge international significance. Leonid Brezhnev stressed in his report on the 50th anniversary of the Great October Socialist Revolution: "The peoples of the world, who witnessed the epic of socialist construction, could from the very outset see that the proletarian revolution was not confined to the destruction of the old. Its underlying purport and grandeur was the building of a new life."[2]

---

[1] V. I. Lenin, "Speech at the First Congress of Economic Councils, May 26, 1918", *Collected Works*, Vol. 27, p. 413.
[2] L. I. Brezhnev, *Following Lenin's Course*, Progress Publishers, Moscow, 1972, pp. 12-13.

Chapter IV

THE MILITARY AND POLITICAL UNION OF SOVIET REPUBLICS IN DEFENCE OF THE GAINS OF THE OCTOBER REVOLUTION

The First Experience of Federation

After approving the Declaration of Rights of the Working and Exploited People, the Third All-Russia Congress of Soviets established the Soviet Russian Republic as a "federation of Soviet national republics", based on a free union of free nations.[1]

This federation united not only the territory of Great Russia but of the entire country. It was a form of union state joining all the sovereign Soviet republics and the first autonomous national-state formations.

At the closing of the Third All-Russia Congress of Soviets, Lenin expressed his deep confidence that "more and more diverse federations of free nations will group themselves around revolutionary Russia".[2]

The triumph of the Soviet power on a nationwide scale and the first socialist transformations in the interest of the working masses made the founding of a federative (union) multinational state possible. Legislatively, the Soviet-type federation was recorded in the documents of the Third All-Russia Congress of Soviets and in the first Constitution of the RSFSR.

At first, it was thought that the federation would be set up and governmental relations between the regions of the Soviet country be worked out under the conditions of peaceful socialist construction.

---

[1] *Decrees of Soviet Power*, Vol. I, pp. 341-43.
[2] V. I. Lenin, "Third All-Russia Congress of Soviets of Workers', Soldiers' and Peasants' Deputies", *Collected Works*, Vol. 26, p. 481.

However, the intervention unleashed by foreign imperialism and the Civil War were responsible for the introduction of changes into the plan for setting up the federation: the Russian Federation (RSFSR) shaped up only on the territory of Great Russia; many of the outlying areas were seized by the interventionists; others formed separate independent Soviet republics. For a number of years, the latter existed "as separate Soviet republics",[1] closely linked to the RSFSR through co-operation and mutual assistance.

This is confirmed by the establishment of fraternal relations between Soviet Russia and the Soviet Ukraine: in the Manifesto to the Ukrainian people of December 3 (16) adopted by the Council of People's Commissars, Soviet Russia recognised the right of the Ukrainian people to secede from Russia or to enter into federative relations with it. The Manifesto also emphasised that "we, the Council of People's Commissars, recognise at once, unconditionally and without reservations everything that pertains to the Ukrainian people's national rights and national independence".[2]

The First All-Ukraine Congress of Soviets held on December 12 (25), declared the Ukraine a Soviet Republic and spoke in favour of a federative link with Soviet Russia.

Even after the signing of the Brest Peace Treaty, the Second All-Ukraine Congress of Soviets which was convened in Ekaterinoslav on March 17, 1918 noted that the treaty disrupted the federative ties of the Ukraine with the Soviet federation only formally.

Having declared the Ukraine an independent federative republic uniting all the autonomous regions, free cities and republics existing in the Ukraine at that time, the congress declared its intention to retain the republic's former relations with Russia.

At the end of April-beginning of May 1918, the Fifth Territorial Congress of Soviets of Turkestan adopted a regulation on the Turkestan Soviet Federative Republic as a component of

---

[1] *The CPSU in Resolutions...*, Vol. 2, p. 73.

[2] V. I. Lenin, "Manifesto to the Ukrainian People with an Ultimatum to the Ukrainian Rada", *Collected Works*, Vol. 26, p. 361.

the RSFSR. A number of autonomous republics as components of the RSFSR had formed on the territory of the latter.

Lenin stressed later on that "the feasibility of federation has already been demonstrated in practice both by the relations between the R.S.F.S.R. and other Soviet republics ... and by the relations within the R.S.F.S.R. in respect of nationalities which formerly enjoyed neither statehood nor autonomy".[1]

The Attack of International Imperialism

The peaceful construction of the Soviet state was disrupted in the second half of 1918 by the attack of the Entente states against the Land of Soviets. The imperialists used bourgeois-nationalistic counter-revolution to try to set up bourgeois nationalistic states in the outlying districts of the country to contaminate peoples' minds with nationalism and chauvinism and to undermine their mutual friendship with the peoples of other nations.

The suppression of the first counter-revolutionary actions in the country's centre and its outlying ethnic regions demonstrated that the Russian and bourgeois-nationalistic counter-revolution could not wage a prolonged civil war against the Soviet republic without support from abroad.

Then the imperialists of the United States, Britain, France, Japan and other countries came to the aid of the internal counter-revolution. Having all this in mind, Lenin noted: "World imperialism ... in reality brought about the Civil War in our country and is responsible for protracting it."[2] Here the imperialists' main aim was "to extinguish the fire of socialist revolution which has broken out in our country and which is threatening to spread across the world".[3]

The wave of revolutionary movements not only in the citadels of imperialism but also in its vast colonies caused great anxiety

---

[1] V. I. Lenin, "Preliminary Draft Theses on National and Colonial Questions", *Collected Works*, Vol. 31, pp. 146-47.

[2] V. I. Lenin, "Fifth All-Russia Congress of the R.C.P. (B.)", *Collected Works*, Vol. 30, p. 171.

[3] V. I. Lenin, "Comrade Workers, Forward to the Last, Decisive Fight!", *Collected Works*, Vol. 28, p. 54.

of the imperialists. Lenin noted that "*owing* to the crisis of imperialism, the flames of national revolt have flared up *both* in the colonies and in Europe".[1]

The victory of the Great October Socialist Revolution and the first acts in the field of nationalities policy adopted immediately after it had a decisive effect on the national liberation movement the world over.

The victory of the dictatorship of the proletariat in Russia signified the advent of a new historical epoch with the working class in the centre and Marxist parties at the head.

The Land of Soviets was in the vanguard of all the forces fighting against imperialism. Therefore, the latter rained blows upon the first country of the dictatorship of the proletariat.

Analysing the experience the Soviet republics gained in more than two years of struggle against the invasion of the imperialists and internal counter-revolution, Lenin wrote: "The world political situation has now placed the dictatorship of the proletariat on the order of the day. World political developments are of necessity concentrated on a single focus—the struggle of the world bourgeoisie against the Soviet Russian Republic, around which are inevitably grouped, on the one hand, the Soviet movement of the advanced workers in all countries, and, on the other, all the national liberation movements in the colonies and among the oppressed nationalities, who are learning from bitter experience that their only salvation lies in the Soviet system's victory over world imperialism".[2]

The key to understanding reasons for the imperialist intervention against the Land of Soviets lies in this proposition of Lenin's.

Plans to Dismember the Land of Soviets

By the close of 1917 and beginning of 1918, the Entente states, working out their plans for a brigand attack against the Soviet country, had established the spheres of military action

---

[1] V. I. Lenin, "The Discussion on Self-Determination Summed-Up", *Collected Works*, Vol. 22, p. 354.

[2] V. I. Lenin, "Preliminary Draft Theses on National and Colonial Questions", *Collected Works*, Vol. 31, p. 147.

against the young state to dismember it and enslave its peoples.

As was noted above, the Ukraine, the Crimea and Bessarabia were declared to be the sphere of France's special interest. England was to secure the overthrow of Soviet power in the North of Russia, in the Don area, in the Kuban and Caucasus, while the United States and Japan were to deal with the Far East and Siberia. US President Woodrow Wilson, who had earned a reputation as a "peacemaker", suggested, as early as the beginning of 1918, that the allies tear the Ukraine, the Caucasus, Central Asia, and the Baltic areas, and a number of other regions away from Russia.

Initially, the organisers of the military intervention planned to make short work of the Land of Soviets with the bayonets of the Austrian and German troops.

But the signing of the Brest-Litovsk Peace Treaty between the RSFSR and Germany frustrated these plans. However, the interventionists did not recognise the Brest treaty, and considered using it as a pretext for military intervention in Russia, supposedly to "help" it as their ally.

In March 1918, British, American and French troops landed in Murmansk. They captured Murmansk and Arkhangelsk and were preparing to advance on Petrograd and Moscow "to finish with Bolshevism once and for all".[1]

In June 1918, the Entente decided to increase the number of troops in the north of Russia and placed them under the command of British General Poole. The Soviet Far East also became an object of intervention by the Entente: at the close of 1917 and beginning of 1918, the US cruiser *Brooklyn*, the Japanese cruisers *Iwami* and *Asahi*, and the British cruiser *Suffolk* appeared in the port of Vladivostok. The intervention was delayed because of the disagreements among the imperialists as to who would be the first to land.

The conference of Prime Ministers and Foreign Ministers of France, Italy and Britain that met in London on March 15, 1918, adopted a decision concerning the Allied intervention in

---

[1] *From the History of the Civil War in Russia*, Collection of Documents and Materials, Vol. I, Sovetskaya Rossiya Publishers, Moscow, 1960, p. 82 (in Russian).

the eastern part of Russia. On the second day of the conference British Foreign Secretary Balfour reported to the President of the United States: "To the conference it seemed that none is possible except through Allied intervention. Since Russia cannot help herself, she must be helped by her friends. But there are only two approaches through which such help can be supplied: the northern ports of Russia in Europe, and the eastern frontiers of Siberia."[1]

The conference suggested that Japan send its troops to the Far East and Siberia and stressed that the intervention would be impossible without the active participation of the United States. On April 4, 1918, Japanese troops landed in Vladivostok.

The counter-revolution mounted its blows. The White Guard detachments of Semyonov and Kalmykov, formed in Manchuria, were active in the Transbaikal area and in the Primorye. In Harbin, Admiral Kolchak began to form White Guard units using British and American money. In the Trans-Baikal area in May and June 1918, Soviet detachments under the command of Sergei Lazo beat back the offensive of Semyonov's bands and drove them across the border into Manchuria. In the Primorye, Soviet detachments battled successfully against the bands of Ataman Kalmykov.

To deal a blow to the very heart of the Soviet republic in May 1918 the Entente provoked a counter-revolutionary mutiny of 45,000-strong Czechoslovak Corps, joining several thousand White Guards to it.

The Entente imperialists did their best to seize the country's southern regions—the Northern Caucasus, Transcaucasia and Turkestan, using the troops of White Guard generals Kornilov, Denikin and Alexeyev for this purpose.

In Transcaucasia, bourgeois-nationalistic and petty-bourgeois parties of Musavatists, Dashnaks and Georgian Mensheviks acted as agents of international imperialism.

In his speech at the joint session of the All-Russia Central Executive Committee, Moscow City Soviet, factory and plant committees and trade unions on July 29, 1918 Lenin described

---

[1] D. Lloyd George, *War Memoirs*, Ivor Nicholson & Watson, Vol. 6, London, 1937, pp. 3175-76.

the military situation as follows: "Murmansk in the North, the Czechoslovak front in the East, Turkestan, Baku and Astrakhan in the South-East—we see that practically all the links in the chain forged by British and French imperialism have been joined."[1]

The Austro-German Occupation after the Signing of the Peace Treaty

It was in the south of the country that the links of the chain were joined by the Austro-German occupation. Violating the Brest Treaty, Austrian and German troops invaded Soviet territory. Signing a treaty with the Ukrainian Central Rada on January 27, 1918 in Brest-Litovsk the German generals moved a 300,000-man occupation army into the Ukraine. It was opposed by individual Soviet Ukrainian units which were later reorganised into the first armies. The supreme command of the Soviet troops in the Ukraine was set up in March 1918 with V. A. Antonov-Ovseyenko at the head. The Soviet Ukrainian detachments put up fierce resistance to the advancing Austro-German troops, but were unable to check their advance. By the beginning of May almost all of the Ukraine had been captured by the Germans. The Central Rada concluded a treaty with the occupiers to deliver to Germany and Austria-Hungary 60 million poods of grain, 2.75 million poods of livestock, 37.5 million poods of iron ore and many other foodstuffs and industrial raw materials.

Having attained these concessions, the occupying authorities no longer had any need for the Rada, and on April 29 disbanded it, proclaiming Ukrainian landowner P. Skoropadsky Hetman of the Ukraine. Under him, the restoration of the bourgeois-land-ownership system began in the Ukraine.

The Ukrainian people under the leadership of the Communists, who had gone underground, rose in a war of liberation against the occupiers and bourgeois nationalists for their social

---

[1] V. I. Lenin, "Speech at a Joint Session of the All-Russia Central Executive Committee, the Moscow Soviet, Factory Committees and Trade Unions of Moscow", *Collected Works*, Vol. 28, p. 23,

and national rights. The Austro-German troops also invaded Transcaucasia, the Don region and the Crimea, Byelorussia, and the Baltic.

Throughout the occupied territory, the rights and freedoms won by the people were liquidated.

In the struggle against the new power, the interventionists and the White Guards resorted to counter-revolutionary White terror which had found its expression in the mass extermination of the civilian population and in the massacre of Soviet and Party workers. By the summer of 1918, foreign diplomats Lockhart, Noulens and Francis plotted with the counter-revolutionary terrorists to overthrow Soviet power, to arrest the members of the Soviet government, and to assassinate Lenin. The Right Socialist-Revolutionaries went over to terror against the Soviet and Party workers: in Petrograd they assassinated prominent Party and Soviet leaders V. Volodarsky and M. S. Uritsky; and on August 30 they made a villainous attempt on the life of the head of the Soviet government, V. I. Lenin.

The White Guards shot the Turkestan Republic's Commissar for Labour P. G. Poltoratsky, and in the desert sands of the Transcaspian area, they murdered the 26 Baku Commissars.

The working people of Soviet Russia demanded that the counter-revolutionary terrorists be punished severely. On September 2, 1918, the All-Russia Central Executive Committee, in response to the actions of the counter-revolution which had attempted to assassinate Lenin, made the decision to introduce Red terror.

The All-Russia Extraordinary Commission for Combating Counter-Revolution and Sabotage headed by Felix Dzerzhinsky dealt shattering blows to the imperialist conspirators and agents.

At the Seventh All-Russia Congress of Soviets, Lenin said: "We have always been accused of terrorism. This is a favourite accusation that is never absent from the columns of the press. We are accused of making terrorism a principle. To this we reply, 'You yourselves do not believe in this slander'."[1]

Explaining the reason for resorting to Red terror against the

---

[1] V. I. Lenin, "Seventh All-Russia Congress of Soviets", *Collected Works*, Vol. 30, p. 222.

counter-revolution, Lenin said: "The terror was forced on us by the terror of the Entente, the terror of mighty world capitalism which has been throttling the workers and peasants, and is condemning them to death by starvation because they are fighting for their country's freedom."[1] As soon as the Soviet power scored successes in the struggle against interventionists and the White Guards, it began to do away with the Red terror. At the beginning of 1920, the death penalty was abrogated on the initiative of Dzerzhinsky.

Bourgeois-nationalistic governments were formed everywhere on occupation territory—in the Crimea, Daghestan, in the Don area and the Kuban, and in Siberia; these governments were united on a common anti-Soviet platform of disuniting people on the basis of nationality.

The RSFSR—the Organising Force Uniting the Peoples

In that difficult period for the country of Soviets, the RSFSR, the first Soviet federative republic, acted as an organising force to unite the peoples of the Soviet republics in defence of the gains of the October Revolution.

After concluding the onerous Brest Treaty, the working people of Soviet Russia had performed their internationalist duty, making it possible to uphold the foundations of the socialist revolution.

Alongside this, the RSFSR played the main role in the movement to unify the peoples for the formation of a union state.

The Russian Federation built its relations with other sovereign Soviet republics on the basis of equality. At the beginning of 1918, Lenin demanded that Antonov-Ovseyenko, the commander of the Soviet troops in the south of Russia, "*eliminate all* friction with the (Kharkov) C.E.C. This is *of the utmost importance*

---

[1] V. I. Lenin, "Seventh All-Russia Congress of Soviets", *Collected Works*, Vol. 30, p. 223. In our time, the US imperialists accuse whole nations fighting for freedom and independence, of terrorism. The authors of these accusations forget the pages of their own history, when the American leaders had to fight for independence.

for the *state*... This calls for *super-tact* on a *national* plane".[1] Later on Lenin stressed that the establishment of proper relations of the Great Russians with the peoples of Turkestan was of immense, epochal importance. He wrote: "The attitude of the Soviet Workers' and Peasants' Republic to the weak and hitherto oppressed nations is of very practical significance for the whole of Asia and for all the colonies of the world, for thousands and millions of people."[2]

Foreign intervention and the intensification of the internal counter-revolution created a mortal danger to freedom and independence of the peoples of Russia and of their first federative state. The working people in the outlying regions, who had won national freedom, did not want to find themselves under the yoke of foreign oppressors once again. They realised that they could preserve their national independence only by uniting with the Russian people.

The Communist Parties of the Outlying Ethnic Regions—Organisers of Struggle

The Communist parties of the outlying ethnic areas came forth as the organisers of the nationwide struggle against the interventionists and the White Guards, as well as against the Austro-German occupiers. They played an important role in exposing the ideology of the bourgeois-nationalistic counter-revolution, and in the internationalist education of the working people.

In June 1918, the Communist Party of Turkestan was founded at the First Congress of the Communist organisations of Turkestan; in July, the Communist Party of the Ukraine came into being; in October, the united Communist Party of Lithuania and Byelorussia; in March 1919, the Byelorussian Communist Party; and in 1920 the Communist parties of Georgia, Armenia and Azerbaijan.

---

[1] V. I. Lenin, "To V. A. Antonov-Ovseyenko", *Collected Works*, Vol. 36, p. 474.
[2] V. I. Lenin, "To the Communists of Turkestan", *Collected Works*, Vol. 30, p. 138.

Lenin paid exceptionally great attention to the setting up of the Communist parties in the republics—inseparable components of the united Party—the Russian Communist Party (Bolsheviks). Thus, on the eve of the First Congress of the Communist Party of Ukrainian Bolsheviks, on July 5, 1918 Lenin met with a group of Ukrainian Party workers, to discuss the most important questions on the agenda and the theses and drafts of the resolutions. Lenin affirmed the idea of creating a Central Revolutionary Military Committee, the task of which was to prepare and conduct an armed uprising against the German occupiers and internal counter-revolutionary forces and to restore the revolutionary unity of the Ukraine with the Soviet Russia.[1] He also gave concrete instructions to the Bolsheviks of the Turkestan, Transcaucasia and other ethnic regions.

A conference of the Communist patries of the Ukraine, Byelorussia, Lithuania, Latvia, Estonia and other occupied regions was held in October 1918 in Moscow. It adopted a decision to prepare an armed uprising against the occupiers with the aim of restoring Soviet power. The CC RCP(B) sent a large group of Party workers to the occupied territory.[2]

The Red Army—an Internationalist Force

The Ukrainians, Byelorussians, Letts, Estonians, Bashkirs, Tatars, Kazakhs and other nationalities fought alongside the Russians against the Austro-German occupiers, against the Entente troups and White Guard Generals Kaledin, Kornilov, Krasnov and Dutov.

A multinational Red Army began to take shape in this struggle of the peoples of the Land of Soviets. In the decree of the Council of People's Commissars and in the first Constitution of the RSFSR all working people regardless of nationality were called upon to defend their country. The decree read: "Everyone should join the Army who is ready to give all his strength and

---

[1] See *Vladimir Ilyich Lenin. Biographical Chronicle*, Vol. 5, pp. 603-04.

[2] A. V. Likholat, op. cit., p. 80.

his life in order to defend the gains of the October Revolution, the power of the Soviets and socialism."[1]

Nearly 40 non-Russian nationalities debarred from military service under the tsar received the right to defend their socialist homeland for the first time.

To build the Red Army and turn it into a large regular army, it was important to introduce general military training of the working people without disrupting their work. According to the decree of the Council of People's Commissars, conscription into the Red Army of the workers and peasants was introduced in June 1918 on the basis of universal military service.

On the other hand, the bourgeois nationalists tried to use national military units for their counter-revolutionary designs. But the Soviet government liquidated these attempts.

The People's Commissariat for Nationalities headed by Joseph Stalin, and its national commissariats and local departments formed national military units in the republics and worked to educate them in the spirit of proletarian internationalism. Their duty was to organise political educational work among soldiers of non-Russian nationalities, to publish and distribute in the military units literature, newspapers and magazines in the languages of the peoples of the country.

In the Ukraine national military units—detachments of Red Cossacks—were already being formed at the end of December 1917. The Cossack regiment under the command of V. M. Primakov fought against the counter-revolutionary Central Rada for the establishment of Soviet power in the Ukraine alongside Russian Red Guard units which arrived from the North.

In the second half of 1918, a regular Red Army was created in the Ukraine. Together with the Red Army of the RSFSR, it waged heavy battles against German troops and Ataman Petlyura's detachments. In the spring of 1918, the Ukrainian Soviet units retreated into Russia and continued their heroic struggle against the occupiers and White Guards.

Insurgent regiments and divisions—the nucleus of the future Ukrainian Red Army—were formed in the so-called neutral zone along the border between Russia and the Ukraine. These units

---

[1] *Decrees of Soviet Power*, Vol. I, p. 356.

played an important role in liberating the Ukraine from the Austro-German occupiers and bourgeois nationalists.

The formation of Muslim military units from among the Tatars, Bashkirs, Chuvashes, Mari, Udmurts and other nationalities played an important role in the internationalist rallying of the working people for the struggle against the interventionists and the White Guards. Party organisations of the Volga area, the Urals and Western Siberia conducted this work in the summer of 1918.

Along with the Red Army units which arrived from the country's centre and consisted of Russians, Ukrainians, Byelorussians and Letts, these newly formed Muslim units fought successfully against White Czechs and Kolchak's White Guard army.

Truly internationalist in composition and spirit, the Red Army units went over to a decisive offensive in the Volga area in August 1918 and liberated Kazan, Simbirsk, and other major cities. These successes on the Eastern Front made it possible to shore up the Southern and Western fronts and increase the aid to the working people of the Ukraine, Byelorussia, the Baltic and other regions in their struggle for liberation from the Austro-German occupiers and bourgeois nationalists.

The Collapse of Austro-German Occupation. Restoration of Soviet Power in the Republics

In November 1918, the Austro-German occupation collapsed: the victorious bourgeois revolution had put an end to monarchy in Germany. In October 1918 the multinational Austro-Hungarian empire disintegrated.

Soviet Russia could annul the onerous Brest Treaty and render direct military aid to the peoples of the occupied regions in driving out the occupiers and their bourgeois-nationalist hirelings.

The All-Russia Central Executive Committee called upon the masses of the occupied regions to drive out the occupiers, liquidate the bourgeois-nationalist governments, and restore Soviet power, promising the peoples "full and complete support to the end in their struggle for the establishment on their lands of the socialist power of the workers and peasants".[1]

The internationalist union of the peoples of Russia, the Ukraine, Byelorussia and the Baltic region shaped up in the joint struggle against the occupiers and White Guards. Its aim was the national and social liberation of the working people from the foreign occupiers. Evaluating the correlation of the national and the internationalist on the example of the Ukrainian people's struggle against the Germans, Lenin wrote: "While the loss of the Ukraine was a grave national sacrifice, it helped to steel and *strengthen* the workers and poor peasants of the Ukraine as revolutionary fighters for the world workers' revolution. The Ukraine's suffering was the world revolution's gain, for the German troops were corrupted, German imperialism was weakened, and the German, Ukrainian and Russian revolutionary workers were *drawn closer together*."[2]

Lenin's proposition is fully applicable to the struggle of other peoples who were victims of Austro-German occupation.

At the close of 1918, the socialist revolution triumphed for the second time—Soviet power which had been overthrown by the occupiers, was restored everywhere.

After Hetman Skoropadsky's flight into Germany, bourgeois-nationalist parties in the Ukraine established the so-called Directory headed by V. Vinnichenko and S. Petlyura. By agreement with the Germans, the Directory seized power in the Ukraine and began to form counter-revolutionary detachments.

The Soviet government of Russia came to the assistance of the Ukrainian workers and peasants who rose against the Austro-German occupiers and the Directory. On November 17, 1918 the Ukrainian Front was established, including the 1st and 2nd Ukrainian insurgent divisions, formed in the autumn of 1918 along the so-called neutral zone at the frontier with Russia, as well as the Moscow workers' division, the 9th Division, and the 2nd Orel Brigade, which all arrived from Russia. V. A. Antonov-Ovseyenko was in command of the Ukrainian Front. On No-

---

[1] *Decrees of Soviet Power*, Vol. IV, Politizdat, Moscow, 1968, p. 18.
[2] V. I. Lenin, "The Proletarian Revolution and the Renegade Kautsky", *Collected Works*, Vol. 28, p. 112.

vember 29, the Ukrainian Soviet Republic was re-established. The Provisional Workers' and Peasants' Government of the Ukraine included V. K. Averin, Y. M. Kotsyubinsky, E. I. Kviring, F. A. Sergeyev (Artyom), K. E. Voroshilov, V. P. Zatonsky, and others. The Ukrainian Soviet Government called on the workers and peasants to step up the struggle to expel the occupiers and the bourgeois-nationalist detachments of the Directory completely and to re-establish Soviet power in the Ukraine.

The working people of Byelorussia stepped up their struggle against the occupying forces and the counter-revolutionary Rada in November and December of 1918. The latter attempted to retain power with the assistance of the imperialists of the Entente, but was unsuccessful. On December 31, 1918, Communists established a Provisional Workers' and Peasants' Government on the liberated territory of Byelorussia which included A. G. Chervyakov, A. F. Myasnikov, D. F. Zhilunovich, and others.

The Byelorussian Soviet Socialist Republic was proclaimed on January 1, 1919. The Congress of Soviets of Byelorussia that met in February 1919 adopted the Constitution of the Byelorussian Soviet Socialist Republic. The Congress resolved to begin negotiations on establishing federal ties with the RSFSR.

The revolution was scoring victories over the occupiers in the Baltic area as well. In November 1918, the working people of Estonia under the guidance of the Communists and with the assistance of the Red Army ousted the Austro-German occupiers from a considerable part of their territory. On November 29, 1918, the Estonian Soviet Republic (the Estland Labour Commune) was proclaimed. Its government included J. J. Anvelt, H. Pöögelmann, J. Kaspert, and others.

The working people of Latvia intensified their struggle against the Austro-German occupying forces in November and December 1918. On November 17, a Provisional Soviet Government was formed, with Stučka at its head, which proclaimed the establishment of the Soviet Republic of Latvia in a manifesto. By January 1919, much of Latvia had been freed from the occupiers and bourgeois nationalists.

In December 1918, Soviet power was proclaimed in Lithuania.

The RSFSR recognised the independence of the young Soviet republics, which in their turn sought to unite more closely around Soviet Russia for the struggle against external enemies. Thus, the military-political union of the Soviet republics gradually began to take shape.

Military Build-Up in the Soviet Republics

Military build-up in the Soviet republics was stepped up. The creation of independent armies in the Soviet republics at the end of 1918 and beginning of 1919 played an important role in this process, enabling the working people in the republics to be drawn into the military defence of their revolutionary gains, to protect the main base of the socialist revolution—the RSFSR. The presence of separate armies in the republics emphasised their sovereignty and independence, robbing bourgeois nationalists of an opportunity to treat the offensive of the Red Army in the outlying areas as an occupation. In the Ukraine, the Provisional Workers' and Peasants' Government showed indefatigable concern for boosting the fighting capacity of the young Red Army units, strengthening the military and political unity of the Soviet Ukraine with the RSFSR and other Soviet republics.

The formation of the Byelorussian Red Army, which included many units of the Western Army composed of Byelorussians, was completed in January 1919.

The 5th Vilnius Regiment, formed in Moscow, which actively participated in the ousting of the Austro-German occupying forces from the Baltic area, became the nucleus of the Lithuanian Red Army formed at the close of 1918.

After the formation of the Estland Labour Commune, the Estonian national detachments were united into the Estonian Red Army. Leaders of the Estonian Bolsheviks J. J. Anvelt, V. E. Kingissepp, I. V. Rabchinsky and others took an active part in its organisation.

The Latvian Red Army was created in Latvia at the beginning of 1919. I. I. Vatsetis, a colonel of the old army, was appointed its commander. Later he became the commander of the Eastern Front, and in September 1918-July 1919—Commander-in-Chief of all the armed forces of the RSFSR. Prominent Latvian revolutionary K. H. Danishevsky, who later became a member of the Revolutionary Military Council of the RSFSR, headed the Latvian Revolutionary Military Council.

In connection with the successful advance of the Red Army units in the regions liberated from occupiers, Lenin proposed to Commander-in-Chief Vatsetis that instructions be issued to Red Army commanders of the corresponding military units for the Red Army to "render all possible support to the provisional Soviet governments in Latvia, Estonia, the Ukraine and Lithuania, but, of course, only to the Soviet governments".[1]

In November-December 1918, the General HQ of the Red Army had transferred from the Eastern Front Byelorussian, Latvian, Estonian and other national units to the Western Front. This created favourable conditions for the establishment of friendly ties between the Red Army and the local population and the speedy restoration of Soviet power. This rapprochement of the army and the population of the outlying areas intensified the desire of the working masses of the ethnic regions to enter into closer unity with the Russian people.

This circumstance alone refuted the contentions of bourgeois falsifiers that Soviet power was allegedly foisted upon the non-Russian peoples with the aid of Red Army bayonets. These contentions reflected the desire of the falsifiers to belittle the importance of the struggle of the working masses of the ethnic regions against the occupiers and White Guards, as well as slur the fact that the Red Army was the only internationalist army in the world in its composition and aims. After defeating the troops of the interventionists and White Guards on the territory of the RSFSR, the Red Army thus rendered invaluable assistance to the outlying areas. On the other hand, the victory over the mounting intervention of the Entente at the close of 1918 and beginning of 1919 would have been impossible without the close union of the RSFSR with the sovereign national republics.

---

[1] V. I. Lenin, "Telegram to Commander-in-Chief", *Collected Works*, Vol. 28, p. 225.

The New Drive of the Entente's Interventionists

The defeat of the Austro-German occupiers was of a dual significance for the Land of Soviets: on the one hand,—positive, since the Soviet Russia could break the onerous Brest Peace Treaty and begin an open struggle for the liberation of all the occupied territories.

But on the other, the position of the Soviet country worsened because of the increased military pressure of the Entente states, which after the victory over Germany were in a position to detach a considerable body of troops for the intervention. Possessing large naval forces, they had all the necessary conditions to organise a blockade.

As before, the aim of the intervention was to smash the state of the dictatorship of the proletariat as speedily as possible and to dismember it into separate regions, headed by the White Guards and bourgeois-nationalistic governments.

The draft worked out in January 1919 by the US State Department for the American delegation at the Paris peace conference pointed out that all of Russia had to be divided into "big natural regions" each of which would have a special economic life of its own, making sure that no region was sufficiently independent to form a separate state.[1]

At the same time the interventionists had worked out a plan to seal off Russia's access to the Ukraine, the Caucasus, and Western Siberia, which, as the French Prime Minister Clemenceau noted, were economically necessary for the new state to hold out.[2]

To keep Soviet power from being restored in the Baltic area, in the Ukraine and Byelorussia, the Entente and the United States decided to retain the Austro-German troops in the occupied regions, counting on their aid in restoring capitalist Russia.

The nationwide war against the occupiers and White Guards

---

[1] Quoted in *History of the Foreign Policy of the USSR*, Vol. I, 1917-1945, Nauka Publishers, Moscow, 1976, p. 98 (in Russian).
[2] See *Russian-American Relations. March 1917-March 1920. Documents and Papers*, Harcourt, Brace and Howe, N.Y., 1920, p. 273.

led to the liberation of the Ukraine, Byelorussia and the Baltic area. Only in the latter did the Entente imperialists with the help of the German troops once again manage to overthrow Soviet power at the beginning of 1919, replacing it with reactionary governments of the Estonian, Latvian and Lithuanian bourgeois nationalists.

The interventionists stepped up their pressure, spearheading it at the main base of the socialist revolution—the RSFSR—in the south, north and in the east, landing more detachments of their troops there.

A large Red Army was needed to repulse the new onslaught of Entente troops. In his letter to the joint session of the All-Russia Central Executive Committee of October 3, 1918, Lenin wrote: "We had decided to have an army of one million men by the spring; now we need an army of three million. We can have it. *And we shall have it.*"[1]

The position at the fronts at the close of 1918-beginning of 1919 demanded the concentration of all resources the peoples of the Soviet republics could muster for the creation of a large regular Red Army which could rely on a sound rear and prompt delivery of arms and foodstuffs to the front for the fighting troops. Chaired by Lenin, the Council of the Workers' and Peasants' Defence which was set up by the All-Russia Central Executive Committee on November 30, 1918, was called upon to concentrate the country's efforts on questions of its military defence.

On the other hand, the growing danger of war demanded ever closer political and economic unity among the republics.

To attain this, all the Communists both in the centre and in the localities had to master the essence of the Leninist nationalities policy and actualise it under the difficult conditions of the Civil War and foreign intervention.

The successes in conducting the nationalities policy were predetermined by strengthening the union of the working class with

---

[1] V. I. Lenin, "Letter to a Joint Session of the All-Russia Central Executive Committee, the Moscow Soviet and Representatives of Factory Committees and Trade Unions, October 3, 1918", *Collected Works*, Vol. 28, p. 103.

the working peasantry of Russia and the ethnic regions. The Party managed to achieve this union on the basis of the realisation of the decisions of the Eighth RCP(B) Congress.

The Eighth Party Congress on the Necessity to Strengthen Unity of the Republics and the Union of the Working Class with the Peasantry

The Eighth Party Congress which convened in Moscow in March 1919 adopted an important decision on the nationalities question.

Bourgeois falsifiers contend that the Soviet power went back on the right of nations to self-determination declared in the first days of the October Revolution, sending its troops to the country's borders to suppress national movements. What troops were sent to the ethnic regions and for what purpose has been stated above.

The history of the Soviet state testifies to the consistent struggle of the Party to consolidate peoples on the basis of the Leninist nationalities policy, the most important aspect of which was the right of nations to self-determination.

At the Eighth Party Congress, Lenin resolutely opposed N. Bukharin and G. Pyatakov, who denied the right of nations to self-determination.

Meanwhile, Lenin stressed, the process of self-determination of nations had just begun in Russia; the unity of the peoples in the struggle against imperialism was a must, but it had to be achieved by means of propaganda, Party influence and the setting up of united trade unions.

The negation of the right of nations to self-determination would only intensify the mistrust of the formerly oppressed nations towards Soviet power. Therefore, an especial caution on the part of the representatives of the Great Russian nation was indispensable in effecting the equality and freedom of nations to secede to eliminate grounds for distrust and allow a voluntary union of all nations.[1]

---

[1] See V. I. Lenin, "Eighth Congress of the R.C.P.(B.)", *Collected Works*, Vol. 29, p. 195.

The Communists were faced with the task of resolutely overcoming even the slightest manifestations of chauvinism and explaining to the working people of the formerly oppressed nations that a closer military and economic union of all peoples was needed to win in the fierce struggle against imperialism.

The separation of working people of different nationalities and intensification of discord only weakened the state of the workers and peasants and strengthened the power of landowners and capitalists.

Therefore, it was recorded in the Party Programme adopted by the Eighth RCP(B) Congress: "The drawing closer together of the proletarians and semi-proletarians of different nationalities for a joint revolutionary struggle to overthrow the landlords and bourgeoisie is the cornerstone of our policy."[1]

Alongside this, Lenin demanded that concrete conditions of the development of various peoples be taken into consideration. ". . .the essence of the question of the self-determination of nations is that different nations are advancing in the same historical direction, but by very different zigzags and bypaths, and that the more cultured nations are obviously proceeding in a way that differs from that of the less cultured nations".[2] One cannot act according to a single pattern even in working for unity. Lenin said that we could not build a socialist society without taking due account of the national question in the Party Programme, of its specific features and ways of solving it.

The latter problem occupied one of the most important places in the work of the Eighth Party Congress: whether the interventionists and White-Guards would win or not depended in large measure on the strengthening of the alliance of the working class with the peasantry of Russia and of the outlying regions.

After the Soviet power realised its agrarian reforms, the middle peasantry became the central figure in the village, and success in the Civil War and in socialist construction depended on how it behaved.

---

[1] *The CPSU in Resolutions. . .*, Vol. 2, p. 45.
[2] V. I. Lenin, "Eighth Congress of the R.C.P.(B.)", *Collected Works*, Vol. 29, p. 195.

Towards the end of 1918, the middle peasantry, which had experienced the oppression of the interventionists and the White Guards, sided with Soviet power. This allowed the Bolshevik Party to go over from a policy of neutralising the middle peasantry to firm alliance with it.

The swing of the middle peasantry testified to a deep differentiation in a petty-bourgeois democracy—from animosity to neutrality and then to an alliance with the state of the dictatorship of the proletariat. Therefore, the proletariat could now seek alliance with it, in particular, with the middle peasantry.

Lenin in his article "The Valuable Admissions of Pitirim Sorokin" (1918) profoundly substantiated the necessity of shifting from the policy of neutralising the middle peasant to an alliance with him. "The task at the present moment is to come to an agreement with the middle peasant—while not for a moment renouncing the struggle against the kulak and at the same time firmly relying solely on the poor peasant."[1]

On the proposal of Lenin, who spoke of the proper attitude towards the middle peasantry, the Eighth Party Congress proclaimed a transition from a policy of neutralising the middle peasantry to a firm alliance with it, while the working class would retain its leading role.

Reality demanded that the policy in the ethnic regions be conducted with due account for class and national peculiarities. Lenin said at the congress: "It would be a mistake to draw up stereotyped decrees for all parts of Russia; it would be a mistake for the Bolshevik Communists, the Soviet officials in the Ukraine and the Don, to apply these decrees to other regions wholesale, without discrimination."[2]

The line of the Party with respect to the middle peasantry adopted at the Eighth Party Congress made it possible to strengthen the alliance of the working class with the peasantry of the central part of Russia and of the ethnic regions, to consolidate millions of working people of different nationalities into a single

---

[1] V. I. Lenin, "The Valuable Admissions of Pitirim Sorokin", *Collected Works*, Vol. 28, p. 191.
[2] V. I. Lenin, "Eighth Congress of the R.C.P. (B.)", *Collected Works*, Vol. 29, p. 158.

militant camp. They came to realise the necessity of strengthening the Red Army which rose to defend their gains from the arbitrariness of the White Guards and the bourgeois-landowner counter-revolution.

The Entente's Diplomatic Manoeuvre

As stated above, after the defeat of Germany, the Entente immediately sent ever new contingents of its troops to the North, the Black Sea ports, and the Far East.

However, it soon came to light that those troops were unfit for action since they became revolutionary after coming into contact with the Russian workers and peasants. A revolutionary solidarity movement sprang to life in a number of capitalist countries under the slogan: "Hands Off Russia!"

The Entente, coming to grief in its attempt to conquer Russia with its own troops, decided to deal the crushing blow with the help of the armies of the White generals and the White Army which it set up in the Baltic area.

In connection with the successes of the Red Army at the end of 1918 and beginning of 1919 on many fronts the leaders of the Entente decided to invite the Soviet government and the bourgeois "governments" of the outlying areas of Russia to a peace conference. It was supposed to take place on the Princes Islands in the Sea of Marmora.

This diplomatic manoeuvre of the Entente was designed to help its allies—the White Guard generals and the governments they had set up. Under cover of negotiations with Soviet Russia, they intended to consolidate the territories they seized.

Thus, the Entente planned to divide Russia among the bourgeois-nationalistic governments and the pretenders to the creation of a unified, indivisible Russia in the persons of Kolchak, Denikin and Yudenich.

Despite the fact that Soviet Russia did not receive an official invitation to attend the conference, its government expressed its readiness to take part in the negotiations in a note to the Entente governments, provided it received an official invitation, in which case it would agree to a truce and the suspension of the successful advance of its troops.

However, the White Guard governments, counting on the success of the offensive of Kolchak's armies, which began their advance from the east, refused to begin talks with the Soviet government. The conference on the Princes Islands was frustrated by the Entente's leaders.

The menace to the Republic of the Soviets in connection with the offensive of the Kolchak armies on the Eastern Front in February 1919 demanded tighter unification of the military forces of the Soviet republics.

The Formation of a Military-Political Alliance of the Republics

In the spring of 1919, the Entente mounted a new major offensive against the Soviet Republic. Kolchak advanced from the east, Denikin—from the south, Yudenich from the west, and Miller from the north. The Entente increased its aid of troops, arms and equipment to the White Guards.

The Soviet republics were threatened with a new foreign enslavement: this called for a closer unity between them.

However, there were serious shortcomings in the activity of the military organs of the Soviet republics. Thus, in the Ukraine, the People's Commissariat for Military and Naval Affairs headed by N. I. Podvoisky, handled the task of mobilising people for the Red Army badly, creating unwieldy formations of internal troops, and failed to make proper use of military equipment stored in the Ukraine.

Upon learning about this, Lenin sent urgent telegrams: On April 22, 1919, he telegraphed Antonov-Ovseyenko and others in Kiev: "From Podvoisky's information I see that there is a mass of war materiel in the Ukraine, even without counting Odessa. It should not be hoarded, and both Donets workers and new units should be formed to take Taganrog and Rostov... At all costs the forces against Denikin must be rapidly and considerably increased."[1] However, despite Lenin's repeated demands that the Ukraine increased its assistance to the Southern Front, Antonov-Ovseyenko, who was then in charge of the Ukrainian Front, and People's Commissar for Military and Naval Affairs Podvoisky failed to comply with Lenin's orders. This was one of the reasons for the success of Denikin's armies, which captured the Donets Coal Basin in May 1919. There were also serious shortcomings in the activity of the People's Commissars for Military Affairs and the commands of the Soviet troops of the Lithuanian, Byelorussian, Latvian and Estonian Soviet republics.

Commander-in-Chief Vatsetis drew the attention of the Council of Defence to this and sent Lenin a memorandum on April 23, 1919 concerning the military situation in the RSFSR and substantiating the necessity of uniting the armed forces of the Soviet republics and subordinating them to a single command. Lenin wrote on Vatsetis's report: "It is necessary *urgently*, at once: 1) to draw up the *text* of a directive from the C.C. to all 'nationals' on army *unity* (integration); 2) to give it *also* to the press for a series of articles. . ."[2]

In a number of his speeches, Lenin determined the main tasks of the Party in the menacing situation and demanded that all political and organisational work in the country be subordinated to defence, turning the country into a military camp, not only in word but also in deed.

At the beginning of May 1919, Lenin wrote Draft CC Directives on Army Unity, which bore his signature and Stalin's as well. This most important document said that "a single command for all contingents of the Red Army, the strictest centralisation of the command of all the forces and resources of the socialist republics" was an essential condition for a successful[3] defensive war, which the Russian Federation was waging in alliance with the fraternal Soviet Republics of the Ukraine, Latvia,

---

[1] V. I. Lenin, "Telegram to V. A. Antonov-Ovseyenko, April 22, 1919", *Collected Works*, Vol. 35, p. 379.

[2] V. I. Lenin, "To E. M. Sklyansky, April 24, 1919", *Collected Works*, Vol. 44, Progress Publishers, Moscow, 1975, p. 216.

[3] V. I. Lenin, "Draft C. C. Directives on Army Unity", *Collected Works*, Vol. 29, p. 404.

Estonia, Lithuania and Byelorussia against world imperialism and the Black Hundred and White Guard counter-revolution supported by it.

The draft also envisaged the centralisation of the entire apparatus of military supply and railway transport as a material factor of prime importance both for conducting military operations and for supplying the Red Army with arms, equipment and food.

The draft directives envisaged practical measures for uniting all the matters of supplying the Red Army under a single leadership of the Defence Council, managing railway transport of the fraternal socialist republics under the leadership of the People's Commissariat for Railways of the RSFSR, and other measures. All decrees adopted in the republics bearing on the management of these branches were to be rescinded if they contradicted the interests of the unity of the Soviet republics.

The Plenary Meeting of the RCP(B) Central Committee, which convened on May 4, 1919, examined the question of military unity, approved the Decree of the Draft Directives on Army Unity, which was then sent to the Central Committees of the Communist Parties of the Ukraine, Lithuania, Byelorussia, Latvia and Estonia. The RCP(B) Central Committee suggested that the republics voice their opinion on the question and adopt corresponding resolutions through the Central Executive Committees of their Soviets.

The Communists and the masses of working people of the Ukraine were among the first to approve the directives of the RCP(B) Central Committee. A joint meeting of members of the CPU(B) Central Committee, representatives of the CC RCP(B), and executives of the Ukrainian central institutions was held in Kiev on May 18, 1919, and the directives of the CC RCP(B) were unanimously approved.[1]

On the same day the Central Executive Committee of the Soviets of the Ukraine, jointly with the representatives of the Kiev Soviet and other workers' organisations, adopted a special resolution "On the Unification of Military Forces of the Soviet Republics", declaring the necessity of coordinating the entire

---

[1] See Likholat, op. cit., p. 85.

armed struggle on a national basis and pooling the material resources of all the republics for the united front.

The Ukrainian Central Executive Committee of Soviets entrusted its presidium to turn to all the Soviet republics with the proposal of working out ways to organise a united front for the revolutionary struggle.

The Soviets of Byelorussia, Lithuania and Latvia adopted similar decisions: the main idea of them all was that the alliance established between the friendly republics should be even closer.

The bourgeois nationalists and petty-bourgeois national-deviationists opposed the military-political alliance of the republics.

In the Ukraine the petty-bourgeois Borotbist Party,* which sided with the Bolsheviks at the time, came out against the proposed alliance.

At the height of the struggle against Denikin, who had seized the Donbas, Poltava, and Ekaterinoslav, when the fate of the Soviets in the Ukraine was utterly dependent on strengthening the military and political alliance with Soviet Russia, the Borotbists came out against military unity, unleashing a slanderous campaign against the CC RCP(B) and the RSFSR.

Having received information about the actions of the Borotbists, Lenin telegraphed Kh. G. Rakovsky in Kiev: "The resolution passed by the Ekaterinoslav Socialist-Revolutionaries shows that those scoundrels are advocates of the kulaks. There must be a newspaper campaign against them on the grounds of their defence of the kulaks and their slogan 'oppose centralisation'; it must be required of them that they expose the kulaks and struggle against the free sale of grain by peasants."[1]

He entrusted the editor of *Pravda* to publish the Borotbists' resolution "with a *circumstantial* and calm analysis, demonstrating *in detail* that *such* waverings of the Socialist-Revolutionaries in the direction of the kulak and of separation from Russia, i.e., of *fragmentation* of our forces in face of Kolchak and Denikin, *objectively* lead to *helping* the bourgeoisie and Kolchak".[2]

---

* *Borotbists*—Ukrainian Left Socialist-Revolutionaries.
[1] V. I. Lenin, "Telegram to the Chairman of the Council of People's Commissars of the Ukraine", *Collected Works*, Vol. 29, p. 327.
[2] V. I. Lenin, "To N. I. Bukharin, April 25, 1919", *Collected Works*, Vol. 35, p. 384.

The working people of the Soviet republics became convinced that the unity of the republics was a vital necessity if they were to be able to defend their existence. This is how one of the organs of the Ukrainian Central Executive Committee of Soviets expressed the thought: "The unification of the armed forces of all Soviet republics is not only expedient and necessary from the point of view of the defence of the revolution, but is also in line with the consciousness and feelings of the masses of workers of all the Soviet republics."[1]

On May 27, 1919, the Plenary Meeting of the Moscow Soviet adopted a decision approving the unification of military efforts of the Soviet republics, proposing that all the workers' organisations of Moscow immediately discuss and adopt effective measures to help the Donbas workers in their struggle against Denikin.[2]

The newspaper of the Ukrainian Bolsheviks, *Kommunist*, appraised this step of the Moscow workers as an effective manifestation of proletarian internationalism, the bearer of which was the internationalist nucleus of the proletarian party "as a counterbalance to those groups in the Soviet Ukraine, including left-oriented ones, which have yet not shaken off their nationalistic mould".[3]

The working people of Lithuania and Byelorussia came out for the speediest possible formation of the military-political alliance of the Soviet republics: in May 1919 the Defence Council of these republics turned to the All-Russia Central Executive Committee of the RSFSR with a proposal to establish a military unity, set up a single command, and station the armies in accordance with their operational assignments and not according to the principle of the national or state boundaries.

Thus, Lenin's idea of a military and political alliance met with general approval in all the republics.

Realising the decision of the Plenary Meeting of the CC RCP(B) of May 4, 1919 on military unity, on June 1, 1919 the All-Russia Central Executive Committee of the RSFSR jointly

---

[1] *The Communist Party Is the Inspirer and Organiser of the Ukrainian People's Unification Movement for the Formation of the USSR,* p. 180.

[2] Ibid., p. 182.

[3] Ibid., p. 185.

with representatives of other independent Soviet republics adopted a decree on the formation of a defensive alliance of the Soviet republics of Russia, the Ukraine, Latvia, Lithuania and Byelorussia to struggle against world imperialism.

The military organisation and military command, economic councils, railway administration and management, finance, and commissariats for labour of the above republics were unified in accordance with this decree. The management of these branches of national life was concentrated in the hands of single boards.[1]

The adoption of this decree gave legislative expression to the nearly two years of experience in the unification movement of the peoples, while the decree itself was in essence a treaty between the Soviet republics on the unification of all their resources under the RSFSR for the struggle against world imperialism.

When this decree had been realised in practice, the separate national units and formations of the Red Army joined into a multinational Red Army with a single command and single organs of supply and management of the home front, transportation by rail in particular.

The unification of the armed forces, means of communication and scarce economic resources of the Soviet republics played a decisive role in the rout of the Entente's forces.

Lenin time and again reminded all the Communists, all the working people of the Soviet land that, unless their efforts were united, there would be no victory over imperialism.

In his "Letter to the Workers and Peasants of the Ukraine Apropos of the Victories over Denikin" (December 1919) he wrote: "If we fail to maintain the closest alliance, an alliance against Denikin, an alliance against the capitalists and kulaks of our countries and of all countries, the cause of labour will most certainly perish for many years to come in the sense that the capitalists *will be able* to crush and strangle both the Soviet Ukraine and Soviet Russia."[2]

---

[1] See *Decrees of Soviet Power*, Vol. V, Politizdat, Moscow, 1963, pp. 259-61.

[2] V. I. Lenin, "Letter to the Workers and Peasants of the Ukraine Apropos of the Victories over Denikin", *Collected Works*, Vol. 30, p. 297.

The year 1919 was a year of decisive victories for the Red Army. In November 1919, Yudenich's army was smashed at the approaches to Petrograd. Denikin's army was routed towards the close of 1919 and the beginning of 1920. The Urals and Siberia were freed from the armies of Kolchak. The Ukraine, Northern Caucasus, Central Asia were also liberated. The White Guards and interventionists were driven out of Arkhangelsk and Murmansk in the North.

The military and political alliance of the sovereign Soviet republics, based on the military and political alliance of Russia's working class with the peasantry of the country's central and ethnic regions, was one of the decisive conditions for the victory over the united forces of internal and external counter-revolution. It was also an important stage in the unification movement of the peoples of the Soviet republics towards the creation of a single federal state.

Further Development of the Federation of Soviet Republics

The establishment of the military and political alliance among the republics in June 1919 meant in fact their closer federation.

In November 1919, the Eighth All-Russia Conference of the RCP(B) adopted Lenin's resolution on Soviet rule in the Ukraine, which pointed to the necessity of the closest possible union among all the Soviet republics in their struggle against international imperialism and stressed that "the R.C.P. maintains that the form of that alliance must be finally determined by the Ukrainian workers and labouring peasants themselves".[1]

This was confirmed by the All-Ukraine Revolutionary Committee which on December 11, 1919 declared: "A free and independent Ukrainian Socialist Soviet Republic is rising again. It will march hand in hand with the free and independent Socialist Soviet Republic of Russia."[2]

---

[1] V. I. Lenin, "Draft Resolution of the C.C. R.C.P.(B.) on Soviet Rule in the Ukraine", *Collected Works,* Vol. 30, p. 166.

[2] *The Communist Party Is the Inspirer and Organiser...,* p. 222.

In January 1920 the All-Ukraine Revolutionary Committee introduced on the territory of the Ukraine all the decrees of the RSFSR concerning military, financial, economic and food supply matters, railway transport, and post and telegraph. In February 1920, this committee was abolished since it had fulfilled all its tasks and was replaced by constitutional organs of power—All-Ukraine Central Executive Committee of Soviets and the Council of People's Commissars of the Ukraine.

The decisions of the Fourth Conference of the CPU(B), which was held in March 1920, and the Fourth All-Ukraine Congress of Soviets convened in May 1920 in Kharkov, were of great significance in terms of defining more specific forms of state relations between the Ukrainian Soviet Socialist Republic and the RSFSR. The decision of the Fourth Conference stated that only Soviet power could give the peoples genuine self-determination and freedom from the rule of the exploiters.

Stressing the role of the RSFSR in the struggle against international imperialism, the conference declared that any separation of the Ukraine from Russia would only be playing into imperialists' hands, while their close alliance would help overcome economic dislocation. The conference mapped out practical ways for the further unification of the people's commissariats of both republics.[1]

The Fourth All-Ukraine Congress of Soviets which opened after the Polish White troops attacked the Ukraine and Russia (in April 1920), affirmed in a special statement that the Ukraine retained both its independence and an agreement with the RSFSR concerning their military alliance. The congress entrusted the Central Executive Committee to pursue a policy of drawing the Ukraine closer together with the RSFSR, expressing confidence that "new allies will join the federation of the Soviet republics of Russia and the Ukraine to form a great international republic of Soviets".[2]

After the war against the Polish White troops and Wrangel came to a successful conclusion, on December 28, 1920 the

---

[1] See *The Communist Party Is the Inspirer and Organiser...*, pp. 260-64.

[2] Ibid., p. 286.

RSFSR and the Ukraine signed a treaty concluding a military and economic alliance between themselves. Their respective military and naval, foreign trade, finance, labour, railways, post and telegraph commissariats, as well as the Supreme Economic Councils were merged. The treaty between the two republics was approved on December 29, 1920 by the Eighth All-Russia Congress of Soviets and on March 2, 1921 by the Fifth All-Ukraine Congress of Soviets.[1]

When the Red Army liberated the territory of Byelorussia from the Polish White troops in July 1920, it became possible to restore Soviet power everywhere, first in the form of revolutionary committees headed by the Byelorussian Revolutionary Military Committee.

The Second All-Byelorussia Congress of Soviets which opened on December 13, 1920 in Minsk formalised the existence of a sovereign Byelorussian Soviet Socialist Republic and the development of federative links with the RSFSR and other Soviet republics.

As a result of the nationwide struggle of the working people of Azerbaijan and with the aid of the Eleventh Army, the Musavatist government was overthrown in April 1920 and Soviet power restored in Azerbaijan; on November 29, the victory was announced in Armenia and in February 1921, Georgia was rewon by the revolution. Azerbaijan, Armenia and Georgia were declared Soviet Socialist Republics.

The possibility of independent development opened up before the working people of the Transcaucasian Soviet republics.

The RSFSR came to the aid of the newly formed Soviet republics: allied treaties were signed on military and economic aid. By decisions of the Ninth All-Russia Congress of Soviets, representatives of Azerbaijan, Armenia and Georgia were included in the All-Russia Central Executive Committee of the RSFSR.

The formation of independent republics led to greater consolidation in the military, economic and political fields and did not weaken in any way the alliance that arose between them.

---

[1] See *The Communist Party Is the Inspirer and Organiser...*, p. 339.

This was a necessary prerequisite for the formation of a single federal state—the USSR.

The treaty relations which arose between the Soviet republics were based on the self-determination and equality of the peoples, encompassed the military, economic, political and cultural fields, and served to preserve peace and restore the national economy.

In March 1921, the Tenth Congress of the RCP(B) substantiated the significance of the federation of Soviet republics as a form of state union, ensuring its economic development as a whole and the development of each individual Soviet republic, and helping to establish fraternal co-operation among the different nationalities which had linked their destinies with the federation. The experience of Russia in the use of varied types of federation "fully proved the expediency and flexibility of a federation as the common form of state union of the Soviet republics".[1] The development of national statehood and the formation of the federation of Soviet republics facilitated the successful realisation of the democratic and socialist transformations for those peoples which by-passed the capitalist stage of development thanks to the victory of the Great October Revolution.

The First Experience of Democratic and Socialist Transformations in the Non-Russian Regions

In the trying years of foreign intervention and Civil War, the Russian Soviet Federative Socialist Republic came out not only as the main unifying force in the struggle of all the peoples of our multinational country for the defence of the gains of the October Revolution, but also as the general organiser of co-operation among the nations and nationalities of the former tsarist empire. The triumph of the Soviets and the establishment of the dictatorship of the proletariat became the main condition for the destruction of national oppression and the establishment of national equality ensuring the national minorities their rights.

The victory over the interventionists and bourgeois-nationalistic governments allowed the finalisation of national-state con-

---

[1] *The CPSU in Resolutions...*, Vol. 2, p. 251.

struction on the territory of the Russian Federation, too. The Autonomous republics—Bashkir, Tatar, Karelian, Kirghiz (later Kazakh), Mountaineer, Daghestan, Yakut—and a number of Autonomous regions were formed in the first years of the revolution.

National state autonomy was the age-old dream of the non-Russian peoples and helped them rapidly liquidate their backwardness. The very fact of their self-determination testified to the consistent internationalism of the Russian proletariat and its vanguard—the Communist Party.

Lenin noted with pride that "we have granted *all* the non-Russian nationalities *their own* republics or autonomous regions".[1]

At the time of the October Revolution, many peoples on the territory of Central Asia had not gone through the capitalist stage of development. Therefore, a number of bourgeois-democratic transformations aimed at the liquidation of patriarchal-feudal relations had to be instituted there. Thus, in 1920, on the territory of the Turkestan ASSR plots of land were taken away from the kulak settlers and given over to the *dekhkans* (poor peasants), the norms of land tenure of the indigenous population and settlers were equalised, the kulak-*bai* organisations disbanded, etc. In August 1920, the All-Russia Central Executive Committee specified the competence of the republican and federal organs of state power in decision-making.

People's democratic revolutions triumphed as a result of the people's uprisings in Khiva, Khorezm (February 1920) and Bukhara (August 1920) supported by the Red Army. In the course of these revolutions, the feudal regimes of the Khiva Khan and the Bukhara Emir were overthrown and Soviet people's republics of Khorezm and Bukhara, which were revolutionary-democratic dictatorships of the people in class nature, were formed. Their class foundation was the alliance of the peasants, workers, handicraftsmen, progressive bourgeoisie and intelligentsia. The major democratic reforms were aimed at the elimination of relations of feudal serfdom: the despotic system, social estates, big land-

---

[1] V. I. Lenin, "Fourth Anniversary of the October Revolution", *Collected Works,* Vol. 33, p. 53.

ownership, and the numerous taxes which made peasants, handicraftsmen and petty merchants suffer, were liquidated.

The government of the RSFSR recognised the full independence and sovereignty of the Bukhara and Khorezm republics and concluded allied treaties and economic agreements with them providing for the coordination of the economic plans of the republics and mutual assistance in the development of trade, industry and culture.

The allied treaty signed on March 4, 1921 by the government delegation of the Bukhara People's Soviet Republic and the Government of the RSFSR read: "The October Revolution, which has overthrown the capitalist yoke that oppressed the working masses in Russia, has established for all the peoples of the former Russian empire the right to free self-determination.

"Guided by this principle and renouncing, in particular, the colonial policy of the former Russian capitalist governments, the objects of exploitation of which were, alongside other nations of the East, the working masses of Bukhara, the Russian Socialist Federative Republic unconditionally recognises the full sovereignty and independence of the Bukhara Soviet Republic with all ensuing consequences and renounces for ever all the rights which Russian tsarism established with respect to Bukhara."[1]

The treaty mapped out ways of coordinating the economic policies and economic plans of the two sovereign republics, including trade, organisation of industrial enterprises, and the provision of materials, equipment, specialists, and credits to Bukhara.

The allied treaty signed between the RSFSR and the KhPSR in Moscow on September 13, 1920 recognised the full independence and sovereignty of the Khorezm People's Soviet Republic, transferring all the property which had belonged to the tsarist government and Russian entrepreneurs to it and determining ways of helping the republic in the construction of schools, hospitals and clinics and in the development of commerce. The Russian Republic extended the Khorezm Republic 500 million roubles in credits.[2]

---

[1] See *History of the Bukhara and Khorezm People's Soviet Republics*, Nauka Publishers, Moscow, 1971, p. 135 (in Russian).

[2] Ibid., pp. 152-53.

These treaties helped the peoples of the Khorezm and Bukhara republics make the transition to the socialist path of development.

In October 1923 the Fourth All-Khorezm *kurultai* and in September 1924, the Fifth All-Bukhara Congress of Soviets proclaimed their republics socialist, based on the principles of the dictatorship of the proletariat.

The road to socialist development opened up before the peoples of the multinational Turkestan, Bukhara and Khorezm republics. The victory of the socialist revolution in Russia and the Leninist nationalities policy, based on the principles of proletarian internationalism and brotherhood, was the chief condition for the successful transition of the peoples to this path.

Peasant Soviets were formed for the first time on the territory of these republics and democratic changes were carried out in the first stage on the way to socialist transformations. These transformations were successful because the Russian proletariat, with Communists in the fore, assumed the leading role. "Experience has shown us," said Lenin at the Second Congress of the Communist International, "that tremendous difficulties have to be surmounted in these countries. However, the practical results of our work have also shown that despite these difficulties we are in a position to inspire in the masses an urge for independent political thinking and independent political action, even where a proletariat is practically non-existent."[1] In pre-capitalist conditions where there was no possibility of a purely proletarian movement, Communists creatively used the tactics of the purely proletarian movement taking place in the central regions of the country, combining it with a democratic, anti-feudal struggle in backward regions of the former "prison of the peoples".

The Communists took into account the existence in the backward regions of the petty-bourgeois prejudices of ethnocentrism and national parochialism, which were slowly dying out and could die out completely only "after the entire foundation of the backward countries' economic life has radically changed".[2]

---

[1] V. I. Lenin, "The Second Congress of the Communist International", *Collected Works,* Vol. 31, p. 243.

[2] V. I. Lenin, "Preliminary Draft Theses on the National and the Colonial Questions", *Collected Works,* Vol. 31, p. 150.

In his address at the Second Congress of Communist Organisations of the Peoples of the East, Lenin praised the successes of Russian Bolsheviks, who, in the "struggle against feudal survivals and capitalism . . . succeeded in uniting the peasants and workers of Russia. . . . Here contact with the peoples of the East is particularly important, because the majority of the Eastern peoples are typical representatives of the working people—not workers who have passed through the school of capitalist factories, but typical representatives of the working and exploited peasant masses who are victims of medieval oppression".[1]

Evaluating the historical significance of the experience of Soviet Russia for the future world revolution, Lenin said that this revolution would consist of a joint struggle of the revolutionary proletarians in each country and "a struggle of all the imperialist-oppressed colonies and countries, of all dependent countries, against international imperialism".[2] This conclusion was based on an analysis of the experience of the combined struggle of the peoples of Russia against internal counter-revolution and foreign intervention in 1918-1920. It showed that the establishment of the Soviet system in Russia, the realisation of the right of nations to self-determination and national statehood destroyed the foundations of national oppression, undermined former national strife and won the Russian workers the confidence of their non-Russian counterparts in Russia, in Europe and Asia. The Russian workers would have been unable to defeat Kolchak and Denikin, Yudenich and Wrangel, the Petlyura bandit detachments in the Ukraine and the *basmach* gangs in Central Asia if national enmity and national oppression had not been liquidated. The confidence and enthusiasm of the working masses of the peoples of the West and East made this victory possible.

The joint struggle of the peoples of Russia in 1918-1920 demonstrated the importance of the unification of their economic efforts for the victory and in restoring the war-ravaged economy. "Despite famine and cold, the peasants and workers stand together, have grown strong, and answer every heavy blow with a

---

[1] V. I. Lenin, "Address to the Second All-Russia Congress of Communist Organisations of the Peoples of the East, November 22, 1919", *Collected Works*, Vol. 30, pp. 160, 161.

[2] Ibid., p. 159.

greater cohesion of their forces and increased economic might," said Lenin. "And it it this alone that has made possible the victories over Kolchak, Yudenich and their allies, the strongest powers in the world."[1] Now the workers and peasants of the Land of Soviets had to show the same "cohesion of their forces and increased economic might" in the restoration of the war-ravaged economy.

[1] V. I. Lenin, "Address to the Second All-Russia Congress of Communist Organisations of the Peoples of the East, November 22, 1919", *Collected Works*, Vol. 30, p. 154.

Chapter V

THE FORMATION OF THE USSR—A TRIUMPH OF THE LENINIST NATIONALITIES POLICY

History has seen the rise and the fall of many multi-ethnic and multinational states. The Empires of Kyros and Alexander of Macedon were created by conquest. The Roman slave-owning state included vast territories presently occupied by the peoples of Italy, Britain, Germany, France, Portugal, Spain, the Balkan countries, Northern Africa, Egypt, the Middle East, and Turkey. Recent history saw the Napoleonic Empire, which united many large and small nationalities by force.

All these empires were created when small, weak peoples were engulfed by larger, stronger ones.

In the Roman Empire, the Roman state served as a single unifying link for enormous masses of people. In time, this state became their bitterest enemy and oppressor. Roman citizenship "did not express any nationality, but only lack of nationality".[1]

The infamous slogan "Divide and rule" born in slave-owning Rome became a programme for enslaving peoples, and the ideal of all subsequent exploitative multinational states and colonial empires of modern times. The so-called dual Austro-Hungarian monarchy of the Hapsburgs under which Slavic peoples—Serbs, Croats, Slovenes, Czechs, Slovaks and Poles—were subjected to national oppression, appeared in the epoch of capitalism. It toppled like a house of cards in 1918 as a result of the peoples' struggle for their national and social liberation.

---

[1] Frederick Engels, "The Origin of the Family, Private Property and the State", in: Karl Marx and Frederick Engels, *Selected Works* in three volumes, Vol. 3, Progress Publishers, Moscow, 1977, p. 308.

186

Tsarist Russia, where the Bolsheviks led by Lenin launched their revolutionary activity, and where many peoples were denied normal conditions for national, economic and cultural development, was no exception in this respect. More than half the country's population consisted of a hundred small and middle-sized ethnic groups and nationalities, a considerable number of which greatly lagged behind the Russian people in their development, having been subjected to national and social oppression by Russian landlords, capitalists, and the local rich.

Tsarist nationalities policy generally followed the old Roman slogan of "Divide and rule", which meant the persecution of "aliens", the organisation of pogroms against the Jews, forbidding Ukrainians, Byelorussians and other peoples to educate their children in their native languages or use them in public and governmental affairs.

There was no genuine community of peoples in these multi-ethnic, multinational state entities due to the violence of the ruling classes with respect to small and weak peoples. In the epoch of capitalism, this community was also obstructed by the disuniting effect of private property. Karl Marx said: "For the peoples to be able truly to unite, they must have common interests. And in order that their interests may become common, the existing property relations must be done away with, for these property relations involve the exploitation of some nations by others."[1]

In Modern Age, the once all powerful British colonial empire, the population of which numbered nearly 400 million at the beginning of World War I and which was composed of different nationalities living in various parts of the world, agonised and disintegrated.

Despite all the distinctions of the multinational state associations of the past due to the nature of the socio-political system which engendered them and to the special conditions and circumstances of their appearance, they all had a common approach to the solution of the highly complicated national question—they

---

[1] Karl Marx and Frederick Engels, "On Poland", in: Karl Marx, Frederick Engels, *Collected Works,* Vol. 6, Progress Publishers, Moscow, 1976, p. 388.

completely ignored the desire of particular ethnic groups to live in a single state with other nationalities or to create an independent state; they saw to the political and economic oppression of the dependent nations, the exploitation of their socio-economic and natural resources in the interests of the ruling class of the dominant nation; and their ruling circles formed alliances with the élite of the oppressed peoples to disunite the working masses.

Naturally, the class and national contradictions made for instability in such state entities; they were plagued by endless conflicts and, as a rule, disintegrated.

The Bolshevik Party and the Soviet government of Russia held to quite different principles. They solved the highly complicated national question, launching a type of national-state development unprecedented in scope and character and made possible by the victory of the October Socialist Revolution. This policy scored its first successes in 1917-1920 on the basis of the military and political alliance of the republics during the Civil War.

The Objective Prerequisites for the Formation of the USSR

The final stage in the unification movement of the peoples of the Soviet republics, which led to the creation of a single multinational state—the Union of Soviet Socialist Republics—began at the close of 1920. Initially, this movement was a form of further development of and perfecting the treaty-based Federation of Soviet Republics during its transition to the restoration of the national economy.

A whole series of political, economic and diplomatic factors characteristic of the position of the Soviet republics by the end of the Civil War spurred their peoples to deepen and expand their co-operation with one another along treaty federative lines.[1]

---

[1] At the end of 1920 and beginning of 1921 there were four Soviet republics which appeared on the territory of the former Russian empire: 1) the Russian Socialist Federative Soviet Republic (RSFSR), the population of which numbered nearly 100 million; 2) the Ukrainian Soviet Socialist Republic with a population of 26 million; 3) the Byelorussian

Lenin substantiated the necessity of a closer federative alliance between the peoples, pointing out the following major factors:

"First, that the Soviet republics, surrounded as they are by the imperialist powers of the whole world—which from the military standpoint are immeasurably stronger—cannot possibly continue to exist without the closest alliance; second, that a close economic alliance between the Soviet republics is necessary, otherwise the productive forces which have been ruined by imperialism cannot be restored and the well-being of the working people cannot be ensured; third, that there is a tendency towards the creation of a single world economy, regulated by the proletariat of all nations as an integral whole and according to a common plan. This tendency has already revealed itself quite clearly under capitalism and is bound to be further developed and consummated under socialism."[1]

The factors which called for a closer federative alliance of sovereign republics—the RSFSR, Ukraine, Byelorussia, and the Transcaucasion Federation (Azerbaijan, Armenia and Georgia)—were not transient, but of lasting importance for the entire period of socialist and communist construction. They arose from the concrete historical position in which the republics found themselves at the end of 1920.

It must be noted that the political situation in all the ethnic regions of the Soviet country at that time continued to be extremely strained. The last battles of the Civil War ended on the territory of Soviet Russia, the Ukraine and Byelorussia only in the autumn of 1920.

The new power of the workers and peasants had to fight against what was left of the counter-revolutionary forces within the country: bands of anarchists under N. Makhno in the Ukraine; a revolt organised by Socialist-Revolutionaries in the Tambov and Voronezh provinces; the Kronstadt counter-rev-

---

Soviet Socialist Republic—1,600,000; 4) the Transcaucasian Socialist Federative Soviet Republic, including Azerbaijan—2,100,000, Armenia—718,000, and Georgia—2,400,000.

[1] V. I. Lenin, "Preliminary Draft Theses on the National and the Colonial Questions", *Collected Works*, Vol. 31, p. 147.

olutionary revolt near Petrograd in March 1921; gangs of bandits who infiltrated the territory of the Ukraine and Byelorussia from abroad; and bands of *basmachi* in Central Asia.

The situation in the Transcaucasian Republics of Azerbaijan, Armenia, and Georgia, where Soviet power had been established later than in the country's centre and west due to the opposition of interventionists and local nationalists, was even more complicated.

Soviet power in these regions was established under conditions of acute political and at times armed struggle against the united forces of the nationalist counter-revolutionaries: the musavatists in Azerbaijan, dashnaks in Armenia, Mensheviks in Georgia, and White Guard bands everywhere, supplied with arms, ammunition and other materiel by the governments of the United States, Britain and France.[1]

In addition, almost throughout 1920, the Entente states blockaded the Black Sea coast of the RSFSR and Georgia.

One of the British Foreign Office documents of April 20, 1920 noted that "the Allied Blockade policy is still in force in the Black Sea."[2] As late as December 1920, British frigates stopped merchant ships heading for the Georgian port of Batumi.[3]

Understandably, the united action and cohesion of the peoples of all the Soviet republics was a *sine qua non* for strengthening the workers' and peasants' power and building a new, socialist society in the name of which the revolution had been accomplished and to which so many sacrifices had been made in the struggle against counter-revolutionaries and interventionists.

---

[1] See G. A. Galoyan, *The October Revolution and the Rebirth of the Peoples of Transcaucasia*, Politizdat, Moscow, 1977, pp. 149-203 (in Russian).

Musavatists—members of the counter-revolutionary bourgeois-land-owner nationalistic party in Azerbaijan; *Dashnaks*—members of the Armenian counter-revolutionary bourgeois-nationalistic party; *Mensheviks* were in power in Georgia in 1918-1921 and conducted a bourgeois-nationalistic policy.

[2] *Documents on British Foreign Policy 1919-1939*, I Series (further referred to as *DBFP*), Vol. XII, Her Majesty's Stationery Office, London, 1962, p. 702.

[3] See V. A. Shishkin, *In the Struggle Against the Blockade*, Politizdat, Moscow, 1979, p. 71 (in Russian).

The economic position of all the Soviet republics, which was extremely difficult as a result of the seven years of war and foreign intervention, demanded concerted efforts. In 1920, the industrial output in Soviet Russia fell to nearly one-seventh of the 1913 level; pig iron output made up 2.4 per cent and iron ore extraction was 1.6 per cent of the pre-war level. Only one-third of all industrial enterprises operating in 1913 functioned in the eastern regions of Byelorussia. In the Ukraine, industrial production fell even lower to approximately one-tenth of the pre-war level.

The economies of Georgia, Armenia and Turkestan were completely ruined. Coal output, with the Donets basin in the Ukraine being the main supplier, was reduced to one-fourth of its pre-war level.[1] Things were no better in the main oil-producing regions—Baku in Azerbaijan and Grozny in Northern Caucasus. At the close of 1920, the oil fields were practically idle. The question of turning them into concessions of foreign firms was quite acute.[2] "Every old-time Baku oil worker is overwhelmed with anguish at the sight of the sad picture which some of our oil fields present today," wrote the Azerbaijan newspaper *Kommunist* in the spring of 1921, calling the most famous and richest oil deposits in the Baku region a "graveyard". The first difficulties of restoring the oil industry were overcome by the joint efforts of the working people of Soviet Russia and Azerbaijan. Nevertheless, oil output in 1921 reached only half of the pre-war level.[3]

The situation of the railways was catastrophic. Industry got its supply of raw materials and fuel by rail. The rural population got consumer goods and the urban population, foodstuffs, by rail too. Thus all sectors of the economy were dependent on

[1] See *The USSR and the Capitalist Countries, Statistical Collection for 1917-1937*, Gosizdat, Moscow-Leningrad, 1938, p. 127; P. I. Lyashchenko, *History of the USSR National Economy*, Vol. III, Politizdat, Moscow, 1956, pp. 77, 79 (both in Russian).
[2] See *Tenth Congress of the RCP(B), March 1921*, Verbatim Report, Politizdat, Moscow, 1963, pp. 610-12; *Lenin Miscellany XX*, pp. 146-48 (both in Russian).
[3] *The USSR National Economy in Figures*, Statistical Handbook, Gosizdat, Moscow, 1925, pp. 442-43, 741 (in Russian).

the operation of the railways, especially given the great distances between the national regions. Thousands of kilometres of railway tracks, hundreds of bridges, railway carriages and roundhouses had been blown up and destroyed in all the republics. Locomotives and carriages, which throughout the seven years of war had been greatly overloaded and frequently operated in combat zones, needed to be replaced or repaired.

The state of agriculture was extremely grave, too. Due to a lack of farmhands and the military situation, the areas under plough in Russia, Byelorussia and in the Ukraine shrank by one-fifth to one-third of the pre-war level, while overall agricultural production dropped to only 67 per cent. The area under cotton in Transcaucasia and Turkestan diminished sharply.

Agriculture was in dire need of farm implements because the output of all types of farm machinery in 1920 did not exceed three per cent of the 1913 level. Villages in Soviet Russia alone needed an extra three million ploughs, one million seeders and so on. The horrible draught and crop failure in 1921-1922 which struck many regions of Soviet Russia, especially the Volga area, and partially the Ukraine, aggravated the crisis in all branches of the national economy, and the food situation was grave: for many years people were underfed, received food by ration card in minimal portions and often suffered from hunger. Of the nearly 30 million people populating these regions, nearly 22 million, or approximately one-sixth of Soviet Russia, suffered from hunger.

The devastation in industry and agriculture and the lack of foodstuffs told on the position of the working class in the country's main economic regions.

Dozens of factories and plants closed down in Petrograd in the winter of 1920-1921 due to a lack of fuel, and many workers went to the villages to feed their families or did odd jobs. The workers of the textile industry of the Moscow industrial region, the metallurgical enterprises of the Ukraine and the Urals, the Donbas miners, and the workers of the manganese mines in Georgia were all in dire straits.

This situation called for co-operation between the peoples of the Soviet republics in the struggle against famine and devastation. Thus the peoples of Russia, the Ukraine, Byelorussia and

Transcaucasia saw co-operation as the way out of the difficult economic situation.

This is how one of the active participants in the unification movement of the peoples of the Soviet republics, delegate to the First All-Union Congress of Soviets and member of the First Central Executive Committee F. N. Matveyev recalled the situation after the end of the Civil War: "It turned out that it wasn't enough to win and uphold Soviet power. We were faced with the task of upholding and preserving it for many years ahead. And what was the situation at that time? Devastation in industry and transport, impoverished agriculture. Metal and coal, like grain, were counted in poods. The work force was dispersed. Qualified specialists had nothing to do, so they sold matches for a living... And there was famine to boot. Nearly 30 provinces were waiting and begging for one and only thing— bread! We could count only on ourselves. That's when the separate republics decided to join their efforts. Did we need oil? It could be found in Transcaucasia. Coal and iron ore? The Ukraine could supply it. Bread and meat? The Don, Kuban and Byelorussia could send it."[1]

The Soviet Republics and the Capitalist Powers

Unity of action on the part of the Soviet republics was necessitated in connection with their difficult position in the international arena. After the Civil War and intervention, even the largest and strongest of them—Soviet Russia—had difficulty in strengthening its international position in the struggle to liquidate the economic and diplomatic blockade by the Entente countries. Its government upheld the principle of peaceful coexistence as the basis of political and economic relations between states with different social systems.

Characterising the attitude of Soviet Russia towards this problem in connection with talks held with the government of Great Britain on the development of the trade between Britain and Russia which had just begun, People's Commissar for Foreign

---

[1] *Leningradskaya Pravda,* April 8, 1972.

Affairs of the RSFSR G. V. Chicherin said: "Our slogan is one and the same: peaceful coexistence with other governments no matter what they are. . . . Economic reality demands the exchange of goods and entering into normal economic relations with the entire world, and that same economic reality demands the same from other governments. . ."[1].

Prominent Soviet diplomat, People's Commissar for Foreign Trade of the RSFSR L. B. Krasin conducted talks with Britain on the conclusion of a trade agreement. On May 31, 1920, a car drove up to the old mansion in 10, Downing Street—residence of the British prime ministers—and L. B. Krasin got out with the secretary of the Soviet delegation N. K. Klyshko. They were ushered into the office of Prime Minister Lloyd George. Besides the Prime Minister, taking part in the talks with the Soviet representatives were British ministers Bonar Law, Robert Horne, Parliamentary Under-Secretary for Foreign Affairs Cecil Harmsworth, Mr. E. F. Wise, Premier's secretary P. Kerr and others.[2] Leonid Krasin shook hands all around.

When Krasin came up to the representative of the Conservative Party in the cabinet, Minister for Foreign Affairs George Curzon, a convinced opponent of establishing diplomatic relations with Soviet Russia, something quite typical occurred. Curzon stood leaning against the fireplace with his hands behind his back. Krasin extended his hand to him, but Curzon did not budge. Lloyd George said irritably: "Curzon, be a gentleman!" After that the British Minister slowly and unenthusiastically shook hands with Krasin.[3]

At the first meeting with the British representatives Krasin suggested a concrete programme for the development of Soviet-British trade.

The talks which began on May 31, 1920 turned out to be very difficult and dragged on with intervals for almost a year. In the course of the talks Leonid Krasin's outstanding diplomatic talent came to light as did his belief in the possibility of coming

---

[1] G. V. Chicherin, *Articles and Speeches on International Policy Problems*, Politizdat, Moscow, 1961, p. 145 (in Russian).

[2] *DBFP*, Vol. VIII, pp. 281-90.

[3] I. M. Maisky, *Reminiscences of the Soviet Ambassador in Britain*, Nauka Publishers, Moscow, 1960, p. 13 (in Russian).

to an agreement with Britain on mutually acceptable terms, which aroused respect in the British ministers who were very experienced in politics.

The Soviet Ambassador to Britain, I. M. Maisky wrote: "Lloyd George told me later that Krasin had made an excellent impression on him at that time, on British ministers and on City leaders alike. Everyone appreciated his calmness, business-like attitude, his ability to keep his word and his understanding that there cannot be agreement without compromise."[1]

On questions of principle concerning the foundations of the domestic and foreign policy of Soviet Russia Leonid Krasin defended the stand of his government firmly and consistently. Thus, for instance, he strongly opposed the illegal financial claims of Great Britain and its subjects.

By June 30, 1920, when the first stage of the talks was finalised, Leonid Krasin, who was leaving for Moscow for consultations, received a memorandum from the British summing up their conditions for re-establishing relations between the two countries.[2] The British government expressed its readiness to conclude an agreement on mutual cessation of the hostilities and revival of trade relations on the following conditions:

a) each side commits itself to refrain from hostile actions and propaganda against the other;

b) the British government agrees not to demand an immediate settlement of the question of debts, postponing the matter of mutual demands until the peace talks.[3]

Before his departure, L. B. Krasin met with Lloyd George and asked him:

"If you receive a positive answer on all points, will Britain resume trade relations?"

"Yes," was the answer.

"And if the position of France remains hostile?"

---

[1] I. M. Maisky, *Reminiscences of a Soviet Diplomat. 1925-1945,* Nauka Publishers, Moscow, 1971, p. 96 (in Russian).

[2] L. B. Krasin, *Questions of Foreign Trade,* Gosizdat, Moscow-Leningrad, 1928, p. 262 (in Russian).

[3] See *Documents on the Foreign Policy of the USSR,* Politizdat, Moscow, Vol. III. pp. 17-18 (in Russian).

"We will resume them all the same, provided all the prerequisites are accepted."[1]

But in actual fact, the talks continued for another eight months since the British government stubbornly tried to secure serious concessions from the RSFSR in relation to bourgeois-landowner Poland, which at that time was in a state of war against Soviet Russia.

On August 4, 1920, after he returned from Moscow to London, Krasin was once again received by Lloyd George.

"Mr. Prime Minister," said the Soviet representative, "I'm authorised to declare that my government is ready to conduct further talks on the conclusion of a treaty on the basis of your conditions."

"Your troops are advancing towards Warsaw—that is the only thing that interests Britain at the moment," Lloyd George cried out nervously. "Unless the Polish question is settled, I refuse to conduct talks on any trade agreements."[2]

The Soviet delegation, demonstrating flexibility and guided by Lenin's instructions, was ready to make concessions which were not of a principled nature and agreed to conduct talks on the basis of the British proposals, resolutely objecting to the unacceptable political and economic concessions.

The British-Soviet agreement, concluded on March 16, 1921, became an important factor in facilitating the establishment of the trade and political relations between Soviet Russia and the capitalist countries.

The CC RCP(B) and Lenin personally guided the actions of the Soviet delegation at all stages of the talks between the two countries. "I must say that we in the Central Committee have devoted a great deal of attention to this question," Lenin said at the 10th Party Congress stressing that the treaty with Great Britain would open the way to the development of the relations with other capitalist countries.[3]

At the concluding stage of the talks in November 1920-March

[1] L. B. Krasin, "British-Russian Talks", *Narodnoye khozyaistvo*, No. 1-2, 1921, p. 4.

[2] Ibid., p. 6.

[3] V. I. Lenin, "Tenth Congress of the R.C.P.(B)", *Collected Works*, Vol. 32, Progress Publishers, Moscow, 1965, p. 181.

1921, the British position reflected the struggle of the two currents of the British bourgeoisie on the "Russian question".

On November 17, 1920 members of the British cabinet gathered at Lloyd George's residence at 10, Downing Street to settle the question of concluding a trade agreement with Soviet Russia. Many of the participants looked just as gloomy as the grey London morning beyond the windows. The intervention of the landowner Poland had fallen through and it had concluded a truce with the RSFSR. And only a few days before news had come of the defeat of the white guard army of General Wrangel.

But even that was not enough for certain ministers in the British government. Curzon tried to intimidate the cabinet members with the threat of a "Red danger" and called for utmost caution in signing the agreement. He was supported by the Chancellor of the Exchequer Lord Chamberlain and Secretary for War Winston Churchill, who later on admitted in the talk with Soviet Ambassador I. M. Maisky: "I thought the Soviets to be the main danger for the British Empire and that is why I fought against you at that time."[1] Lloyd George himself, President of the Body of Trade Robert Horne, and other members of the government thought that "the fall of the Soviet government" was nowhere in sight and advised that trade be used as a means of "taming" or "toppling Bolshevism". On the next day, November 18, 1920, the British cabinet of ministers adopted by the overwhelming majority of voices a decision to "entrust the minister for trade to conclude a trade agreement with Russia."[2]

The British government was interested in developing trade with Russia, since British trade was in the state of stagnation, while the country was threatened with unemployment.

Replying to the opponents of the conclusion of an agreement, who hoped that the Soviet power would soon topple, Prime Minister Lloyd George said that he heard more than once during the last two years predictions about the fall of the Soviet Government. He went on to say that Denikin, Yudenich and

---

[1] I. M. Maisky, *Reminiscences of a Soviet Diplomat,* p. 301.
[2] See *History of the Foreign Policy of the USSR,* Vol. I, pp. 127-28.

Wrangel had suffered defeat and that he did not believe in the immediate prospect of the collapse of the Soviet government.

But the British government was in no hurry to conclude the talks, trying to secure maximum concessions from Krasin.

In connection with the counter-revolutionary revolt in Kronstadt, which began on February 28, 1921, the differences between the British ministers flared up again.

However, four days before the revolt was crushed, the futility of the anti-Soviet venture became evident even to the opponents of the agreement with Soviet Russia. The British government held a secret meeting on March 14, in the protocol of which was recorded the following: "The cabinet has received information that ... despite recent events in Russia, the position of the Soviet government remains without any reservations firm and stable."[1] After two days the trade and political agreement was signed.

This was the first *de facto* recognition of the Soviet state by one of great Western powers. On the same day Krasin wrote to the Deputy Minister for Foreign Trade A. M. Lezhava: "The trade agreement of the RSFSR with the British Empire was signed today in the version proposed by me in Moscow... We fought nearly a year to reach this agreement. Now we are faced with a new struggle for the actual realisation of an opportunity to supply the Republic of the peasants and workers with the foreign-manufactured goods, and to sell the Western countries our raw materials and foodstuffs. ... New path, new tasks and new dangers are opening up before the Republic of Soviets."[2]

In 1921, Soviet Russia established relations with other European countries after being recognised by them—Germany, Italy, Austria and Poland. The establishment of relations with Italy was particularly difficult although its government had agreed to receive a Soviet mission way back in the summer of 1920.

Despite the agreement, the Italian government impeded the exchange of delegations. Only a branch of the Soviet joint-

---

[1] See V. A. Ryzhikov, *Zigzags of London Diplomacy (from the History of the Soviet-British Relations)*, Politizdat, Moscow, 1973, p. 30 (in Russian).

[2] L. B. Krasin, *Questions of Foreign Trade*, pp. 286-88.

stock company Arcos in London operated in Rome starting in October 1920. When appointing head of the economic delegation to Italy, G. V. Chicherin stressed especially that "this must be a prominent personality".[1] The choice fell on V. V. Vorovsky. But while waiting for permission to enter the country, he fell ill. When Vorovsky was beginning to recover, Lenin asked doctors for permission to visit him in the hospital. Business Manager of the Council of People's Commissars V. D. Bonch-Bruyevich recalled the meeting as follows: "Vladimir Iliych walked in and approached him in an especially affable way, shaking his finger at him from afar.

" 'We want you to be absolutely healthy! Italy is waiting for you and you're behaving badly,' Lenin joked.

"Vatslav livened up and began to talk energetically.

" 'Easy, easy, that won't do,' Lenin said softly. 'You just keep quiet and I'll tell you everything. You mustn't waste your strength.' "[2]

Soon Vorovsky recovered and left for Italy at the head of the Soviet economic delegation. On March 14, 1921 they were met at the Rome central terminal Termini by a few Soviet employees of the Italian branch of Arcos. In Moscow there was still snow on the ground, but in Rome the southern sun blazed brightly. However, those who met Vorovsky did not conceal their concern: "You have arrived at an unhappy time: the reaction has taken the offensive."[3]

Soon the delegation met with the threats of fascists and the ill-disposed attitude of the authorities. Hostile acts against the members of the Soviet economic delegation followed one after another. It all began at the customs-house where, despite the agreement with the Italian government on the immunity of the delegation's baggage, it was opened and subjected to an exami-

---

[1] S. Zarnitsky, A. Sergeyev, *Chicherin*, Politizdat, Moscow, 1975, p. 162 (in Russian).

[2] V. D. Bonch-Bruyevich, *At a Glorious Post*, Politizdat, Moscow, 1971, p. 12 (in Russian).

[3] N. N. Lyubimov, A. N. Erlikh, *Genoa Conference (Recollections of the Participants)*, Politizdat, Moscow, 1963, p. 139; V. V. Vorovsky, *Articles and Materials on Questions of Foreign Policy*, Politizdat, Moscow, 1959, p. 230 (both in Russian).

nation. As a sign of protest, Vorovsky refused to attend an appointment previously arranged with Minister of Foreign Affairs Count Sforza. The Soviet diplomat acted firmly and resolutely. He refused to send a representative of the delegation to be present when the baggage was opened and forwarded several notes to the Italian government demanding the observance of those diplomatic privileges which the Soviet representatives in Italy were vested with in accordance with the agreement.

The class struggle in Italy had intensified sharply. The fascists, whom the bourgeoisie used to stifle the revolutionay movement, were striving for power. The *Londra Hotel*, where the Soviet delegation stayed, was the object of provocations. As one of its members, Y. Strauyan, recalled, "we were annoyed every night. At late hours, groups of young idlers strolled to and fro past the *Abergo di Londra*, singing and shouting all kind of threats at us and at Soviet Russia. Vatslav paid no attention to these trifles. In the morning he usually joked about the night escapades of the Italian sissies."[1] On March 23, the fascist Serventi managed to get inside the *Londra* and insulted Vorovsky. In its note of March 24, the Soviet economic delegation demanded "an immediate investigation of the case and the trial of the executors and organisers of the attack against an official".[2] Serventi was arrested and tried but found not guilty.

Seeing that the Italian government did not wish to adopt the necessary measures to ensure the normal functioning of the Soviet economic delegation, limiting itself to formal apologies and promises, Vorovsky sent a note to the Ministry for Foreign Affairs of Italy on May 23, 1921, in which he stated that in the circumstances that had developed "the delegation could do nothing but inform the ministry that it was leaving the territory of Italy".[3] This resolute step finally had an effect, and on May 29, Count Sforza replied that the Italian government was prepared "henceforth to agree to granting the desired privileges, which will be included in the agreement."[4] As a result, Vorovsky

---

[1] V. V. Vorovsky, *Articles and Materials. . .*, p. 230.
[2] *Documents on the Foreign Policy of the USSR,* Vol. IV, pp. 64-65.
[3] Ibid., p. 135.
[4] V. V. Vorovsky, *Articles and Materials. . .*, p. 210.

wrote to his friends on June 15, 1921, "now passions have died down. We've won the right to existence at the cost of our nerves."[1]

Despite the complicated situation, Vorovsky and his colleagues, as Chicherin put it, virtually "smashed" the way for normal relations with Italy. Vorovsky has played an important role in the establishment of relations with different representatives of the Italian business world. They came to him with apprehensions resulting from the fabrications about the Land of Soviets that filled the bourgeois press. Instead of a tough secret police agent with a Mauser in his hand, businessmen and industrialists unexpectedly met a thin, slightly stooped intellectual with a greying beard, simply but immaculately dressed. He spoke European languages fluently. His speech was flavoured by witty, light, refined humour. Chicherin later said that when he met Italian businessmen, "who were interested in close economic relations with Soviet Russia", he saw "how deep Vorovsky's influence was in Italy."[2]

The work of the Soviet economic delegation was finalised in the conclusion, on December 26, 1921, of an agreement between the two countries.

All these trade and political agreements of Soviet Russia with the capitalist countries envisaged the exchange of official representatives vested with diplomatic privileges and trade officials, and contained articles ensuring the safety and inviolability of the goods and property brought to these states in the course of mutual trade.

Also of importance was the establishment and development of friendly contacts between Soviet Russia and the neighbouring states—Iran, Afghanistan and Turkey. The Soviet government annulled all the unequal treaties of the tsarist government with these countries and signed new treaties with them, based on the principles of mutual diplomatic recognition, equality and respect for each other's sovereignty. The Soviet-Iranian treaty was signed on February 26, 1921, Soviet-Afghan—on February 28, and a

---

[1] I. Verkhovtsev, *Life Dedicated to the Great Cause,* Politizdat, Moscow, 1959, p. 131 (in Russian).
[2] Ibid.

treaty on friendship between the RSFSR and Turkey—on March 16.

Thus, in 1921 the RSFSR's diplomacy scored obvious successes. Soviet Russia emerged from the state of political and economic isolation, which had engulfed it during the Civil War and the intervention. "Russia has sprouted, if one may so express it, a number of fairly regular and permanent commercial relations, missions, treaties, etc. True, we are not yet recognised *de jure* ... the relations, however, are a fact."[1]

The Necessity of a Uniform Foreign Policy

However, the consolidation of the positions of the other Soviet republics in the international arena and in the world trade market would be impossible unless they conducted a uniform foreign policy and international economic policy and unless they closely co-operated with each other and with Soviet Russia in this field. The experience of 1918-1921 proved conclusively that uncoordinated actions by individual republics would not have been successful in the face of the capitalist encirclement.

The imperialist states tried to make use of the slightest possibility for infiltrating the markets of those republics where foreign capital had had any firm positions before the Revolution and hoped to create new bridgeheads for economic and political expansion.

This especially applied to the Transcaucasian Republics. The separatism displayed by the leaders of certain Soviet republics, who at times did not realise the importance of the united and consolidated actions in the field of foreign policy and foreign economic ties, played a large role in these plans.

The September 29, 1920 telegram of Sergo Orjonikidze, Secretary of the Caucasus Bureau of the Party CC, from Baku, addressed to Lenin, is extremely illustrative in this respect. It informed Lenin that certain leading workers in Azerbaijan failed to realise the importance of ensuring the export of oil in a cen-

---

[1] V. I. Lenin, "Ninth All-Russia Congress of Soviets", *Collected Works,* Vol. 33, p. 152.

tralised way in order to counter the Western monopolies successfully. The telegram said further that after discussing this question at a session of the CC of the Communist Party of Azerbaijan, a decision was adopted with the support of the head of the republic's government, N. Narimanov, that it was "in the interests of strengthening" all the Soviet republics on the international market to grant the Russian Federation exclusive export rights. The leaders of Azerbaijan agreed to grant such rights to the People's Commissariat for Foreign Trade of the RSFSR "on the basis of the military-economic alliance concluded between Azerbaijan and Russia."[1]

There were cases of rash actions by the leaders of foreign trade organs in certain other Soviet republics which seriously weakened their positions in the international arena.

In Georgia, for instance, agreements were concluded in 1921 to grant Standard Oil concessions for the Batumi oil reservoirs and to open a branch of the Ottoman Bank on the territory of the republic. These agreements, which violated the foundations of Soviet political and economic legislation, were later cancelled.

When he received the text of the agreement on a new concession for the development of tracts of forest land, concluded by the Georgian government, Lenin suggested in a note to V. A. Smolyaninov that they had "to find out whether the Georgian comrades have abided by the condition (there has been one, hasn't there? a Party one?) not to sign any concessions without our consent?"[2]

Naturally, if there had been unity of action in our foreign affairs, there would have never been agreements and treaties with the capitalist countries which were so disadvantageous for the Soviet republics.

The trip of the commercial delegation from Soviet Turkestan to Iran in the autumn of 1918 is another example of how difficult it was for the Soviet republics to try to resolve international problems independently. The aim of this mission, which

---

[1] See V. A. Shishkin, *V. I. Lenin and the Foreign Economic Policy of the Soviet State (1917-1923)*, Nauka Publishers, Leningrad, 1977, p. 297 (in Russian).

[2] V. I. Lenin, "To V. A. Smolyaninov", *Collected Works*, Vol. 45, Progress Publishers, Moscow, 1981, p. 276.

had the status of a diplomatic delegation, headed by the chairman of the Kokand Soviet of Workers' Deputies E. A. Babushkin, was to establish trade relations with the northern provinces of Iran in order to buy the food Turkestan so desperately needed. Although the trip had been agreed upon with the British representative in Turkestan, F. M. Bailey, as soon as the delegation arrived in Meshhed, its members were arrested on the instructions of the British military authorities influential in this region. Members of the mission spent a long time in prison, where they were subjected to humiliation, then they were deported to the British colony, India. Only in November 1920, after prolonged efforts on the part of Soviet diplomats and the representative of the RSFSR in London, L. B. Krasin, were the members of the delegation allowed to return home via London —nearly two years after their departure from Tashkent.[1]

And vice versa, the united and concerted efforts of the Soviet republics, their mutual assistance in international affairs allowed them to make progress even on the basis of those early federative relations, grounded merely on treaties.

This vividly came into view on such a complicated matter as the establishment of normal political and economic relations with Turkey, a matter of interest not only to the RSFSR but also to the Soviet Ukraine and all the Transcaucasian republics.

As it has already been noted, a treaty of friendship between the RSFSR and Turkey was concluded in Moscow on March 16, 1921. It ensured the development of normal relations between Soviet Russia and Turkey and enabled the former to counter more resolutely the pressure of the Western powers which were trying to impede the rapprochement between the Soviet republics and Turkey. Moreover, it helped rebuff the territorial and political claims of the reactionary circles with respect to Georgia, Armenia and Azerbaijan. The following historical facts testify to this. A Soviet-Ukrainian trade delegation arrived in Constantinople (Instanbul) in February 1921, representing Tsentrosoyuz, a cooperative association which was to establish

---

[1] See *Documents on the Foreign Policy of the USSR*, Vol. II, Politizdat, Moscow, 1958, pp. 130-71; M. V. Popov, *E. A. Babushkin's Mission in Iran (Little-Known Page of History of the Soviet Diplomacy)*, Politizdat, Moscow, 1964, pp. 34-99 (both in Russian).

economic relations with Turkey and organise the shipments of Soviet goods via the Black Sea and the Mediterranean. The situation was very complicated: Constantinople was under the control of British troops. The Soviet delegation established business contacts with the Turkish commercial and financial circles, examined the market, and began its work.

At the beginning of July, Reuter news agency spread a sensational story: a plot had been uncovered in Constantinople, the aim of which was to "organise revolution" with the use of terrorist methods, including the assassination of Commander-in-Chief of the British troops in this region, General Harrington. Allegedly, the Soviet trade delegation (according to British authorities in Constantinople) played the main role in this "plot."[1]

What actually happened? On June 29, 1921 at 5:30 a.m. the premises of the Soviet trade delegation were occupied by a detachment of British troops. Naturally, no one was there at such an early hour. The night watchman, a Turk, was arrested, the premises were searched, the keys from the desks, many documents, contracts, money and a car were confiscated. Members of the delegation who came to work were searched and then arrested without even a search warrant. Some of them were placed under house arrest.

Among the 12 people arrested was a seven-year-old boy. On July 2, all the "plotters" were put into a motor boat, towed out into the open sea and left far from shore with an engine which had been damaged beforehand. They got to shore with great difficulty. The premises of the Soviet trade delegation were vacated and documents and property returned only after repeated protests by the Ambassador of the RSFSR in London, L. B. Krasin. Only then could members of the delegation return to Constantinople and resume their work.

The delegation was subjected to numerous provocations after this first incident. A number of trade officials who came to Constantinople on business from the Caucasus, the Ukraine and the Crimea were subjected to arrest and deportation. On July 19, 1921 an unknown person assassinated Azerbaijan foreign trade

---

[1] *Documents on the Foreign Policy of the USSR,* Vol. IV, pp. 202, 214.

representative, M. Jevanshiev. On August 1, deputy of the head of the Soviet delegation V. Kuznetsov was arrested groundlessly. He was freed after several resolute protests by the chargé d'affaires of the RSFSR to the British commissar in Constantinople and to the Secretary of State for Foreign Affairs of Great Britain in London.

The fact that the government of Soviet Russia defended the interests of all other friendly republics improved the working conditions of the Soviet trade delegation in Constantinople to some extent.[1]

The 1921 Moscow Treaty with Turkey envisaged the conclusion of agreements between Turkey and the Soviet Transcaucasian republics. The clauses of this treaty and resolute actions by the government of the RSFSR allowed these republics to come out jointly against Turkish nationalistic plans, aimed at tearing away Batumi from Georgia and of certain regions of Azerbaijan and Armenia.

After a prolonged diplomatic struggle and with the direct and active help of the RSFSR, on October 13, 1921 the Transcaucasian republics signed the Kars treaty with Turkey, which settled the political and economic relations of the parties on a mutually advantageous basis.[2]

A decision was also adopted in August 1921 that famous Civil War commander and Commander-in-Chief of the armed forces of the Ukraine and the Crimea M. V. Frunze would take a trip to Ankara as head of a delegation of the Ukrainian Soviet Socialist Republic to consolidate friendly relations between Turkey and all the Soviet republics. This mission was regarded as a means for further deepening Soviet-Turkish relations. Frunze's mission was based on the foreign political course of the Soviet republics directed at the support of the national liberation revolution in Turkey, with Kemal Pasha (Gazi Mustapha), an outstanding state leader, at the head. Before his departure, M. V. Frunze had a long talk with People's Commissar for Foreign Affairs of the RSFSR G. V. Chicherin, who acquainted the Ukrainian mission with the basic principles of the Soviet

---

[1] *Documents on the Foreign Policy of the USSR*, Vol. IV, pp. 484-85, 545-47, 673.

[2] For more details see G. A. Galoyan, op. cit., pp. 208-18.

policy in the East and with the "line of friendship with Kemalist Turkey" ensuing from it, which he recommended them to maintain at the talks in Ankara.[1]

Frunze's diplomatic mission which left Kharkov in November 1921, slowly travelled southeast by train to Batumi, where Frunze and his diplomatic and military advisers boarded an Italian ship incognito and made their way to Trabzon—a port at the extreme northeast of Turkey. Then they were joined by others in the mission and their Red Army security guard, and the group sailed on the Soviet ship *Georgi* for the Turkish port of Samsun in the west closer to Ankara.

From Samsun it took the mission several weeks on horseback and by wagon to reach Ankara travelling across Anatolia (Eastern Turkey). Their choice of route was dictated not by any passion for the exotic, but by the extremely complicated political and military situation in that region of Asia and by the difficult tasks with which the Soviet governments of the Ukraine and Russia entrusted the Frunze mission. The most obvious way to reach Turkey via the Black Sea straits and Istanbul was barred to the Soviet delegation because at that time the country's western part was controlled by interventionist forces, the reactionary sultanate and the troops of the British emissary General Harrington.

In his talks with Mustafa Kemal Atatürk in December 1921, Frunze coordinated with him the main clauses of the Turkish-Ukrainian Treaty On Friendship and Fraternity,[2] and also discussed in detail the question of the Soviet government providing financial aid to Turkey. On his return to Moscow, Frunze submitted a report to the government of the RSFSR on February 9, 1922 in which he outlined the basic suggestions on Soviet-Turkish co-operation.

After Frunze's trip Soviet-Turkish relations became closer and friendlier.[3]

[1] See I. Gorokhov, L. Zamyatin I. Zemskov, *G. V. Chicherin—Diplomat of the Leninist School,* Politizdat, Moscow, 1973, pp. 119-20 (in Russian).
[2] See *Documents on the Foreign Policy of the USSR,* Vol. V, Politizdat, Moscow, 1961, pp. 9-14.
[3] See A. N. Kheifets, *Soviet Diplomacy and the Peoples of the East. 1921-1927,* Nauka Publishers, Moscow, 1968, pp. 185-86 (in Russian).

Talks on an armistice and peace with Poland took place on October 12, 1920 and on March 16, 1921 on the basis of the common position of several of the Soviet republics. The RSFSR and the Ukrainian governments appointed a joint delegation, which was entrusted by the government of the Byelorussian Soviet Republic to represent Byelorussia's interest as well. As a result a treaty on the armistice and preliminary peace conditions with Poland[1] was signed in Riga by A. A. Ioffe, S. M. Kirov, D. Z. Manuilsky and L. L. Obolensky who, representing the RSFSR and the Ukrainian SSR, had upheld the stand of the three Soviet republics.

On February 22, 1922 the Soviet republics concluded the first Agreement on the Representation and Defence by the Government of the RSFSR of the Interests of the Soviet Republics of Azerbaijan, Armenia, Byelorussia, Bukhara, Georgia, the Ukraine, Khorezm and the Far Eastern Republic at the Genoa Conference. Under this agreement, all the eight independent republics authorised the RSFSR to represent and defend their interests at conferences and to sign treaties and agreements with other countries in their name.

Attached to the agreement was the statement of the All-Russia Central Executive Committee signed by M. I. Kalinin expressing satisfaction with the decision and the readiness of the RSFSR government to take all measures to defend the interests of these republics.[2]

As well as the RSFSR representatives G. V. Chicherin—who headed the delegation to the Genoa Conference—L. B. Krasin, V. V. Vorovsky and A. A. Ioffe, the delegation included Kh. G. Rakovsky, N. N. Narimanov, P. G. Mdivani, A. A. Beksadyan, F. Khojaev, and others representing the Ukraine, Byelorussia and Transcaucasia.

Further Treaty Relations Between the Republics

From the end of 1920 to mid-1922, the movement of unification of the peoples of the Soviet republics, which was stimulat-

---

[1] See I. Gorokhov, L. Zamyatin, I. Zemskov, op. cit., p. 113.
[2] See *Documents on the Foreign Policy of the USSR*, Vol. V, pp. 110-12.

K. E. Voroshilov and Bela Kun (1920)

The Chapayev division forcing the Belaya River (June 1919)

Soviet troops entering Riga (1919)

V. I. Chapayev and V. I. Zakharov (1919)

Hungarian internationalists (1919)

An international battalion on parade (Vitebsk, 1919)

Smash Yudenich! (Petrograd, 1919)

Red Army units entering Kiev (1919)

Proclamation of the Uzbek Soviet Socialist Republic (1925)

M. I. Kalinin in Central Asia (1925)

Land and water reform in Central Asia (Ferghana, 1925)

At a communist *subbotnik* (Verkh-Isetsk, 1921)

A Soviet soldier among townsfolk of Vilno (1940)

Moscow working people's demonstration against the Curzon ultimatum (1923)

Demonstration of friends of the Soviet Union in the USA (1925)

The Congress of the Peoples of the East (Baku, 1920)

Soviet diplomats M. M. Litvinov and V. V. Vorovsky (Genoa, 1922)

In the presidium of the First Congress of the Communist International (1919)

Proletárdiktatura!
Éljen az oroszokkal
szövetséges magyar
SZOVJET
KÖZTÁRSASÁG

Soviet diplomats at the Genoa Conference (1922)

Hungarian internationalists supporting the revolution in Russia (1919)

The delegation of the RSFSR in Genoa (1922)

The embassy of the Ukrainian Soviet Socialist Republic in Ankara during the arrival of a delegation headed by M. V. Frunze (1922)

Soviet delegation headed by K. E. Voroshilov in Turkey

Bernard Shaw among members of a commune (Tambov Province)

A conference of foreign workers' delegations in defence of Soviet Russia (1920)

A protest demonstration in connection with the assassination of V. V. Vorovsky

Moscow workers' demonstration against the imperialist war

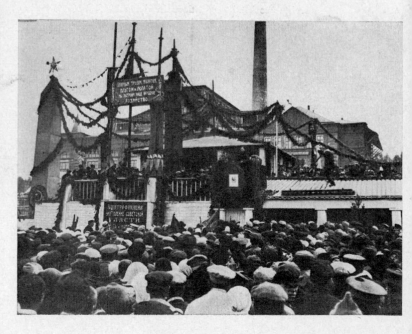

The first Soviet tractors

Commissioning of the Kashira Hydroelectric Power Station

M. I. Kalinin speaking at a meeting of builders of the Volkhov Hydro-electric Power Station (June 1924)

M. I. Kalinin among workers of the Putilov Works (June 1924)

Devastation (1920)

Zhenya Romanko with a concrete layers team at the Dnieper Power
Station building project.

At the construction site of the Big Ferghana Canal (1939)

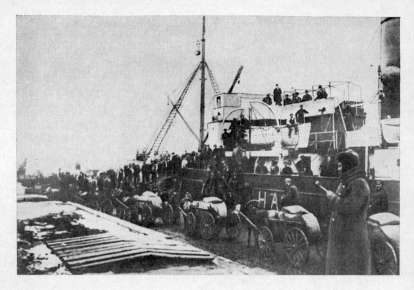

Bread for the famine-stricken Volga area (Burgass, 1921)

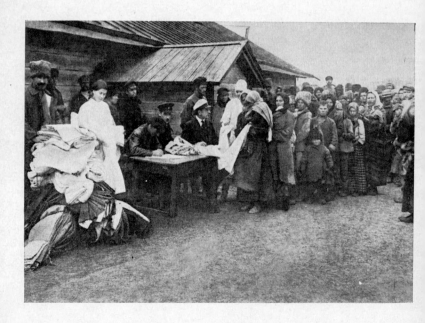

At a collective farmers' meeting (Ukraine)

Distributing clothing to the hungry population of the town of Samara (1921)

At a collective farm field camp (1930)

ŞƏRK KADЬNЬ

Learning to read and write (Azerbaijan, 1920)

They have found their home here (Vladivostok)

Illiteracy abolition courses (Dnepropetrovsk Region)

Coming to see the doctor (Kazakh Soviet Socialist Republic, 1925)

Their first books

Lecturers of the Tashkent State University (1922)

Delegation of the All-Union Central Executive Committee among delegates of the Congress of Soviets (1923)

Soviet diplomats at Genoa (1922)

ed by political, economic and diplomatic factors, was based on Union treaties, concluded between the RSFSR and other Soviet republics.

The first of these treaties, as mentioned above, was concluded on September 30, 1920 between the RSFSR and the Azerbaijan Soviet Socialist Republic. It was subsequently supplemented by a treaty on the coordination and unification of the economic policy of the two fraternal republics.[1]

On December 29, 1920 the Eighth All-Russia Congress of Soviets approved a treaty between the RSFSR and UkSSR, and on March 2, 1921 it was ratified by the Fifth All-Ukraine Congress of Soviets. It noted "that while recognising the independence and sovereignty of each party, and realising the necessity to unite their forces for defence, as well as in the interests of their economic construction", their governments "decided to conclude a genuine workers' and peasants' treaty envisaging the creation of a military and economic union between the two republics".[2]

In 1920-1921 the RSFSR concluded similar Union treaties with the Soviet republics of Byelorussia, Armenia and Georgia, as well as with the Khorezm and Bukhara Soviet republics which existed in Central Asia at the time.

The essential feature of these treaties was their recognition of the equality of the Soviet republics and the greater integration of their military and economic efforts to win peace and get the economy functioning again.

Closer collaboration between the Soviet republics, primarily in the economic field, was the outstanding feature of the development of the federation based on these treaties. They proclaimed unified commissariats of foreign trade, finance, railways, labour, post and telegraph and the organs of industrial management—supreme economic councils. Alongside this, each republic continued to be a sovereign state with a constitution, organs of power and management of its own. Certain republics (the Ukraine, Azerbaijan and Georgia) had diplomatic and trade rep-

---

[1] See *Soviet Community of the Peoples. (The movement of unification and the formation of the USSR). Collection of documents. 1917-1922*, Nauka Publishers, Moscow, 1972, pp. 158-60 (in Russian).
[2] Ibid., pp. 175-77.

resentations abroad. The Union treaties, therefore, were based on Lenin's principles of sovereignty and equality of peoples, and envisaged uniting their efforts to successfully build socialism .

The decisions of the Tenth Congress of the RCP(B) held in March 1921 were instrumental for the planned reconstruction of the economy of all the Soviet republics, as well as for the further development of their treaty-based federation. The RCP(B) united Communists regardless of nationality or residence in any republic. Therefore, the decisions of its congresses, which were the Party's highest organs, reflected the opinion and interests of the Communists and of the broad masses of working people of all nations and nationalities who, led by the Communist Party, were building a new society.

The Tenth Congress of the RCP(B) adopted an important decision on a new economic policy, which envisaged several measures to establish a solid union of the working class and the working peasantry on an economic basis, which created the prerequisites for rapidly putting agriculture, industry and transport on their feet again, and opened the way to involving the urban and rural working people in the constructive work of building socialism. Lenin underlined the necessity of creatively realising the importance of the new policy[1] in the Transcaucasian republics which took the road of socialist development later than Russia, the Ukraine and Byelorussia.

The Tenth Congress of the RCP(B) also approved the resolution "On Current Tasks of the Party in the National Question". It contained a profound analysis of the condition of various nations and nationalities and noted that the RSFSR and other independent Soviet republics, bound to it by treaties, numbered nearly 140 million people, 65 million of them non-Russians.

The congress noted the expediency of preserving the federation as the general form of the state union, which would allow the national question to be ultimately resolved, as well as the mutual trust and voluntary agreement on co-operation between

---

[1] See V. I. Lenin, "To the Comrades Communists of Azerbaijan, Georgia, Armenia, Daghestan, and the Mountaineer Republic", *Collected Works,* Vol. 32, p. 316.

the Soviet republics as being a prerequisite for ensuring power of such a federation.

The resolution expressed the idea that building socialism in a multinational country could not succeed unless the actual inequality of the peoples was overcome, first of all, in the economic field, and it was resolved "to help the working masses of the non-Great Russian peoples to catch up with the Central Russia which progressed far ahead".[1]

The ideas of fraternity and mutual assistance of the peoples in the struggle to rebuild the economy and build a new society grew and strengthened within the framework of the treaty-based federation bound by the Union military-economic agreements between the Soviet republics. Many documents of the period testify to the coordinated efforts by these republics and to the tremendous help which the RSFSR provided to other peoples in dealing with the priorities in overcoming the economic crisis. In January 1921 *Pravda* wrote about the shipment, on the instructions of the Council of Labour and Defence of the RSFSR, of electric bulbs, electric motors, picks, shovels, steam boilers, foodstuffs and clothing from Soviet Russia to help get the coal industry in the Donbas functioning again.[2] On April 5, 1921 the People's Commissar for Foreign Affairs of Azerbaijan telegraphed Lenin: "Today on April 5, at 1 p.m. head of the Azerbaijan Soviet government Comrade Narimanov ... announced the opening of navigation. Then an oil caravan, consisting of 33 vessels carrying nearly 3.5 million poods of oil products, sailed out of the port of Baku for Astrakhan... Realising Soviet Russia's acute need of fuel and taking into consideration the great importance of oil in the struggle aginst economic dislocation, the Baku proletariat ... sacredly vow that they will spare no effort to make the coming campaign a success and provide Soviet Russia with as much oil as possible."[3]

On April 9, 1921 Lenin informed G. K. Orjonikidze, leader of the Communists in the Transcaucasian republics, by telegram that in response to news about the grave food situation, the So-

---

[1] *The CPSU in Resolutions...*, Vol. 2, pp. 248-56.
[2] *Pravda*, January 29, 1921.
[3] *Soviet Community of the Peoples*, p. 206.

viet government of the RSFSR had adopted several measures to organise assistance to Armenia and had given corresponding instructions to the People's Commissariat for Food.[1] On decision of the government of the RSFSR, Armenia received 1.5 million roubles in gold.[2]

A decision of the Council of People's Commissars of June 18, 1921 allocated 30 million roubles for buying foods and consumer goods in Poland to create a special fund for the Byelorussian Economic Council and the Byelorussian Trade Union Council to reward deserving workers and office employees.[3] The Ukrainian, Azerbaijan, Armenian and Georgian Soviet republics aided the famine-stricken people of the Volga area; the Soviet Ukraine sent food to Georgia, Armenia and Azerbaijan; Soviet Russia helped Azerbaijan develop the Mugan Steppe for cotton-growing, restore the cement mill and oil fields, and to train specialists; it helped Byelorussia restore its industry and Turkestan to develop horse-breeding and cotton-growing,[4] etc.

The report of the Council of People's Commissars of Armenia noted that "economic and financial assistance from Soviet Russia allows the government to begin on a modest scale the initial intensive work of regulating the melioration system, of reviving work at some enterprises, and of supplying the village poor, who had suffered most, with bread, as well as with grain for sowing, agricultural implements, draught animals and manufactured goods. The present ... policy makes the people confident in the morrow and stimulates them to the calm work of reconstructing their devastated economy..."[5]

Thus, the development of the federation based on treaties served to expand and deepen the economic ties between the republics, and to rebuild and gradually stimulate economic growth. Alongside this experience was gained in national-state construction. As of the end of 1920 representatives of other Soviet republics participated in the Council of People's Commissars of

---

[1] See V. I. Lenin, "Telegram to G. K. Orjonikidze, 9.4.1921", *Collected Works*, Vol. 35, p. 483.

[2] *Soviet Community of the Peoples*, p. 209.

[3] Ibid., pp. 221-22.

[4] Ibid., pp. 233-89.

[5] Ibid., p. 292.

the RSFSR and in several commissariats; there were united people's commissariats, representing the interests of not only Soviet Russia but of the Union Soviet states as well. The Supreme Economic Council of the RSFSR helped to coordinate the industrial development of all the republics. All this created conditions for the emergence of the all-Union organs of management and for the transition to a new stage in the construction of a united multinational state. In the summer of 1920 representatives of the Ukraine and Byelorussia were seated on the All-Russia Central Executive Committee.

The Ninth All-Russia Congress of Soviets took a new step in establishing the organs of power of the RSFSR based on representation of other Soviet republics. The congress session on December 26, 1921 adopted a proposal of the Transcaucasian republics concerning their representation in the All-Russia Central Executive Committee so that they could express their solidarity with Soviet Russia and "continue to learn from the rich experience of building socialism in Russia".[1] The All-Russia Central Executive Committee elected at the Ninth Congress of Soviets included 20 representatives from the Azerbaijan Republic, 20 from the Georgian and 15 from the Armenian.[2]

National-State Construction. Necessity of Closer Integration

The experience of establishment in 1920-1922 of eight autonomous Soviet republics and eleven autonomous regions in the composition of the RSFSR was essential in preparing the transition from the federation based on treaties to a multinational union state.

The creation and development of several different forms of Soviet autonomy, specification of constitutional rights and adjustment of the mutual relations between the autonomous com-

---

[1] *Ninth All-Russia Congress of Soviets of Workers', Peasants' and Cossacks' Deputies,* Verbatim report, Gosizdat, Moscow, 1922, p. 186 (in Russian).

[2] *Soviet Community of the Peoples,* p. 250.

ponents and the federation helped regulate national co-operation in building socialism.

Of great importance was the establishment of firmly demarcated autonomous republics and regions with due consideration of their ethnic groups and the economic community of nations.

This created the conditions for the national consolidation of nationalities—in the feudal or pre-feudal, clan-tribe stage of development—into socialist nations.

Thus, at the end of May 1920 the All-Russia Central Executive Committee issued a decree on the formation of the Tatar ASSR, which included several districts of the Kazan, Ufa, Samara, Vyatka and Simbirsk provinces populated by Tatars. The Chuvash autonomous region, which included several districts of the Kazan and Simbirsk provinces, was formed in June 1920. The Karelian Labour Commune uniting the Olonets and Arkhangelsk provinces populated by Karelians was formed at the same time.

Decrees on the formation of the Udmurt (Vyatka), Kalmyk and Mari autonomous regions were adopted in November 1920. The Daghestan ASSR, uniting over 30 nationalities, the Mountaineer Autonomous Republic in the Northern Caucasus and several other national state association were formed at the same time. The Russian Federative Republic became an example of a multinational state.

By the beginning of 1922 the RSFSR included: the Bashkir, Tatar, Mountaineer, Daghestan, Kirghiz, Crimean, Turkestan and Yakut Autonomous republics as well as the Buryat, Udmurt, Kalmyk, Kabardin-Balkar, Karachai-Circassian, Komi, Mari, Oirot, Circassian (Adygei), Chechen and Chuvash autonomous regions, and the Karelian and Volga Area German labour communes.

A formation at Lenin's suggestion in March 1922 of the federative union of the Transcaucasian republics of Georgia, Armenia and Azerbaijan, which in December 1922 was reconstituted into the Transcaucasian Socialist Federative Soviet Republic consisting of three equal Soviet republics, was a major step in strengthening the unity of the Transcaucasian peoples, in consolidating their fraternal union with the Russian and other peoples.

Lenin proposed the idea of forming the Transcaucasian Republic when in April 1921 he said he was confident that close union "will serve as a model of national peace, unprecedented under the bourgeoisie and impossible under the capitalist system".[1] The interests of rebuilding the republics' economy demanded unification.

The Communist Parties of Azerbaijan, Armenia and Georgia wholly supported Lenin's idea of unifying the three republics into a Soviet federation. An economic organ for the entire Transcaucasia had already been created in the summer of 1921, railways and foreign trade were integrated and border customs between the Transcaucasian republics, Daghestan and Soviet Russia set up by nationalists were abolished. Economic mutual assistance between these republics and the RSFSR intensified to combat economic dislocation. On March 11-12, 1922, in Tbilisi, the authoritative representatives of Azerbaijan, Armenia and Georgia signed a Union treaty on the formation of the federative union of the republics, envisaging close political, economic and military co-operation.

In December 1922 the First Congress of Soviets of Transcaucasia adopted the decision to reconstitute the union into the Transcaucasian Socialist Federative Soviet Republic.

This is how, in Soviet national-state construction, the idea of the union federation, uniting independent and equal Soviet republics, was put into practice. The formation of the Transcaucasian Socialist Federative Soviet Republic was an important step on the way to the formation of the USSR.

The development of the treaty federation, which from one stage to another was characterised by increasingly closer relations between the Soviet republics and the expansion of the sphere of joint endeavour, led their Party and the Soviet leaders to the gradual realisation that a federative union was necessary since many economic and political factors demonstrated that links based on treaties alone were insufficient.

The key element in determining the necessity of replacing

---

[1] V. I. Lenin, "To the Comrades Communists of Azerbaijan, Georgia, Armenia, Daghestan, and the Mountaineer Republics", *Collected Works*, Vol. 32, p. 316.

links based on treaties between the Soviet republics by a new form of socialist federation was the heightened significance of the principal economic and political factors, which Lenin had drawn attention to in the summer of 1920, first of all, by the impossibility of defending the existence of the Soviet republics in the face of a hostile capitalist world without close union.

As the treaty-based federation developed, it became clear that the economic restoration of all the republics and creating the foundations of a socialist economic structure demanded a more solid and closer mobilisation of efforts than simply coordinated action in the framework of co-operation based on union treaties.

A single economy, based on the traditional specialisation of national regions and on the division of labour between them had evolved in Russia long before the October Revolution. Coal, iron ore and iron-and-steel production in the Ukraine and the oil industry in Azerbaijan were closely integrated with the engineering industry in several regions of Russia; the cotton growing in Turkestan and flax growing in Byelorussia with the textile industry of the Central industrial region. There was also specialisation in the production and consumption of agricultural and industrial products in all the other national regions of the former Russian Empire which made up a single economic organism. Rail transport linked practically all regions of the country.

The New Economic Policy facilitated the restoration of the market links and of the specialisation and co-operation of the national regions that had been disrupted by the Civil War. However, economic rehabilitation and building socialism demanded economic links on a higher level, the deepening of the historically evolved specialisation in the national regions, the more rational distribution of the productive forces, the location of manufacturing industry closer to the raw material sources, electrification, etc. Inequality, especially in economic development between the Soviet republics, could not be overcome unless this was done.

Rebuilding the country's economy and bringing it to a qualitatively new stage, and the creation of the material and technical base of socialism demanded the planned development of all the branches of the economy, of single state legislation in the socio-economic field, and a very precise definition of the functions and competence and wholly coordinated actions by the organs of power and management of the RSFSR and the other Soviet republics (Council for Labour and Defence, Supreme Economic Council, Economic Councils of the republics and many commissariats). But such a high level of interaction between the Soviet republics was impossible within the framework of the treaty federation. Attempts to coordinate economic planning by creating a body of representatives from the republics on economic construction under the government of the RSFSR, as was done to coordinate efforts between the RSFSR and the Ukraine in September 1921,[1] could not change the situation in any real way.

The insufficiency of the treaty system was seen in the fact that several questions were unresolved and unsettled: the rights of certain federal organs of management, unified planning, financial relations, budget allocations, differentiation, frontiers, equality of legislation, etc.[2] Under the treaty federation complete unity had not been reached in foreign policy either. The experience of the Genoa Conference, at which Soviet republics presented a consolidated front and granted the RSFSR the right to speak for them all demonstrated how difficult it was to defend their integrity when in the position of alien capitalist encirclement. Genoa showed that it was time to move forward from temporary agreements on diplomatic unity to the permanent realisation of the foreign functions of all the Soviet republics as a single and coordinated policy which was possible only within the framework of a single state.

Finally, the fact that the union treaties of 1920-1921 stipulated that general federal functions would be executed by the highest state organs of primarily one republic—the RSFSR— was yet another shortcoming of the treaty federation. It reflected the acknowledgement of the great authority of Soviet Russia

---

[1] *Soviet Community of the Peoples*, pp. 236-39.
[2] See V. M. Shapko, *The Union Is 50 (The 50th Anniversary of the Formation of the USSR)*, Politizdat, Moscow, 1971, pp. 39-40, 42-46; *History of the USSR from Ancient Times to Our Days*, Vol. VIII, Nauka Publishers, Moscow, 1967, pp. 93-95, 98-99 (both in Russian).

as the biggest and most important economic and political force among all other union republics allied to it.

However, the RSFSR's position and the practice followed by several of its commissariats not stipulated by the union treaties as united (justice, agriculture, etc.) to extend their functions to other republics, gave rise to nationalist sentiment among many local officials, resulting in attempts by them to ask whether it was really possible for these republics to retain their sovereignty in a treaty federation.[1]

This made it imperative to go ahead with the complicated problem of the transition from federative relations between the republics, based on treaties, to a closer federative union that would better ensure the combination of cohesion and centralisation with equality and independence of the nations and peoples, and the retention of their sovereignty. It was extremely difficult to resolve this problem because it had never been done anywhere before.

Meanwhile, there were all the necessary political and economic conditions to move forward to the federative union and to create a single multinational state: the political power of the working class in the form of the Soviets as the basis of the state system of all the Soviet republics; the experience of their alliance and mutual assistance within the framework of treaty federative relations; public property and the socialist way of life as the economic foundation of each of the republics.

Movement of Unification

In the spring of 1922 a proposal was moved on the initiative of the Communist Party of the Ukraine on the resolving and concretisation of the federative relations between the RSFSR and the USSR. A special commission of representatives of the central committees of the Communist parties of the RSFSR and the Ukraine, chaired by Frunze, was established in May 1922; it prepared several drafts and suggestions on relations between

---

[1] V. M. Shapko, *The Union Is 50*, p. 47; *History of the USSR*, Vol. VIII, p. 100.

certain people's commissariats and departments of the two republics.

However, attempts to deal with these matters came up against the fact that the general questions of the treaty federation of the two republics had not been resolved.

Decisive steps were taken in the second half of 1922 towards the formation of the USSR. In the summer of the same year, the Party organisations of the Transcaucasus, the Ukraine and Byelorussia authorised their delegates to go to Moscow and bring up the question with the CC RCP(B) of the specification and concretisation of federative relations between the RSFSR and other Soviet republics. On August 10, 1922 the Politbureau of the CC RCP(B) adopted a decision to set up a commission to draft the principles of the federative relations of the republics and to determine the structure of the future federation. On it were J. V. Stalin, V. V. Kuibyshev and G. K. Orjonikidze (RSFSR); S. A. Agamali-ogly (Azerbaijan); A. F. Myasnikov (Armenia); P. G. Mdivani (Georgia); G. I. Petrovsky (Ukraine); A. G. Chervyakov (Byelorussia), and others.

At its sessions of September 23 and 24, 1922 the commission adopted an initial draft of the resolution "On the Relations of the RSFSR with the Independent Republics", which was known as the "autonomisation" plan. Basically, the idea was that the RSFSR would be declared a single multinational union state, while all the other independent republics would become parts of it and enjoy autonomous rights; the competence of the highest organs of power and management (All-Russia General Executive Committee and the Council of People's Commissars) of the RSFSR would extend to the corresponding institutions of the Ukraine, Byelorussia and Transcaucasus. The problem was that the plan was one-sided as it only provided for the requirements of strict unity and centralisation, while those of the independent republics retaining their sovereign rights were insufficiently regarded. Representatives of several Soviet republics spoke for it, but it still had to be discussed further.[1]

---

[1] *History of the USSR*, Vol. VIII, pp. 107-08; V. M. Shapko, op. cit., pp. 54-56; S. I. Yakubovskaya, *The Construction of the Union Soviet Socialist State. 1922-1925*, Nauka Publishers, Moscow, 1960, pp. 143-59, 174-82 (all in Russian).

Lenin's Plan for the Formation of the USSR

At the time when the question of the character of federative relations between the Soviet republics was being examined, Lenin, the leader of the Party and the head of the RSFSR's government, was ill.

Towards the end of 1921, Lenin's health began to be a matter of grave concern. He was plagued by headaches and insomnia, the result of long and difficult years of revolutionary endeavour, of tremendous personal exertion as the Party and state leader, as well as of the grave wound he had received in 1918. However, although he had to rest from time to time, Lenin continued with his political activity. In the spring of 1922 he flung himself into the preparations for the 11th Congress of the RCP(B) and attended the sessions. He also guided the activities of the Soviet delegation on the eve of and during the Genoa Conference. This caused his health to further deteriorate. On May 23, on doctors' advice, Lenin moved to Gorki to rest, and on May 25-27 his health took a serious turn for the worse: partial paralysis of the right hand and leg, and speech disturbance.[1]

Gorki was Lenin's permanent residence from the autumn of 1918 to 1924.

Lenin first lived in a small and modest room on the first floor of the northern wing, and only after endless persuasion agreed to move to one of the rooms of the big house, where he used to spend long hours on the balcony enjoying the fresh air. Together with him in Gorki were his wife N. K. Krupskaya, and sisters M. I. Ulyanova and A. I. Ulyanova-Elizarova.[2]

When he recovered somewhat, Lenin began to take strolls along the park lanes in his well-worn semi-military tunic with its big leather buttons, and his slightly rumpled cap.

Lenin's rest schedule in Gorki at that time was, as usual, quite peculiar. He felt the ban on reading, especially newspapers, which the doctors had imposed during his first weeks of

---

[1] V. I. Lenin, *Collected Works*, Vol. 33, p. 551.
[2] L. A. Fotieva, *From the Life of V. I. Lenin*, Politizdat, Moscow, 1967, pp. 178-79 (in Russian).

illness, very keenly. An acquaintance, who visited Lenin in July, later recalled: " 'I'm not allowed to read the papers,' Lenin said ironically, 'I can't discuss politics. I carefully avoid any scrap of paper on the desk, afraid that it might happen to be a piece of newspaper and make me break discipline.' "[1] M. I. Ulyanova notes in her *Recollections:* "When, in an attempt to distract him a little, doctors suggested that he see some of his friends, but on the condition that he not discuss politics, Lenin flatly refused, and once the doctors had left, told us: 'They think that political leaders who haven't seen each other for several months can talk about anything else but politics, which they lived with all their lives.' "[2]

As Lenin overcame illness and grew stronger, he greeted every new relaxation of medical discipline with glee. On July 13 he wrote to his secretary at the Council of People's Commissars L. A. Fotieva: "You can congratulate me on my recovery. . . . Start preparing books for me (and sending me lists) of 1) science, 2) fiction, 3) politics (the latter last of all, because it is not yet allowed)."[3] In a note of July 18 to J. V. Stalin he wrote: "You can congratulate me: I have been permitted *to read the papers!* Old papers from today, and *new ones* from Sunday!"[4]

"The creation of the USSR is a living embodiment of the ideas of Vladimir Ilyich Lenin and of the Leninist principles of the national policy,"[5] as stressed in the CPSU Central Committee Resolution on the 60th anniversary of the Union of Soviet Socialist Republics.

On September 25, 1922, he learned of the decision of the special commission; he spent two days discussing the question with representatives of the RSFSR and other republics, and then

[1] *At the Helm of the Land of Soviets,* Vol. 2, Politizdat, Moscow, 1980, pp. 213-14 (in Russian).

[2] Quoted in V. V. Volkova, *Lenin in Gorki,* Politizdat, Moscow, 1969, pp. 56-57 (in Russian).

[3] V. I. Lenin, "To Lydia Fotieva", *Collected Works,* Vol. 45, p. 560.

[4] V. I. Lenin, "To J. V. Stalin", *Collected Works,* Vol. 45, p. 561.

[5] "Resolution of the Central Committee of the Communist Party of the Soviet Union on the Sixtieth Anniversary of the Formation of the Union of Soviet Socialist Republics", *Pravda,* 21 February 1982.

sent a letter to the Party Politbureau, strongly critical of the "autonomisation" plan. In his letter of September 26 and in another of October 6, 1922, Lenin proposed the unification of the Soviet republics into a new Union state founded on full equality and on the retention of sovereignty by each. "We consider ourselves, the Ukrainian S.S.R. and others, equal, and enter with them, on an equal basis, into a new union, a new federation, the Union of the Soviet Republics of Europe and Asia."[1]

He also proposed that the other propositions be formulated differently, drawing specific attention to the necessity of creating an All-Union Central Executive Committee and of setting up several All-Union people's commissariats. So it was Vladimir Lenin who conceived the idea of creating the Union of Soviet Socialist Republics based on the voluntary union of equal and sovereign republics. It was a major contribution to Marxist theory and to national state building.

Lenin substantiated a new type of multinational socialist state, a totally new kind of federation, based on the principles of proletarian internationalism.

On October 6 the Plenum of the CC RCP(B) used Lenin's proposal as the basis of a resolution envisaging the conclusion of a treaty between the RSFSR, the Ukraine, Byelorussia and the Transcaucasian Federation on their unification into the Union of Soviet Socialist Republics with each retaining the right freely to secede from the Union state. From October 1922 through December, Lenin's concept, which was embodied in the decisions of the October (1922) Plenum of the CC RCP(B), was discussed extensively in all the republics, and received the total approval and support of the Party and the Soviet organisations, of the working people in each. At the same time a special commission, established by decision of the Plenum of the CC RCP(B), prepared the materials for drawing up a Union treaty. A draft of the main points of the Constitution of the USSR was also elaborated. Despite his progressing illness, Lenin continued to be extremely interested in the question of the formation of a Union state.

---

[1] V. I. Lenin, "On the Establishment of the U.S.S.R.," *Collected Works*, Vol. 42, pp. 421-22.

On November 29, 1922 he was informed that the Politbureau would dedicate a coming session to this question, and on December 14, 1922 he planned to dictate another letter about the Union of Socialist Republics.

On December 27-28, the national question and internationalism appeared in his plan for future articles.[1]

Congresses of the Soviets of the Republics

On December 10 Lenin sent greetings to the Seventh All-Ukrainian Congress of Soviets: "One of the most important problems which the Congress has to solve is that of uniting the republics. The proper solution of this problem will determine the future organisation of our machinery of state...."[2]

The Congress met from December 10 to 14, 1922 in Kharkov, the capital of the Ukrainian Soviet Republic.

One of the delegates, I. V. Miroshnichenko, who was elected by the workers of the Izyum railway shops, recalled: "At last came the opening day. In the presidium was the Ukrainian 'elder statesman' Grigori Ivanovich Petrovsky.... He delivered the opening speech. We listened to him very attentively. He said that the question was not about the strength of the Soviet power —it was quite strong—but the ways the workers and peasants would choose to make it a reality and to better organise their lives.

"Mikhail Frunze, Vice-Chairman of the Council of People's Commissars of the Ukraine, was to report on the activities of the republic's government. He was just heading for the podium when Petrovsky was handed a telegram. He glanced through it, gestured to Frunze, and said excitedly:

" 'Comrades! A telegram from Lenin!'

"It seemed that the walls trembled from the applause. The

---

[1] "Journal of Lenin's Duty Secretaries", in V. I. Lenin, *Collected Works,* Vol, 42, pp. 470, 480; V. I. Lenin, *Complete Works,* Vol. 45, p. 596 (in Russian).

[2] V. I. Lenin, "To the All-Ukrainian Congress of Soviets", *Collected Works,* Vol. 33, p. 454.

gathering was overjoyed to receive the greetings, as it meant that Lenin, although not very well, was working."[1]

The Congress sent Lenin a telegram of reply: "At this moment, to the strains of the *Internationale*, the All-Ukrainian Congress of Soviets unanimously adopted a resolution on the government's report about the immediate creation of a new state formation under the name of the 'Union of Soviet Socialist Republics'. The Congress has no doubts that the initiative of the Ukrainian workers and peasants will receive the full sympathy and approval of the working masses of Russia and of all the fraternal Soviet lands. In warmly greeting you as our ideological leader, the Congress is confident that it will see you in the near future at the head of the All-Union Soviet government."

On December 13, the Congress adopted a declaration with an appeal to the other Soviet republics to "immediately begin forming a single Union state".[2]

In Byelorussia, the idea of forming the USSR received total support at the Party conferences, six *uyezd* and 116 *volost* congresses of Soviets, and at many public meetings. Party conferences, *volost* and *uyezd* congresses of Soviets and public meetings in Georgia, Armenia and Azerbaijan gave it similar support.[3]

Resolutions on creating the USSR were adopted on December 13, 1922 by the First Transcaucasian Congress of Soviets, held in Baku, and five days later by the Fourth All-Byelorussian Congress of Soviets, which met in Minsk. These congresses, like the Seventh All-Ukrainian, elected delegates to the Tenth All-Russia Congress of Soviets and gave them the authority to participate in the formation of a single Union state.

Thus, the highest organs of state power of the three Soviet republics declared themselves in favour of the creation of a single Union state through voluntary unification on the basis of the principles of equality, sovereignty and proletarian internationalism. Now it was the turn of the largest Soviet republic— the RSFSR, which by that time had a population of nearly 100

---

[1] *Pravda,* December 1, 1972.
[2] *Soviet Community of the Peoples,* pp. 293-95.
[3] *History of the USSR,* Vol. VIII, p. 112.

million that was predominantly (up to 80 per cent) Russian and which had a considerable number of autonomous republics and national areas.

In the second half of 1922 the Russian Federation was preparing for its Tenth Congress of Soviets. Lenin's deteriorating health did not allow him to take part, although up to December 16 he thought of making the government's report and wrote a summary of the speech he hoped to give at the Congress.

The Tenth All-Russia Congress was to open at 18:00 on December 23, 1922 in the Bolshoi Theatre. As the hands of the clock drew nearer and nearer to the hour, the livelier it became on Sverdlov Square and nearby streets. The Congress delegates converged on the Bolshoi in groups and singly, showed their credentials to the Red Army men wrapped up in huge bulky sheepskin coats, and, quickly peeling off their coats, filled the pit, boxes and balconies. There was a new element in the outward appearance of the delegates, in the way they carried themselves and talked, compared to those attending the congresses of Soviets held two or three years previously. Then the prevailing mood among the delegates was nervous fatigue and tension: pale faces, feverish burning eyes, and abrupt movements.

The atmosphere was quite different at the Tenth All-Russia Congress: broad smiles, calm eyes, confident and unhurried movements, cheerful voices, laughter and jokes.

Some delegate from Moscow, as he approached the Bolshoi Theatre that evening, might have been thinking: How time flies! Only five years ago, in November 1917, the detachments of Red Guards and revolutionary soldiers of the Moscow garrison concentrated here at the theatre for the decisive storming of the Kremlin, and wheeled two three-inch guns into position for firing at the City Duma and the *Metropol* Hotel—the strongholds of the counter-revolutionary cadets. And just four and a half years ago, during the Socialist-Revolutionary mutiny in July 1918, a machine-gun placed on the pediment of the Bolshoi Theatre between the bronze horses kept all Teatralnaya Square under fire, while armoured cars and Lett Red Army men were positioned near the building. Here in the Bolshoi only two years previously, in December 1920, delegates to the Eighth All-Russia Congress of Soviets—pale, emaciated and singed by the flames of the Civil War—responded to Lenin's appeal for the electrification of the country with an avalanche of applause, and stood for a long time in front of the map, reflecting on what had to be done to realise this grandiose plan.

And now in December 1922, it was the Tenth All-Russia Congress of Soviets. Congress delegates and guests had years of revolution behind them. Civil War and the 1921-1922 famine were things of the past. The country was getting on its feet, life was reviving and the economy finding its way again—it was a sign of time, the initial successes of the new economic policy: the Kashira Electric Power Station near Moscow and the "Krasny Petrograd" electric power station in Petrograd having been commissioned, the beginning of construction at the Volkhovstroi and the building of the Shatura Electric Power Station, the rapid restoration of the textile industry and preparations for the First All-Russia Agricultural Exhibition. Life was still hard, the country was still backward and illiterate, but there was already confidence that, as Lenin put it in November 1922, "Russia will become socialist Russia".[1] This confidence engulfed the delegates to the Tenth All-Russia Congress of Soviets, which opened on December 23, 1922 at the Bolshoi Theatre.

First All-Union Congress of Soviets

Six p.m. The theatre, filled to capacity, seated 2,215 delegates—1,727 representing the Russian Federation, and 488, honoured guests from the Ukraine, Byelorussia and Transcaucasia.

The orchestra pit was occupied by Soviet journalists, and, what was rather unusual, by foreign correspondents from the major capitalist countries.

M. I. Kalinin, Chairman of the All-Russia Central Executive Committee, mounted the podium. "Comrades," he said, "we may regard the Tenth Congress as a jubilee congress, because it finalises to a certain degree what all the previous congresses have

---

[1] V. I. Lenin, "Speech at a Plenary Session of the Moscow Soviet, November 20, 1922", *Collected Works*, Vol. 33, pp. 443.

achieved in one of the fields, placing on the agenda the unification in a closer union of all the Soviet socialist republics." Greeting the representatives of the Ukraine, Byelorussia and Transcaucasia, Kalinin continued with emotion in his voice: "They are here now as guests of honour. And in a few days they will be here as full-fledged delegates at a new congress of the Soviet Socialist Republics... The might of the congresses of Soviets lies in this infinite solidarity..."[1]

Lenin was not physically present at the congress, but he was present in the delegates' thoughts, in the speeches and reports. As soon as the chairman gave the floor to the speaker who would deliver the report of the All-Russia Central Executive Committee and the Council of People's Commissars of the RSFSR, the love and respect for Vladimir Ilyich Lenin that were present in the huge auditorium burst forth. This can be seen from an excerpt of the congress records: "*A Voice*: Greetings to Comrade Lenin on behalf of the congress! (Prolonged and stormy applause). The delegates rise from their seats and sing the Internationale.

"*Chairman*: Comrades, regretfully, doctors have prescribed a regime for Comrade Lenin which does not allow him to go out. The presidium proposes on behalf of the congress to send Vladimir Ilyich Lenin a telegram with the hope that this ban will be lifted in the immediate future. (Applause.")[2]

The New York Times had good reason to write on December 25, 1922, in a report from Moscow: "Two things in the first session stood out—their nationalism and their devotion to Lenin, although he was not present. Perhaps the two are one—nationalism being their firm belief in the new Russia and Lenin the man who personifies it."

Lenin's thinking and his central propositions concerning the formation of the USSR were fully set forth at the end of the congress.

Discussion of the sixth point on the agenda—"Propositions of the treaty Soviet republics on the formation of the Union of

---

[1] *Tenth All-Russia Congress of Soviets*, Verbatim Report, Gosizdat, Moscow, 1923, p. 2 (in Russian).

[2] Ibid., p. 4.

Soviet Socialist Republics" — began at the evening session of December 26 and ended on the following day.

J. V. Stalin, who delivered the report on the question, explained the main factors and circumstances, both domestic and international, that impelled the Soviet republics to unite into a single multinational state.

The draft resolution on the question which the delegates were to consider reflected Lenin's idea that had been approved by the Plenary Meeting of the CC RCP(B) of October 6, 1922. It acknowledged that the unification of the RSFSR, the Ukrainian SSR, the Transcaucasian Socialist Federative Soviet Republic and the Byelorussian SSR into a single Union state was dictated by the times, with unification based on the principle of voluntariness, the equality of the republics and on the retention by each of full sovereignty and the right to secede from the Union. The draft also envisaged the election by the congress of a delegation from the RSFSR which would be instructed to elaborate jointly with the delegations of the Ukraine, Transcaucasia and Byelorussia a draft of the Declaration on the Formation of the USSR and to conclude a Treaty with these republics on the formation of a single Union state.

In their speeches to the congress, delegates representing the Soviet republics, such as M. V. Frunze (Ukraine), G. Musabekov (Azerbaijan), M. G. Tskhakaya (Georgia), V. Lukashin (Armenia) and A. G. Chervyakov (Byelorussia), spoke about the decisions of the congresses of their republics to seek immediate formation of the USSR. At the evening session of December 27, the draft resolution of the Tenth All-Russia Congress of Soviets on the question was adopted unanimously.[1]

Summarising the congress results, especially the decision to form the Union of Soviet Socialist Republics, M. I. Kalinin drew this expressive picture in his concluding speech: "I see flying above us a red banner with five sacred letters—RSFSR. (Applause.) We who are delegates to the Tenth Congress of Soviets, plenipotentiary representatives of the entire Soviet Russian Federation, dip our cherished banner, covered with the

---

[1] See *Tenth All-Russia Congress of Soviets*, pp. 184-89, 190-98, 216-17.

glory of battles and victories, strengthened by the sacrifices of workers and peasants to the Union of Soviet Republics. (Applause.) We see a new red banner of the Union of Soviet Republics being hoisted. I see this banner in the hands of Comrade Lenin. (Prolonged applause.)"[1]

The Tenth All-Russia Congress of Soviets, an important milestone on the road to the formation of the Union of Soviet Socialist Republics, ended on December 27, 1922. Two days later, on December 29, 1922, a conference of the plenipotentiary representatives of the delegations of the RSFSR, the Ukrainian SSR, the Transcaucasian SFSR and the Byelorussian SSR met in the Andreyevsky Hall of the Grand Kremlin Palace; it was chaired by M. I. Kalinin. It examined the drafts of the Declaration and of the Union Treaty on the Formation of the USSR, then approved and signed them. The conference then decided to convene on the following day—December 30, 1922—in the Bolshoi Theatre, the First Congress of Soviets of the Union of Soviet Socialist Republics so that all the delegates of the united congress could adopt a Declaration and a Treaty.[2]

The historic day of December 30, 1922 was the concluding stage of the movement to unify the peoples of the Soviet republics. It was the day the First All-Union Congress of Soviets met at the Bolshoi Theatre.

The same 2,215 delegates who had attended the Tenth All-Russia Congress of Soviets, some as plenipotentiary representatives of the RSFSR and the others as guests of honour, assembled again. At the First All-Union Congress of Soviets the RSFSR was represented by 1,727 delegates, the Ukraine by 364, the Transcaucasian Federation by 91, and Byelorussia by 33.[3]

In the first hour p.m. P. G. Smidovich, the oldest delegate, on the instruction of the conference of the plenipotentiary representatives of the RSFSR, the Ukrainian SSR, the Transcaucasian SFSR and the Byelorussian SSR, opened the congress. By unanimous decision of the delegates of the four republics,

---

[1] *Tenth All-Russia Congress of Soviets*, p. 217.
[2] See *Soviet Community of the Peoples*, pp. 302-03.
[3] See *The First Congress of Soviets of the USSR*, Verbatim Report, Gosizdat, Moscow, 1922, p. 19 (in Russian).

delegate A. S. Enukidze proposed that V. I. Lenin be elected honorary Chairman of the First All-Union Congress of Soviets. This proposal was met with stormy applause and shouts: "Long live leader of the world proletariat, Comrade Lenin!" The congress unanimously adopted a message of greeting to Comrade Lenin.

J. V. Stalin delivered the report on the formation of the USSR, briefly summarising the principal inner and external reasons for the formation of a single multinational state. Then he read out the Declaration and the Treaty on the Formation of the Union of Soviet Socialist Republics that the conference of the authoritative delegations had adopted the day before.

The Declaration set forth the main reasons for the decision to form the USSR: the necessity of the republics one and all to restore the economy and to build socialism; military and defence considerations; proletarian internationalism, and the class essence of Soviet power.

The Treaty reflected Lenin's idea of the unification of the equal Soviet republics—the RSFSR, the Ukrainian SSR, the Transcaucasian SFSR and the Byelorussian SSR—in a single Union state: the Union of Soviet Socialist Republics; it stipulated the areas of competence of the supreme organs of the Union, their structure, the procedure of election, the character of the relations between the Union and republican organs of power, and established a single all-Union citizenship. Each of the Union republics retained the right to secede from the USSR.

These documents established the constitutional foundations of the multinational Union of Soviet Socialist Republics both on the general political level and in organisational and legal form.[1]

Recollections of the delegates to the First All-Union Congress of Soviets convey an idea of the festive atmosphere and special significance of that historic event. V. M. Verkhovnykh, a member of the CPSU from 1913, recalled: "December 30, 1922. We delegates to the Tenth All-Russia Congress of Soviets headed, en masse and with the same mandates, for the initial session of the First All-Union Congress of Soviets, whose responsibility it was to create a new state, the highest form of Soviet federation

---

[1] See *The First Congress of Soviets of the USSR*, pp. 3-11.

—the Union of Soviet Socialist Republics. We will never forget the Bolshoi Theatre—cold, unheated and half-lit. Delegates talked among themselves in many languages, and presented a picturesque sight as they sat in their furcoats, greatcoats or national robes... Delegates were extremely friendly and warm. In the recesses and then in the hotel, both acquaintances and people who had never met were saying: 'Brothers, comrades! We're creating a powerful and solid union which no one will ever break.' "[1]

"Those were wonderful days for us delegates," wrote another participant, A. Nukhrat. "It was still hard times in Moscow, but no one felt tired or tense. You could meet a mountaineer in his Circassian tunic or a Ukrainian in a wide coat. Music was played in the recesses between sessions. Everyone felt wonderful! What other emotion could they be savouring, as the Civil War had ended, the country's international prestige had grown and other countries now took us very seriously. And from now on we were not just a republic but a new kind of state—the Union of Soviet Socialist Republics. It is difficult to convey the feelings of joy and pride that gripped us..."[2]

The report of the Petrograd delegation which was presented to the Petrograd Soviet on January 10, 1923 on the results of the Tenth All-Russia and First All-Union Congresses of Soviets gives a rather good idea of the spirit of fraternal friendship and solidarity of the representatives of the many nationalities who gathered at the Bolshoi that day: "The session at which delegates spoke about the formation of a single union of Soviet republics was, probably, the most interesting moment for foreign diplomats. The diplomatic box was packed to capacity. The starched shirtfronts thought that, echoing their own conferences, they would now see the representatives of the different republics try to strangle and choke each other, try to pull the wool over one another's eyes. But they were absolutely astonished to see that they were mistaken, and that an equal union had been formed."[3]

Discussion at the congress was brief. The question had been

---

[1] *Pravda*, April 26, 1972.

[2] *Izvestia*, September 27, 1977.

[3] *Krasnaya gazeta* (Petrograd), January 11, 1923.

long imminent and clear for each of the 2,000 delegates, and had been prepared by the entire course of historical development.

The Ukrainian delegate M. V. Frunze proposed that the Declaration and the Treaty on the formation of the USSR be approved in principle and, considering their special importance, that they be turned over for additional consideration to the Central Executive Committees of the Union republics so that a final text could be adopted by the Second All-Union Congress of Soviets. The proposal was accepted unanimously.

V. Kolarov read the greeting from the Communist International to the congress, which then heard the representatives of the Bukhara and Khorezm people's republics and of the Red Army.

Peasant M. Odinets drew an allusion as might befit a faithful Christian when he spoke on behalf of the Ukrainian peasants of the Chernigov Province: "...By common effort we shall erect the building of our union, and Comrade Lenin will be its guardian angel."[1]

The congress elected the Central Executive Committee of the USSR of 371 members and 138 alternate members. In accordance with Lenin's previously expressed suggestion, four representatives of the Union republics—M. I. Kalinin (RSFSR), G. I. Petrovsky (Ukrainian SSR), A. G. Chervyakov (Byelorussian SSR) and N. N. Narimanov (Transcaucasian SFSR)— were elected chairmen of the Union CEC.[2]

Closing the First Congress of Soviets, M. I. Kalinin said with deep feeling: "Taking place today, in rather modest circumstances, is an event of world significance. Perhaps now, at this particular moment, its importance is not as yet felt in full measure, but with every passing day its magnitude on the political horizon will grow. There is no doubt about it."[3]

In the evening of December 30, 1922 the First All-Union Congress of Soviets was declared closed.

[1] *The First Congress of Soviets of the USSR,* pp. 16-18; *Izvestia,* December 31, 1922.

[2] Ibid., pp. 19-24.

[3] Ibid., p. 24.

The acts proclaiming the formation of the Union of Soviet Socialist Republics are of outstanding historical and international significance. They were the triumph of the Leninist nationalities policy, based on the principles of proletarian internationalism, of equality, and of the fraternal friendship and unity of the sovereign peoples of the Land of Soviets.

For the first time ever, a multinational state was created which did not establish the rule of one nation over another, a state without ruling and oppressed nations. It proclaimed the full equality of all peoples, big and small, which chose the road of co-operation and mutual assistance in building a new and just socialist society.

Chapter VI

THE SOVIET MULTINATIONAL STATE BY THE MID-1920s. THE GROWING INTERNATIONAL PRESTIGE OF THE USSR

Lenin's Plan for Building Socialism

On October 2, 1922 Lenin came back to Moscow from Gorki; he chaired a meeting of the Council of People's Commissars on October 3, and two days later the RCP(B) Central Committee met for a three-day plenary session. Lenin attended the first meeting of the session, but poor health kept him away on the subsequent days. On October 6, the session, as was mentioned above, adopted a fundamental decision based on Lenin's proposals which called for a treaty to be concluded between the Soviet republics on the establishment of the USSR.

This final period of Lenin's active political life was to last until mid-December 1922, when his health again took a turn for the worse. Essentially, he had worked as hard as ever. His secretary noted that during the period Vladimir Ilyich "wrote 224 business letters and notes, received 171 people (on 125 different occasions), and chaired 32 meetings and conferences of the Council of People's Commissars, Council of Labour and Defence, of the Politbureau, and committees".[1]

Lenin continued to work on practical problems of the New Economic Policy, to direct the building of the economy and cultural progress, and to deal with various matters associated with the development of industry, transport, agriculture, finance and trade, the state structure, foreign trade and foreign policy.

After two and a half months of strenuous work Lenin's health

---

[1] *Vladimir Ilyich Lenin. Biography.* Politizdat, Moscow, 1967, p. 599 (in Russian).

deteriorated considerably. He suffered a serious relapse on December 16. Once he recovered somewhat, although confined to bed, he asked the doctors to allow him to dictate notes to his secretaries, outlining the tasks and ways of development of Soviet society.[1]

Between December 23, 1922 and March 6, 1923 Lenin dictated his final letters and articles which are occasionally referred to as his political testament.

The central ideas of these letters, articles and notes were a tremendous contribution to final elaboration of the plan for building socialism in the Soviet Union. They also contained measures for realisation of the plan.

In essence, Lenin's last works expressed the following idea: the Soviet state had everything it required to successfully build a socialist society. Many factors, including the relatively low level of economic development, made building socialism difficult, but hard work could overcome them. With the words, "Russia will become the socialist Russia" which concluded his final public speech on November 20, 1922, Lenin expressed his solid confidence that socialism would in fact be successfully built in the USSR.

Lenin believed that the creation of the material and technical base of socialism was one of the primary conditions for the triumph of the new society. Only highly developed heavy industry that was to be founded on planned electrification and industrialisation could be the nucleus of that base. At the same time, Lenin emphasised that the country must adopt a policy of industrialisation preserving and strengthening the alliance between the working class and the peasantry.

In his final works, particularly the article "On Co-operation" Lenin outlined the ways of remodelling agriculture along socialist lines. At the time there was an infinite patchwork of small individual farms which were economically weak and did not have enough efficient agricultural machinery or tools. He considered the absence of compulsion, the development of co-operation from lower to higher forms, and the combination of the personal interests of the peasants with those of society as a whole

---

[1] See *Vladimir Ilyich Lenin. Biography*, pp. 620-21.

to be the paramount principles of the co-operative movement—the sole path to highly-developed large-scale farming. There would be gradual transition to the most advanced methods of agriculture and to the organisation of production co-operatives (collective farms) as peasants became convinced that collective forms of working the land were more advantageous than individual private farming. Lenin linked both industrialisation and the collectivisation of agriculture with a cultural revolution (the elimination of illiteracy, development of primary secondary and higher education, the assimilation of the best of the world's cultural heritage, the growth of socialist culture, science, literature and the arts).

Prominent in Lenin's final works were matters related to improving all the links of the Party and state apparatus. He felt that the cohesion and unity of the Party as the leading and guiding force in the construction of new socialist society had to be strengthened in every possible way and suggested concrete ways in which the Party could extend its links with the workers and peasants, and could enhance the authority of its Central Committee. Lenin suggested that rank-and-file workers be involved in the administration and management of the state apparatus so that manifestations of red tape alien to the essence of a socialist state could be combated more successfully.

In one of his last articles, Lenin also outlined the prospects for the development of the Soviet multinational state, and expressed his opinion about the principal objectives in finalising the national question.[1]

On December 30, 1922, the day the First All-Union Congress of Soviets opened, Lenin, although ill in his Kremlin apartment, began dictating to M. A. Volodicheva, an aide to the secretary for the Council of People's Commissars and the Council of Labour and Defence, one of his famous last articles entitled "The Question of Nationalities or 'Autonomisation'". The theme was the creation of the Union of Soviet Socialist Republics. It took two sessions of dictation on the following day to complete.

---

[1] See *Vladimir Ilyich Lenin. Biography*, pp. 621-49; V. I. Lenin, *Collected Works*, Vol. 33, pp. 462-502; Vol. 36, pp. 593-611.

This article was a programme for the Party and state for consolidating and developing the multinational Union of Soviet Socialist Republics. "...we must maintain and strengthen the union of socialist republics. Of this there can be no doubt. This measure is necessary for all of us and it is necessary for the world communist proletariat in its struggle against the world bourgeoisie and its defence against bourgeois intrigues".[1]

Lenin was insistent about the consistent implementation of the principles of proletarian internationalism as the new state was being built and felt that both Great-Russian chauvinism or local nationalism had to be prevented from being manifested in any way.

He said that representatives of the great nation had to display concern and understanding towards the formerly oppressed peoples and spoke out sharply against the haste, high-handed actions and pressure which some Party workers and state administrators tended to use in the national question.

Lenin said the Party's main objective, in addition to abolishing the formal inequality between the peoples of the Soviet republics, should also be overcoming the real inequality inherited from the past. The economic and cultural backwardness of the formerly oppressed peoples would have to be overcome, they would have to move forward to higher socialist forms of economic organisation and culture, and in this way the genuine equality of all nationalities and peoples inhabiting the USSR would be achieved.

First Constitution of the USSR

The year following the First Congress of Soviets of the USSR was a year of tremendous organisational work by the Party and the government in pursuit of Lenin's directives. The Union's Central Executive Committee formed a Constitutional Commission in January 1923 to draw up a draft Constitution of the USSR. At the same time, the Presidium of the Central Execu-

---

[1] V. I. Lenin, "The Question of Nationalities or 'Autonomisation'", *Collected Works*, Vol. 36, p. 609.

tive Committee suggested that the Central Executive Committees of the republics study and discuss the Declaration and Treaty on the Formation of the USSR and present their comments.

The Constitution was based on Lenin's directives contained in the article "The Question of Nationalities or 'Autonomisation'". Recommendations on how to deal with the main problems of national building in accordance with Lenin's ideas had also been presented by the 12th Congress of the RCP(B) in April 1923, which adopted a special resolution on the national question.

This resolution contained proposals on the nature of the Union's highest bodies of state authority which were to reflect not only the general needs and requirements of all the nationalities of the USSR but the interests of the individual peoples as well. It was proposed that the Union's executive bodies should be also structured in a way that would ensure the real participation of representatives of the republics.[1]

After many proposals and amendments which were forthcoming as the draft Constitution of the USSR was discussed in the republics, and was studied by the highest bodies of state authority of the Soviet republics and the highest Party bodies, the draft all-Union Constitution was approved by special sessions of the Central Executive Committees of the Russian Soviet Federative Socialist Republic, the Ukrainian SSR, the Transcaucasian Socialist Federative Soviet Republic and the Byelorussian SSR in late June and early July 1923.

On July 6, 1923 the draft was unanimously approved by the Second Session of the USSR Central Executive Committee, which decided that the Constitution (Fundamental Law) of the Union of Soviet Socialist Republics came into force immediately and instructed the Presidium of the Central Executive Committee to prepare the statutes of the central bodies of power and administration for the Union state.[2]

The session elected a new Union government—the Council of People's Commissars of the USSR, headed by V. I. Lenin.

---

[1] See *The CPSU in Resolutions...*, Vol. 2, pp. 440-41.
[2] See *The 2nd Session of the CEC of the USSR*, Verbatim Report and Resolutions, Gosizdat, Moscow, 1923, p. 21 (in Russian).

Several constitutional acts of that year established the All-Union bodies of state power and administration and their functions: the Central Executive Committee, the Council of Labour and Defence, the USSR Council of People's Commissars, and the commissariats dealing with foreign affairs, military and naval affairs, foreign trade, railways, and post and telegraph, the State Bank, and the Supreme Court.[1] The Second Session of the Central Executive Committee decided that the Constitution be submitted to the Second Congress of Soviets of the USSR for final approval once it had been ratified by the congresses of Soviets of the Union republics.

On January 21, 1924 V. I. Lenin died.

Moscow. January 26, 1924. In the bitter cold of 30°C below a mournful and silent queue of hundreds of thousands marched slowly to the Hall of Columns in the House of Trade Unions to pay last respects to Lenin. People from Petrograd, Kaluga, and Ryazan thawed out the frozen ground in Moscow's Red Square with campfires and attacked it with picks, crow-bars and spades. Beam and boards of Arkhangelsk pine were brought from a timber-yard of Sokolniki to build a temporary wooden mausoleum designed by the architect A. V. Shchusev in one night which would house the casket with the body of Vladimir Ilyich Lenin on the following day.

Mourning shrouds draped the Bolshoi Theatre, where delegates to the Second All-Union Congress of Soviets had gathered to finally approve the new Constitution of the USSR. Its first session on January 26 was wholly dedicated to the memory of V. I. Lenin. CEC Chairman M. I. Kalinin paid tribute to Lenin's great contribution to the creation of the USSR: "...Vladimir Ilyich was not only the first to issue the appeal, but was also the first to achieve complete national liberation in practice. And now right here ... we are demonstrating to the entire world the solidarity of all the peoples inhabiting our Union, where every nationality feels itself under no constraints and where every worker and peasant of the smallest nationality considers himself an equal citizen of the great Union of Soviet Socialist

---

[1] See *The Constitution and Constitutional Acts of the USSR (1922-1936)*, Politizdat, Moscow, 1940, pp. 3-42 (in Russian).

Republics. . . . Vladimir Ilyich left with us his behest that in our national policy we, the large nationalities, should provide an opportunity for the rest of the peoples in our Union to develop, that we should help them to raise their cultural level."[1]

On January 31, 1924 A. S. Enukidze made a report on the Constitution of the USSR. Having dwelt upon the main provisions of the Declaration and Treaty on the Formation of the USSR which made up the two parts of the Constitution, he concluded with these words: "Comrade Lenin is no more, but the Union of Soviet Socialist Republics that he inspired and created, and whose Constitution we shall approve today, will remain the best and the most dependable leader of all oppressed peoples."[2]

The Second All-Union Congress of Soviets ratified the USSR Constitution on that day, thereby formalising the fact of the establishment of the multinational Soviet state.

The Constitution of the USSR consisted of two parts: the Declaration on the Formation of the USSR, and the Treaty on the Formation of the USSR. The first all-Union Constitution did not include clauses referring to the gains of the socialist revolution, to the class nature—the principles underlying the organisation and functioning of the Soviet state. These issues had already been reflected in the Constitution of the RSFSR of 1918 discussed previously and in the Constitutions of other Soviet republics.

The 1924 Constitution set forth the principles of building a unified multinational Union state. It expressed Lenin's ideas of the complete equality of the republics in the framework of the Union state, and formalised the two-chamber system of the USSR Central Executive Committee as the supreme state authority between the All-Union Congresses of Soviets, which were the highest bodies of power.

The two equal legislative chambers were the Soviet of the Union which represented the entire population of the USSR, and the Soviet of Nationalities, a body which represented the

---

[1] *The Second Congress of Soviets of the USSR,* Verbatim Report, Gosizdat, Moscow, 1924, pp. 5-6 (in Russian).
[2] *The Second Congress of Soviets of the USSR,* p. 128.

special national interests of the Union and autonomous republics, as well as the autonomous regions.

The 1924 Constitution gave the supreme bodies of power in the USSR and the all-Union administrative bodies authority over defence, state borders and boundaries between republics, foreign policy and foreign trade, planning on an all-Union scale and direction of the economy as a whole, establishment of monetary and credit systems, approval of the state budget, Union legislation, and certain other fields. Accordingly, the people's commissariats (ministries) were divided into all-Union, whose competence extended for the entire USSR, and combined bodies which functioned within both the Union and the individual republics.

The chapter "On Sovereign Rights of Union Republics and on Union Citizenship" stated that each Union republic exercised state power independently, and the USSR safeguarded the sovereign rights of the republics. They reserved the right to secede freely from the Union, while the territory of a republic could not be altered without its consent.[1]

Thus the 1924 Constitution of the USSR formalised the main Leninist principles of creating a unified socialist multinational state: proletarian internationalism, co-operation of peoples on the basis of genuine and unqualified equality, free will and the preservation of their sovereign rights, guaranteed by the right to secede from the Union, and consideration for the interests of large and small nationalities alike.

This created conditions for the free political, economic, and cultural development of all the nations and nationalities living in the USSR, for overcoming the backwardness of the former national outlying areas and for the peoples of the entire multinational Union state to successfully build socialism.

Further Development of National-State Structure

Following the adoption of the 1924 Constitution of the USSR, the process of organising the national-state structure within the

---

[1] See *Congresses of Soviets of the USSR, Collection of Documents, 1922-1936*, Vol. III, Yurizdat, Moscow, 1960, pp. 40-54 (in Russian).

framework of the single Union state continued. The national and territorial boundaries of some nationalities were defined more precisely and new Union and autonomous republics were created.

In the Turkestan Autonomous Soviet Socialist Republic and in the Bukhara and Khorezm Socialist Republics, complex problems involving the national-state structure where administrative boundaries did not coincide with ethnic, were tackled. They were resolved through free national demarcation.

In June of 1920 Lenin had outlined the need of making preparations for democratic changes in his comments on the Central Committee's draft decision on the tasks of the RCP(B) in Turkestan, and gave instructions "to draw up a map (ethnographic and so on) of Turkestan, dividing it into Uzbekia, Kirghizia and Turkmenia" and to ascertain in detail the terms of fusion or division of these three parts without predetermining the partition itself.[1]

Democratic and socialist changes in those three republics (referred to previously) had prepared the way for national demarcation. The issue was discussed by the central and local bodies of the Party and government organisations of Turkestan, Khorezm and Bukhara, and by the people themselves.

On June 12, 1924 the Politbureau of the RCP(B) Central Committee adopted a resolution "On the National Demarcation of the Central Asian Republics" to eliminate the sources of national hostility—the administrative boundaries established by the tsarist empire—and to conduct a new national demarcation which would strengthen the national statehood and unity of the peoples of the area.

The preparatory stages of national demarcation were carried out by the Communist parties of Turkestan, Khorezm and Bukhara under the leadership of the Sredazbureau (Office for Central Asian affairs) of the RCP(B) Central Committee.

The Third Extraordinary Session of the Turkestan Central Executive Committee, the Fifth All-Bukhara Kurultai (Con-

---

[1] V. I. Lenin, *Complete Works*, Vol. 41, p. 436 (in Russian); see also "Draft Decision for the Politbureau of the C.C., R.C.P.(B.) on the Tasks of the R.C.P.(B.) in Turkestan", *Collected Works*, Vol. 42, p. 198.

gress) of Soviets and the Fifth All-Khorezm Kurultai of Soviets adopted historic decisions in September 1924 to grant the Uzbek, Kazakh and Turkmen peoples the right to secede from these republics and to form their own national republics. The decisions were subsequently approved by the All-Russia Central Executive Committee of the RSFSR and the 12th All-Russia Congress of Soviets.

On October 27, 1924 the Central Executive Committee of the USSR granted the republics' request for national-state demarcation and instructed its Presidium to formalise the existence of the newly formed Central Asian republics.

The result was the appearance of new republics: the Turkmen SSR, encompassing the Transcaspian region of Turkestan, western Bukhara and southern Khorezm where Turkmens predominated; and the Uzbek SSR in the remaining lands of Turkestan, Bukhara and Khorezm where Uzbeks predominated.

October also saw the formation of the Tajik Autonomous Republic (as part of the Uzbek SSR), and the Kara-Kirghiz autonomous region (it became part of the RSFSR and was renamed the Kirghiz autonomous region in May 1925, and then became the Kirghiz ASSR on February 1, 1926). The unification of the Kazakh lands in the single national Soviet state was completed at the same time: the Syr Darya and Semirechye regions with a predominantly Kazakh population were included in the former Kirghiz ASSR, whose capital was transferred from Orenburg to Kzyl Orda. The historically correct name of the Kazakh people was restored in April 1925, and the republic was named the Kazakh ASSR.

The Gorno-Badakhshan autonomous region was formed as a part of the Tajik ASSR in January 1925, while in May the Kara-Kalpak autonomous region came into being within the Kazakh ASSR. The Third Congress of Soviets of the USSR approved the entry of the Turkmen and Uzbek republics into the USSR in 1925.[1]

The national-territorial demarcation of Central Asia and the peaceful reunification of formerly scattered national lands into

---

[1] See *Congresses of Soviets of the Union of Soviet Socialist Republics. Collection of Documents, 1922-1936,* Vol. III, pp. 72, 75-77.

independent republics was one of the great triumphs of the nationalities policy of Soviet power. It could only have been achieved thanks to the equal rights and friendship of the peoples achieved on the basis of the Leninist nationalities policy.

Territorial demarcation was dictated by the desire to utilise correctly the entire territory of the USSR as the common property of all the Soviet people in accordance with the national composition of the population. An important step in settling the question was the enlargement of the Byelorussian SSR in 1924 and 1926 by incorporating in it some lands with a predominant Byelorussian population which were formerly part of the RSFSR. The area of the Byelorussian SSR doubled, and its population increased from 1.5 to 4.2 million.

The RSFSR government gave the Ufa Gubernia to the Bashkir ASSR, reunifying the western and eastern Bashkirs. The republic's area and population doubled.

Autonomous republics and regions with ethnically homogeneous populations emerged in all the Union republics.

The Moldavian Autonomous Soviet Socialist Republic was formed in October 1924 as part of the Ukrainian SSR. The Declaration on the Formation of the Autonomous Moldavian SSR issued by the All-Ukraine Central Executive Committee on October 12, 1924 stated that the formation of the Autonomous Republic conformed to the firmly expressed will of the workers and peasants of Soviet Moldavia. This step was crucial to the consolidation and development of the Moldavian socialist nation.

It intensified the struggle of the working people in Bessarabia, which had been seized by boyar Romania, for their reunification with Moldavia.

By the end of 1925, the Soviet multinational state consisted of six Union republics—the RSFSR, the Ukrainian SSR, the Byelorussian SSR, the Transcaucasian Socialist Federative Soviet Republic (comprising the Azerbaijan, Georgian and Armenian republics), the Uzbek SSR and the Turkmen SSR—fifteen autonomous socialist republics, of which there were ten in the RSFSR, two in Georgia and one each in the Ukrainian SSR, the Azerbaijan and Uzbek republics, and sixteen autonomous

244

regions. Small and large peoples of the USSR from the Baltic Sea in the West to the Pacific in the East, from the Arctic Ocean in the North to the Black and Caspian seas in the South acquired national statehood, many for the first time in their long history.

Paths of the New Economic Policy. Normalisation of Finances

The emergence of the Union of Soviet Socialist Republics enabled the economic resources of the Soviet republics to be combined and ensured the conditions for the gradual rehabilitation and development of the country's economy within a single state. But the economy could not be put on its feet again without radically overhauling the financial system.

The State Bank of the RSFSR had been established in October 1921, and made responsible for restoring "correct money circulation" in Soviet Russia.[1] The state of Soviet finances at the time had become disastrous. By January 1922 the money supply had exceeded 17 trillion roubles (17×10^{12}), but a year later, even with attempts to halt the currency emission, the money supply reached the astronomical figure of one quadrillion 800 trillion roubles. But the real value in terms of pre-war gold roubles was barely 100 million. In other words, there had been a colossal emission of money leading to devaluation and an increase in prices.[2] Therefore, a monetary reform was instituted in 1922. It lasted until the spring of 1924, and produced excellent results. Even in mid-1923 when the monetary reform was already apparently producing results and especially once it was completed in 1924, the West was extremely interested in its results.

The Western press wrote that the USSR was determined to "normalise its currency", and that financial stabilisation would

---

[1] *Izvestia Narkomfina,* No. 16, 1921, pp. 40-44.
[2] See *Finances of the USSR for 30 Years. 1917-1947,* Finansy Publishers, Moscow, 1947, pp. 18-19 (in Russian); *Vestnik finansov,* No. 2 (47), 1923, p. 9.

have a favourable impact on the rehabilitation and development of the economy. It noted the solid backing for the new Soviet currency—the *chervonets*—with gold and other precious metals, the quotations for it in relation to Western currencies which first appeared on the Moscow stock exchange, and the expanding international activities and growing authority of the USSR State Bank.

Significantly even the eminent British businessman Leslie Urquhart, chairman of the Russian-Asian society, whose factories in Soviet Russia had been expropriated and who, therefore, could not be expected to look favourably on the Soviet government, had effusive words of praise for the results of the monetary reform, when he described the measures taken by the People's Commissariat for Finance to overcome terrible difficulties in balancing the state budget and stabilising the currency as a splendid example to be admired by any unprejudiced man.

The monetary reform came to a successful close in February and March of 1924, and the old banknotes were no longer accepted as legal tender as of July 1. One point worth mentioning is that the stabilisation of the monetary system and subsequent rebuilding and development of the Soviet economy was done without any financial support from the Western powers, which refused loans to the Soviet government.

In an interview given to the British press in London on October 1, 1926 L. B. Krasin said that although the USSR had received short-term credits from foreign companies and banks, these could not replace long-term credits or monetary loans over a 15-20 year period, which would enable the country to build new industry, to get it producing, and to obtain the profits necessary to completely pay off the principal and interest on loans received abroad.

Krasin aptly concluded that the Western policy of denying loans made the Soviet Union "the sole example of a large country restoring its economy without any assistance from outside".[1]

---

[1] *Documents on the Foreign Policy of the USSR*, Vol. IX, Politizdat, Moscow, 1965, pp. 466-69.

The capitalist countries' refusal to resolve the problem of loans for rehabilitation of the national economy on the basis of compromises during negotiations with Britain in 1924 and with France from 1925 to 1927 compelled the Soviet government to rely on domestic loans as an additional source of financing the economy. The funds which the people contributed to the state through buying bonds covering domestic loans and credit transactions grew each year. This public debt was 367 million roubles on October 1, 1925, and exceeded 417 million roubles on October 1, a year later. At the same time, the number of domestic bond holders increased from several hundred thousand in 1925 to ten million in 1928. The supplementary financing of economic growth gradually became a popular cause.[1]

The consolidation of the Soviet republics into a single multinational state and the monetary reform helped to steadily and rapidly get all the branches of the USSR economy on their feet again.

Agricultural Progress

The New Economic Policy allowed peasants to dispose freely of their surplus produce and sell it on the market. The state had also taken the course of culting the taxes levied on peasants and of collecting taxes in cash, which suited the peasants best. When there was a poor season, many peasant households were exempted from taxation or paid lower taxes. The Union state also provided tremendous financial assistance. The Central Agricultural Bank, established by decree of the Second All-Union Congress of Soviets in early 1924 to encourage agricultural development, offered low-interest credits to peasant households. The decree stated that "the tremendous and difficult task of organising agricultural crediting can be accomplished only provided there is a powerful tide of initiative from the peasantry

---

[1] See *USSR. One Year in the Work of the Government,* Materials for the Report on the 1927/1928 Fiscal Year, Gosizdat, Moscow, 1929, p. 115 (in Russian); *Ekonomicheskaya zhizn,* April 6, 1928.

itself in response to the efforts and funds of the Soviet government".[1]

Crucial to agricultural redevelopment was the supply of farm machinery and implements. The Union state made every effort to increase their domestic manufacture while imports of farm machinery had risen sharply since 1923. By the 1925-1926 season, the productivity of the agricultural machine industry exceeded the pre-war level. However, the countryside still lacked efficient agricultural machines. Obsolete implements like wooden ploughs were still used. There were only 11,000 tractors, most of them foreign-made, in 1925. Nevertheless, it was at that moment that a decisive step forward was made in providing machinery and implements. While in 1920 only two or three per cent of requirements were covered compared to the time before the war, the domestic manufacture and import of farming machines and implements covered 60 per cent of the pre-war consumption in the 1924-1925 agricultural season. The growth of production was especially great from 1924 to 1926.[2]

In 1921, when agriculture was in the depths of crisis, many, wrote G. M. Krzhizhanovsky, Chairman of the USSR State Planning Commission, thought that "that path of raising our agriculture at least to its modest pre-war level would be a very long one and could not be accomplished within the first decade".[3] But in spite of a disastrous crop failure and the famine of 1921 and 1922, followed by another crop failure in 1924 in many areas of Soviet Russia and the Ukraine with a population of about 8 million, agriculture was being restored at a rapid pace, ever closer approaching the pre-war level. The rapid growth and expansion of cultivated land started in 1923. For the USSR as a whole, the cultivated land area was 81 per cent of

[1] *Decisions of the Party and Government on Economic Questions*, Vol. 1, Politizdat, Moscow, 1967, p. 403 (in Russian).

[2] See *USSR. One Year in the Work of the Government*, Materials for the Report on the 1924/1925 Fiscal Year, Gosizdat, Moscow, 1926, pp. 286, 290 (in Russian).

[3] G. M. Krzhizhanovsky, *Ten Years of Economic Construction of the USSR, 1917-1927*, Gosizdat, Moscow, 1927, p. 34 (in Russian).

the 1913 figure in 1924, increased to 86 per cent in 1925, and to 91 per cent in 1926.[1] The percentage was even greater in the Soviet Ukraine and Byelorussia, where by 1925 more cropland was being farmed than before the war. That year's grain harvest in the Ukraine was over 90 per cent of the pre-war level.

Key to the agricultural development of the republics in Transcaucasia and Central Asia was the rapid expansion of cotton, which, in 1925, was grown on eight times the area it was in 1922. Extensive reclamation was begun, and introduction of better, high-yield cotton in the Mugan lowlands of Azerbaijan, in Uzbekistan and Turkmenistan (Ferghana, the Golodnaya Steppe, the Chirchik River valley) helped increase the supply of necessary raw materials to the country's textile industry. There were 592,000 hectares of cotton in 1925-1926 (701,000 in 1913) —84.5 per cent of the pre-war level—while domestic production that same year came to 62 per cent of imports (54 per cent in 1913), which showed the USSR was beginning to free itself of the necessity of bringing cotton in from abroad. The funding to irrigate cotton in the Transcaucasian and Central Asian republics came primarily from the state budget of the Union and from the budget of the RSFSR.[2]

Cattle farming also expanded rapidly from 1923 to 1925, when the pre-war level of cattle farming for the USSR as a whole had been reached and even exceeded. This branch of agriculture was especially fruitful in Byelorussia and the Ukraine, as well as in central and northwestern Russia.

Rapid agricultural redevelopment enabled the Soviet state not only to completely overcome the damage wrought by the famine, but also to resume exports of grain and other agricultural produce. L. B. Krasin, People's Commissar of Foreign Trade, said that, in the autumn of 1922, the Soviet Union began offering "exports of a country producing a certain amount

---

[1] *USSR. One Year in the Work of the Government*, Materials for the Report on the 1925/1926 Fiscal Year, Gosizdat, Moscow, 1927, p. 238 (in Russian).

[2] See *Industrial Import, Results and Prospects*, Gosizdat, Moscow-Leningrad, 1930, pp. 14, 29, 32 (in Russian).

of surplus".[1] There were 2.6 million tons of grain exported in 1923 and 1924, and exports continued to rise.[2] The appearance of Russian and Ukrainian grain on the world market after a long interval greatly impressed the Western business community, and enhanced the prestige of the Soviet Union.

Small plots of land individually owned by peasants still prevailed through 1925 and 1926. Though there were agricultural co-operatives, embracing about 6 million peasant households, they were usually based on the simplest forms of co-operation— the sale and supply of products. The number of production co-operatives (collective farms) had increased from 14,000 in 1922 to 22,000 in 1925 and embraced 300,000 peasant households. Although small in number, they accumulated experience, strengthened and increasingly presented an example to follow for individual peasants convincing them in the advantages offered by a large collective economy over a petty individual one.

Industrial Growth

In Soviet history, the first half of the 1920s is usually called the rehabilitation period to underline the fact that recovery was then the main aspect of economic development. Generally speaking it is a correct definition considering that truly decisive steps in restoring agriculture and industry had been taken between 1921 and 1925. However, it does not provide a totally accurate description of the nature of industrial development, especially during the period of the construction and further growth of the Soviet state from 1923 and 1924 onwards.

In 1927, G. M. Krzhizhanovsky, Chairman of the USSR State Planning Commission, made the apt point that during the years of the "conventional rehabilitation" period, "we laid a new foundation under our edifice".[3] The conventional nature of the

---

[1] *Bulletin of the 2nd All-Russia Conference of Representatives of the People's Commissariat for Foreign Trade*, No. 2, 1924, p. 2 (in Russian).

[2] See *Foreign Trade of the USSR in 1918 to 1940*, Politizdat, Moscow, 1960, p. 84 (in Russian).

[3] *15th Congress of the CPSU(B)*, Verbatim Report, Politizdat, Moscow, 1962, p. 890 (in Russian).

term "rehabilitation period", particularly when referring to the industrial development of the mid-1920s was also underlined by other leading figures of the Party and government.

How then did Soviet industry develop and what were the results in the mid-1920s?

Industrial production for the Union as a whole grew steadily and rather rapidly, reaching 75.5 per cent of the 1913 level in 1925 and almost equalling it with 98 per cent in 1926. In manufacturing at large plants and factories, the pre-war level was exceeded by 8 per cent.[1]

The Ukraine's industry had almost reached the pre-war level in 1925/1926, and exceeded the figure for the whole country which was 90 per cent in the production year beginning with October 1925. In 1925/1926 Byelorussia's industry had surpassed the pre-war level, but it contributed a small percentage of the country's total and its principal branches were the light and handicraft industries.

Transcaucasia was very successful in rebuilding and developing its petroleum industry which surpassed the pre-war level in 1926. It should be noted that in this period no substantial changes had yet been made in distribution of industries country-wide.

Old economic centres continued to be rebuilt and to grow, while many national republics and regions still had to look ahead to the time when they would have up-to-date factories and plants, and sophisticated industries would start developing. Thus, for example, in 1925/1926 the national districts of the RSFSR accounted for only 5 per cent of all industry in Soviet Russia in terms of the overall cost of products and the total work force.

But, on the other hand, industrial development in the USSR between 1924 and 1926 was already not just recovery, because the ratio of growth between various branches had changed considerably from that prior to the revolution, aside from the fact

---

[1] See *The USSR and the Capitalist Countries,* Book of Statistics, p. 127; *National Economy of the USSR*, Book of Statistics, Gosstatizdat, Moscow, 1955, p. 45; *Industry of the USSR,* Book of Statistics, Statizdat, Moscow, 1957, p. 32 (all in Russian).

that by that time almost all heavy industry was different from the social-class point of view, as it was state-owned and socialist. There was still some privately-owned heavy industry, but it accounted for less than 5 per cent of industrial production.

Trends towards modernisation and a dramatic improvement in technological standards, that would be fully developed later during the industrialisation of the country in the pre-World War II five-year plans, were already obvious after 1923-1924 in some industries.

An editorial in October 27, 1925 issue of *Izvestia*, the official newspaper of the USSR Central Executive Committee, entitled "From Rehabilitation to Reconstruction" provided a typical appraisal of the economy's development process in the mid-1920s. It said that "there is something conventional in the distinction made between a period of simple rehabilitation and that of reconstruction when industry is raised to a higher technological level. In the preceding production year (1924/1925—*Auth.*) and even earlier in certain industries, the very relativity of the dividing line has already become especially obvious".

The editorial went on to point out that in electrical engineering and electrification "we have not so much restored as created anew, built almost from scratch", that extensive modernisation enabled the petroleum industry to dramatically increase oil production, that the manufacture of the latest and powerful locomotives was just about underway and that the tractor industry was in the making. "Indeed," the newspaper concluded, "rehabilitation is even now largely interwoven with the reconstruction of the economy on a new technological basis."

In fact, the reconstructive trends in industrial development had become distinct as early as the 1924-1926 period. Twenty-eight underground mines and 117 factories were in the planning or in the initial construction phase by the end of 1925. Totally new industries such as the tractor, automobile, airplane, and production of machines for the power and textile industries were either being built or about to start, while shipyards for marine and river vessels were being built.[1]

---

[1] See *History of the Communist Party of the Soviet Union*, Vol. 4, Book 1, Politizdat, Moscow, 1970, p. 374; F. E. Dzerzhinsky, *Selected Works*, Vol. 2, Politizdat, Moscow, 1977, p. 329 (both in Russian).

All in all, the Soviet Union built 379 new factories, power plants, mines, etc., between 1922 and 1926.[1]

Progress of Electrification

In accordance with Lenin's electrification plan (GOELRO), construction of power plants was proceeding very rapidly. As early as 1925 the generation of electricity in the country considerably exceeded the 1913 level. On the heels of the Krasny Oktyabr thermal power plant near Petrograd and the Kashira plant near Moscow, both launched in 1922, came other regional power stations, rather large for the time, which were built in different parts of the USSR between 1924 and 1926, such as the Kizel, Nizhni Novgorod (Balakhna), Shatura, Yaroslavl and Volkhov power plants in the RSFSR, the Shtera plant in the Ukraine, and the Zemo-Avchal power plant in Transcaucasia.

The feasibility study and design of the 500,000 kilowatt Dnieper Hydroelectric Power Station in the Ukraine—the biggest at the time—was completed during 1925 and 1926, and on December 3, 1926, the Council of Labour and Defence decided to start construction. The Dneproges became the pride of the Soviet people, and it was put into operation during the First Five-Year Plan.[2]

Progress in Basic Industries

The building of power plants stimulated the manufacture of electrical machinery, which had already exceeded the pre-war production level in 1924/1925. Radio engineering was also developing rapidly. I. P. Zhukov, Chairman of the radio industry trust (industrial association), said that it had not only managed

---

[1] See Main Features of Reconstruction of the USSR Industry, Essays, Gosizdat, Moscow, 1930, p. 106 (in Russian).

[2] See USSR. One Year in the Work of the Government, 1925/26, Gosizdat, Moscow, p. 201; USSR. One Year in the Work of the Government. Materials for the Report on the 1926/1927 Fiscal Year, Gosizdat, Moscow, 1928, pp. 176-78 (in Russian).

to close the gap, "but also to keep pace with foreign countries".[1]

The petroleum industry, concentrated primarily in Soviet Azerbaijan, was one of the first to embark on reconstruction, which it did in 1923-1924. On the initiative of its chief, A. P. Serebrovsky, who had been an active figure in Russia's revolutionary movement and then became a leading economic executive in the USSR, the Azneft (Azerbaijan Central Oil Department) adopted new, technically advanced methods of drilling and extraction. In 1925-1926 the pre-war level of oil production and processing had been far surpassed. The export of petroleum products also considerably exceeded the 1913 figures and helped to improve the country's balance of trade.

The petroleum industry was re-equipped both by increasing the import of equipment and by manufacturing it domestically on a growing scale. And production was on the rise not only at the traditional RSFSR engineering centres like Leningrad, Moscow, Gorky and Bryansk, but also at the Azneft enterprises: the F. E. Dzerzhinsky Works and N. Schmidt Works in Baku.[2]

The re-equipment and mechanisation of the coal industry begun during the same period was especially extensive in the Donets Coal Basin in the Ukraine, and stimulated the rebuilding and development of the Ukraine's iron-and-steel and machine-building industries. The New Economic Policy envisaged, in its first stage, the rehabilitation of light industry, and, therefore, led to the creation of a totally new industry producing textile machinery. Factories in Leningrad, Tula, Podolsk and other cities began manufacturing ring spinning frames, carding machines and other textile equipment. Production was already 85 per cent greater than the 1913 level in terms of cost in 1924/1925, and 130 per cent in 1925/1926[3]. The AMO Plant in Moscow was getting ready to turn out the country's first trucks, and the manufacture of tractors was beginning in the RSFSR and the Ukraine.

The emergence of the USSR was a factor that facilitated and accelerated the economic restoration and development of the

---

[1] *Izvestia*, January 9, 1925
[2] See *Industrial Imports of the USSR*, pp. 130-35.
[3] Ibid., pp. 136-38, 153.

country as a whole and of its national districts, republics, and regions. The single Union state was able to very efficiently distribute funds and budget allocations, taking into account the importance of an industry for the overall economy. Thus, about 60 per cent of all investment in the iron-and-steel industry between 1922 and 1926 went to the Ukraine, which had suffered most of all during the Civil War. In turn, coal and grain from the Soviet Ukraine were instrumental in overcoming the crisis in fuel and food supplies that gripped the country in 1921 and 1922. The reconstruction of Soviet Azerbaijan's petroleum industry was financed primarily from the all-Union budget. In turn, increased oil production in Azerbaijan and the export of petroleum products was key to restoring industry throughout the country and to bolstering its position on the world market. Growing production of manganese ore in the Ukraine and in Georgia also helped. Assistance provided by the RSFSR and the Ukraine was infinitely important for reconstruction and economic growth which had begun in formerly backward national republics and regions. The RSFSR and Ukraine sent engineers and workers to organise production, and supplied the equipment for the factories and plants that were going up.

Getting the Railways Rolling Again. First Engineering Achievements

There was also impressive progress in getting the railways, which were in extremely bad shape by the end of the Civil War, rolling again. The length of track had already surpassed the 1913 figure by 1923/1924, and the number of railway cars was about the same. In 1925/1926 the railways hauled almost 90 per cent of the freight they did in 1913.

Although reconstruction and the introduction of new technology in certain industries was only beginning by the mid-1920s, quite a number of engineering achievements of Soviet industry and transport drew the attention of the West and even drew the praise of experts and businessmen. There was great interest in a turbodrill invented by the engineer M. A. Kapelyushnikov in

255

1922, which led to the new and very efficient method for oil-well sinking called turbodrilling.

A new automatic brake invented by F. P. Kazantsev was adopted by the railway industry in 1924. This brake was more efficient than the one manufactured by Westinghouse, which was widely used at the time. Applications for licences to manufacture the Kazantsev brake came from the USA, Germany, France, Czechoslovakia and Japan as early as 1926.[1]

After examining the first diesel engines made in the USSR and designed by Y. V. Lomonosov and Y. Gakkel, the president of the Baldwin Locomotive Company of the USA said that Russia had done more than anybody in the world in diesel-engine building.[2] The USSR built its first large all-metal airplane, designed by A. N. Tupolev and developed by his design office at the Central Aero-Dynamics Institute (TsAGI) in 1925. The following year, M. M. Gromov flew the Tupolev plane from Moscow to Berlin and then to Paris, Rome, Vienna, Warsaw and back to Moscow in 34 hours flying time. In this way, the Tupolev planes "entered the wide European road", as newspapers wrote then.[3]

The Central Institute of Labour, the world's first institute on problems of industrial engineering, was founded in the 1920s. After sitting in on training courses and examining its laboratories in various fields, three American visitors from the Ford Company specialising in tractor operation and maintenance training wrote in the guest book in April 1926 that it was the best trade school they had ever seen.[4]

Socialist Planning

The unification of the Soviet republics in a single Union state paved the way for developing socialist planning of the economy. The first long-term development plan was produced in Soviet

[1] See *Ekonomicheskaya zhizn,* June 24, July 27, 1926.
[2] See *Izvestia,* May 6, 1926
[3] See *Izvestia,* September 4, 1926
[4] *Izvestia,* April 25, 1926

Russia in 1920—it was Lenin's GOELRO plan, ambitious project with electrification as its main target, and in addition, providing for a considerable increase in industrial production based on it. The State Planning Commission (Gosplan) was established in the RSFSR in 1921. In 1922, on the eve of the Genoa Conference, Gosplan was instructed to produce a long-term (three or five years) plan of the Soviet Republic's economic growth so that the Soviet delegation to the Conference could use it in its quest for long-term loans for restoring Soviet Russia's economy. Later, G. M. Krzhizhanovsky wrote: "In the spring of 1922, the Gosplan was preparing materials for the Genoa Conference and tried to produce the first outline of prospects for launching the industry. This sketch, however rough, still outlines the general scope of capital construction."[1]

In 1925, after the Union of Soviet Socialist Republics had been established, the Gosplan drew up long-term plans for individual industries (such as metallurgical or machine-building) in which what had to be done to restore their operations in all the Soviet republics was outlined. Major projects, which later became targets of advanced long-term development plans for the entire economy and of five-year plans, were envisaged even then. The first integrated annual plan for Soviet economic development entitled "The Planned Targets for the Development of the USSR National Economy in 1925/1926" made its appearance in the mid-1920s. It signified the move forward from sectoral planning to a new stage of socialist planning—integrated economic plans. The targets which were set for each successive year from 1925 until 1928/1929 prepared the ground for five-year economic development plans. The first five-year plan, based on the experience, was adopted for 1928/1929 through 1932. The ten five-year plans which the Soviet people had carried out by 1980 were each distinctive stages in the country's economic growth which turned the USSR into the highly-developed industrial power it is now.

---

[1] G. M. Krzhizhanovsky, *Selected Works,* Gospolitizdat, Moscow, 1957, p. 424 (in Russian).

Development of Soviet Democracy

The recovery and development of the economy of the single Soviet state was not an end in itself. Progress along this path was accompanied by a great stride forward in raising the living and cultural standards of the peoples of the USSR, and in developing education and science.

The 1926 census indicated that there were 147 million people in the USSR, an increase of 13 million over 1923 and of 16 million over 1920. Accounting for the rapid population growth was that the war had ended and the famine of 1921-1922 had been overcome. The rural population was still far larger than the urban, the latter accounting for only about one-fifth of the total. However, the urban population had already started to grow as a result of the incipient industrial development. This demographic trend subsequently became even more pronounced.

Peasants were the largest sector, accounting for about three quarters of the country's population. There were approximately 5.6 million workers and around four million white-collar workers.

The political system in the mid-1920s was firmly based on the gains of Soviet democracy. The state system was determined by the fact that political power was in the hands of the working class, with this power being exercised through the Soviets—elected central and local bodies of state. Three all-Union congresses of Soviets—the supreme body of state power in the country—had met between late 1922 and 1925 after the Union of Soviet Socialist Republics had been established. Four all-Russia congresses of Soviets, five all-Ukrainian, five congresses of Soviets of Byelorussia, and three of Georgia had met during the same period. Azerbaijan and Armenia had held four congresses each, and there were congresses of Soviets in the Transcaucasian Federation, the Uzbek SSR and Turkmen SSR.

The All-Union Communist Party (Bolsheviks)—CPSU(B)—was the party of the working class, the only political party in the country because of the specific features of its historical development, and the leading and guiding force of Soviet society. The supreme bodies of the Party—its congresses—elaborated and defined on the basis of scientific Marxist-Leninist theory, the general directions and paths of development of the state, and the measures to be taken to carry out the course. By late 1925, the Communist Party had over one million members,[1] the best representatives of the working class, working peasants and working intellectuals of all nationalities. The Party congresses met annually then, so five of them were held between 1921 and 1925 (the 10th to the 14th). Trade unions played an important part in the country's political life, being the largest organisations of industrial and office workers and designed to protect their interests; in addition, in Soviet society, the trade unions directly participate in managing production, in improving the organisation of work in industry and the state apparatus, etc. Trade union membership exceeded nine million in mid-1926.

Young people of progressive conviction who shared communist views could join a mass organisation—Russia's Leninist Young Communist League or Komsomol—which had had over 1.6 million members by the end of 1925. These young people were actively involved in the country's political and economic life, helped the Communist Party in its ideological, cultural and educational work with the people. The Komsomol directed the activities of the mass children's organisation set up in May 1922—the Young Pioneers, which had 1.5 million members by mid-1925.

Many public organisations appeared and were active in the country along with the above. These were co-operatives of various types, branches of the International Red Aid, the Down-with-Illiteracy Society, Society of Friends of the Air Fleet, the Red Cross and Red Crescent Society, Friend-of-Children Society, Radio Fans Society, the Union of Atheists, etc. The total membership of all these organisations in 1925 was 10 million.

In the first half of the 1920s, the people's diet was improving rapidly thanks to the successful growth of agriculture; the number of calories consumed already conformed to pre-war standards. The real wages received by all hired workers and state employees also approached the 1913 figure. Working people's living standards were steadily rising, due to the introduction of a system of social security for factory and office workers, free medical service, low rent in the state-owned dwellings, and increased spending on public education. Particularly striking were the changes

---

[1] See *History of the CPSU*, Vol. 4, Book I, p. 414.

in the situation of the peoples of Central Asia and of certain autonomous republics of the RSFSR, who had been nomads before the revolution and had not been the beneficiary of any medical aid. A network of medicosanitary facilities was established in those national regions financed by the central budget, while similar facilities in the central regions of the RSFSR and Ukraine were financed by local authorities. The improvements in medical service led to a decrease in the toll taken by epidemic deseases. For example, the typhus rate was slashed by 66 per cent, while the overall death rate was reduced by one-third compared with the pre-war period.

Progress of the Cultural Revolution

As was mentioned earlier, Lenin considered that making culture accessible to the people and developing of education were an integral part of economic rehabilitation and the building of socialism. "There must be a veritable revolution—the entire people must go through a period of cultural development," he wrote.[1] According to the 1920 census, less than a third of the population of Soviet Russia were literate. So the elimination of illiteracy was a vital task in the early half of the 1920s. It could not be done quickly, but Soviet power did a great deal in five years to raise general educational standards. The anti-illiteracy campaign was gone about in a planned way, based on special decisions of the All-Union Central Executive Committee and the Council of People's Commissars, with the effective participation of the public Down-with-Illiteracy Society founded in the autumn of 1923.

Lenin was one of the first to join this society, along with the Central Executive Committee Chairman M. I. Kalinin, N. K. Krupskaya and other leading statesmen and Party figures such as A. V. Lunacharsky, M. N. Pokrovsky, N. I. Podvoisky and A. S. Bubnov. Kalinin was appointed the Chairman of the society's Central Council.

---

[1] V. I. Lenin, "On Co-operation", *Collected Works*, Vol. 33, p. 470.

The society opened thousands of centres and schools where adults were taught their ABCs by students, teachers and just adequately educated people. Many thousands of men and women learned to read and write that way.

A peasant from the village of Boyevo in the Voronezh Province who had completed the course at one of these centres, sent the following letter to M. I. Kalinin: "I, citizen Ivan Vasilyevich, was poor and illiterate before the revolution but thanks to Soviet power ... we got an anti-illiteracy centre here. I was the first to enter and many others, too. They taught us for three years and now I read and write well. Whenever I find a book or newspaper, I gather people around and read to them, and they thank me very much for it. All, old and young, alike, come to me and ask me to read them something and to answer questions. ... Let everybody know how Soviet Russia educates villagers. . ."[1]

While less than 500,000 attended the centres and schools for elimination of illiteracy in 1922, by 1925 they already had almost 1.5 million adult students.

According to the 1926 census, more than half the country's population aged nine and over were literate, including 53 to 57 per cent in the RSFSR, Ukraine and Byelorussia (compared with 32 per cent in the RSFSR in 1920). Literacy had also increased considerably in the Georgian, Armenian and Azerbaijan republics, and ranged from 25 to 47 per cent. It was still low in the Tajik ASSR, in the Turkmen and Uzbek Union Republics. Besides, the literacy rate was far higher among the urban population than the rural.

Over 75 per cent of city dwellers were literate while the figure was only 45 per cent for the countryside.

General education had been strengthened considerably. A stable school system had emerged in the mid-1920s, consisting of four-year elementary (first-stage) schooling, seven-year schooling in the cities, schools for peasant youth and factory apprentice schools on the basis of the elementary schools, and the second-

---

[1] V. A. Kumanev, *Socialism and Universal Literacy. Elimination of Illiteracy in the USSR,* Nauka Publishers, Moscow, 1967, p. 152 (in Russian).

stage school (from fifth to ninth form). At that period the state was able to spend more on education than in 1921-1922 when, as N. K. Krupskaya wrote, pupils "had to have lessons without textbooks, paper or ink, to sharpen pencils with axes, and to study by the light of a burning wooden splinter".[1]

More than ten million children attended elementary and secondary school in the 1925/1926 school year, a third more than in the school years of 1914 and 1922-1923.[2] Higher education was also stimulated. To make it more accessible to children of workers and peasants, so-called Workers' Faculties were set up everywhere so that people could acquire secondary school knowledge at an accelerated rate to allow them to enter higher educational establishments. Workers' Faculties were established by higher schools themselves. There were almost 60,000 people in 1925/1926 at these faculties. At the time the Soviet Union had 145 institutions of higher learning with a total of 167,000 students (Russia had 91 institutions and 112,000 students in 1914).

The accomplishments of Soviet science were equally impressive. As early as the mid-1920s, A. V. Lunacharsky, People's Commissar for Education of the RSFSR, was able to say proudly: "European scientists say that during the years of famine and tribulation our science contributed such great achievements, made so many scientific discoveries, conclusions, and provided so many guiding ideas that they cannot move forward without Russian scientists. They now apply to us all the time, asking for our assistance in various forms."[3]

The West recognised the originality and significance of the works of a real galaxy of Soviet physicists such as A. F. Ioffe, V. A. Fok and I. E. Tamm; of the outstanding shipbuilding expert Academician A. N. Krylov; of chemists V. N. Ipatyev and A. N. Bakh, and of the mathematician V. A. Steklov and his school.

---

[1] N. K. Krupskaya, *Elimination of Illiteracy,* Politizdat, Moscow, 1938, p. 87 (in Russian).

[2] See *History of the USSR*, Vol. VIII, pp. 273-76; V. A. Kumanev, *Revolution and Education of the Masses,* Nauka Publishers, Moscow, 1973 (both in Russian).

[3] A. V. Lunacharsky, *About Culture in the West and Here,* Gosizdat, Nizhni Novgorod, 1927, p. 33 (in Russian).

Major discoveries were made by geologists I. M. Gubkin and A. E. Fersman, by the eminent natural scientists and engineers I. P. Pavlov, S. A. Chaplygin, S. I. Vavilov and D. N. Pryanishnikov, and by scores of others. The works of the orientalists and linguists V. V. Bartold, I. Y. Krachkovsky, N. Y. Marr and S. F. Oldenburg were world-famous. The number of scientific journals issued by two Soviet publishing houses alone had reached 62 titles in 1926, with the titles of scientific books and articles being published at the same time amounting to about 2,000.[1]

By the mid-1920s many research institutes, design offices and laboratories had been organised, among them top scientific centres, which would later become universally recognised such as the L. Y. Karpov Chemical Institute, the Leningrad Physico-Technical Institute directed by A. F. Ioffe, the V. I. Lenin Nizhni Novgorod Radio Laboratory headed by M. A. Bonch-Bruyevich, the N. E. Zhukovsky Central Aero-Dynamics Institute, and about 40 others.[2]

Thus, the internal political and economic development of the Soviet Union had by the mid-1920s shown both the usefulness and vital importance of fusing the many nationalities and peoples of the Soviet republics into a single multinational state.

Thanks to this unity, in just three or four years, the USSR had managed not only to get the economy on its feet again but also to prepare the ground for further rapid and dynamic economic progress through industrialisation and formation of agricultural co-operatives and for considerably raising cultural and educational levels. The overall advance of Soviet society during those years did not rule out but, to the contrary, implied and made real the political, economic and cultural development of every national republic or region, of every—even the smallest and formerly deprived—people, such as the nomads of the Far North and of the vast steppes of Kazakhstan and Kirghizia, the mountain dwellers of Daghestan and Altai, and the hunters and

---

[1] See *Ten Years of Soviet Science*, Collection of Articles, Gosizdat, Moscow-Leningrad, 1927, pp. 21, 109-11, 142, 445 (in Russian).
[2] See *Torgovo-promyshlennaya gazeta*, November 7, November 16, 1927.

fishermen of Yakutia and Kamchatka. The creation of the single Soviet state equally had an impact on the consolidation of the USSR's international positions.

At the Genoa Conference

Even the initial joint action on the international scene by the Soviet republics at the Genoa Conference (in April-May 1922) on the basis of the previously mentioned "Agreement on Representation and Defence by the Government of the RSFSR" of the interests of the other republics bound to it by treaties bore witness to consolidation of their positions once unity was achieved.

It should also be pointed out that the Genoa Conference demonstrated the insufficiency of temporary agreements on diplomatic unity, as well as the necessity of having the Soviet republics act closer together in foreign affairs, which was possible only within the framework of a single Union state.

The Soviet objective in taking part in the Genoa Conference, which was supposed to iron out relations between Soviet Russia and the capitalist world, was to have these relations established on an equal and mutually beneficial footing.

In the Political Report of the Central Committee to the 11th Congress of the RCP(B), Lenin said: "We are going to Genoa not as Communists but as merchants. We must trade and they must trade." The Soviet delegation, therefore, was given the job of establishing normal diplomatic relations with the capitalist countries and, if that proved impossible, "of expanding trade and of creating the most favourable conditions for its successful development on the widest scale".[1] The stance taken by the Western powers was quite different. They intended to talk with the Soviet republics in the language of winners and wanted to put them into the position of dependent states. This was the general line in the report of the Western delegates prepared in March 1922 in London which would be used as their platform

---

[1] V. I. Lenin, "Eleventh Congress of the R.C.P.(B.)", *Collected Works*, Vol. 33, p. 264.

of negotiations. As the former Italian premier F. Nitti put it, the report was a programme for the "conquest by plutocrats" of the Soviet lands.[1]

Lenin headed preparations to the Genoa Conference and was appointed Chairman of the Soviet delegation by the All-Russia Central Executive Committee, and G. V. Chicherin, Vice-Chairman.

Taking into account Lenin's ill health, and the many letters from across the country expressing concern for the security and life of the leader of the Party and the Soviet state, as well as diplomatic considerations, the Central Committee of the RCP(B) adopted a special decision under which Lenin did not go to Genoa, but directed all the steps of the Soviet delegation from Moscow.[2]

The Soviet delegation left for Italy in late March 1922, and was to go via Latvia, Lithuania, Germany and Austria. As Chicherin said later, the very fact that Soviet Russia had been invited to Genoa reflected in more ways than one the views of major European politicians like Lloyd George, who believed that the New Economic Policy heralded the beginning of the restoration of the bourgeois order in Russia. That is why the conference "was initially regarded by foreign governments as some sort of the return of the prodigal son to his father's house".[3] The prodigal son was supposed to repent and accept any terms dictated to him. However, Leo Lederer of the Austrian newspaper *Neue Freie Presse,* who managed to find a spot in Chicherin's compartment in Berlin and to travel with the People's Commissar as far as the Italian border, was astonished at his "sudden" statement: "The Russian delegation is going to Genoa with great determination, and has no intention of playing the beggars."[4]

Lloyd George himself was equally astonished when in response

---

[1] F. Nitti, *The Decadence of Europe: The Paths of Reconstruction,* T. Fischer Unwin Ltd., London, 1923, pp. VIII, 158.

[2] See *Documents on the Foreign Policy of the USSR,* Vol. V, pp. 716-17; M. I. Trush, *Soviet Foreign Policy and Diplomacy in the Works of V. I. Lenin,* Politizdat, Moscow, 1977, p. 136 (in Russian).

[3] G. V. Chicherin, *Articles and Speeches on Foreign Policy,* p. 326.

[4] S. Zarnitsky, A. Sergeyev, *Chicherin,* Politizdat, Moscow, 1975, pp. 179-80.

to Chicherin's statement at the conference that "the popular masses of Russia refer the tsar's debts to the old historical period which is absolutely a thing of the past", he laughed incredulously and said: "Do they think that they won't have to pay anything? If you came to Genoa with this you might as well not come at all."[1]

However, this was all to become clear later, but for the present both parties were anxiously waiting for the conference to begin. It opened in Genoa on April 10, 1922 with 34 countries attending. At about 3 in the afternoon, the representatives of Soviet Russia arrived at Príncipe, the Genoa railway station, from the resort of Santa Margerita where the delegation had been staying in the posh Palazzo Imperiale Hotel. They left the train, crossed the square decorated with the flags of the participating countries and, accompanied by a deputy of the conference high commissar, passed the guard of honour of carabiniers and sailors, who presented arms, and entered the San Giorgio palace where all was ready for the talks to begin at the Hall of Transactions.

One by one, they walked to their seats amid murmurs and shouts: "Bolsheviks! Bolsheviks!"—G. V. Chicherin and L. B. Krasin were in tails, while M. M. Litvinov, V. V. Vorovsky and the other delegates were wearing dark suits.[2]

Long tables covered with green cloth were arranged in a square. The seats at the head were taken by the representatives of the member states of the Entente Supreme Council, while the tables perpendicular to them were occupied by the delegations of the other countries in alphabetical order.

At 3:05 p.m. the Italian Prime Minister Luigi Facta declared the first plenary meeting of the Genoa Conference open. He was followed by the heads of governments or ministers who made their opening statements, among them Lloyd George of Great Britain, Louis Barthou of France and Josef Wirth of Germany. The procedure was extremely long and tedious. The official languages were English and French, and the speakers used either of

---

[1] G. V. Chicherin, *Articles and Speeches,* p. 328.
[2] See N. N. Lyubimov, A. N. Erlikh, *Genoa Conference (Recollections of the Participants)*, pp. 37-40.

them or German. Each speech, therefore, had to be translated into one or two of the official languages because there were no facilities for simultaneous translation at the time.[1]

It was at 5:30 that Chicherin rose to speak. The People's Commissar of the RSFSR spoke fluent English, French and German, and could get along in Italian, Czech, Polish, Serbian, and Spanish.[2]

He made the statement of the Soviet delegation first in French and then, after a brief pause, repeated it in English. "The effect and impression made by Chicherin's speech," participants recall, "which was understood by the entire audience, were so irresistible that the storm of applause which broke all the barriers of diplomatic etiquette was a natural response to this very profound speech and to Chicherin's exceptional linguistic talent."[3]

Chicherin underlined the "imperative necessity" of establishing economic co-operation between the states representing two different property systems, as well as the Soviet state's willingness to engage in "business-like relations with governments and commercial and industrial circles of all countries on the basis of reciprocity, equality and complete unconditional recognition". He went on to point out that the Soviet delegation intended to put forward a proposal on general arms reduction, and stated that the Soviet government was willing to discuss all positive proposals made by other countries on disarmament and the elimination of the threat of war.[4]

All the attempts by the capitalist politicians to impose unequal trade and political terms on Soviet Russia at the Genoa Conference and the Hague Conference held in June and July 1922 were to no avail.

The Soviet delegation's uncompromising and, at the same time, constructive stand at the Genoa Conference won the Italian people's profound interest and respect. As the conference continued, affection for the envoys of the young Soviet republics grew, and the moral isolation of certain Western diplomats was increasingly felt.

---

[1] See N. N. Lyubimov, A. N. Erlikh, op. cit., pp. 40-46.
[2] See I. Gorokhov, L. Zamyatin, N. Zemskov, op. cit., p. 82.
[3] N. N. Lyubimov, A. N. Erlikh, op. cit., pp. 45-46.
[4] See *Documents on the Foreign Policy of the USSR*, Vol. V, p. 192.

In May 1922, Italy's cinemas showed newsreels on the conference which became quite popular. And the same scene was witnessed in all the cinemas—from the cheapest, with low ceilings and heavy cigarette smoke enveloping the rows of seats, to the most fashionable where the spectators were of the upper classes. Whenever members of the Soviet delegation appeared on the screen, the audience all rose and applauded unanimously. And when the head of the French delegation, who was the most stubborn opponent of establishing equal relations with Soviet Russia appeared, there was such a deafening whistling that the show had to be stopped. Those who were there recall that the Rome cinemas found a solution: they showed all the delegations except the French.[1]

The Treaty of Rapallo

The astute and energetic conduct of Soviet diplomacy split the united anti-Soviet front, leading, while the Genoa Conference was in session, to the conclusion of the first equal economic and political treaty with a major European power. It was the Treaty of Rapallo with Germany.

The Treaty of Rapallo, signed by the RSFSR and Germany on April 16, 1922, was based on the principles of peaceful co-existence between states with different social systems, and of resolving all political and economic issues on the basis of complete equality and mutual benefit.

Under this treaty, the two countries were to resume diplomatic relations; their governments renounced all financial and material claims against each other issuing from the war period, all promissory notes, or nationalisation of German property in Soviet Russia. Also envisaged was the granting to each other of the most favoured nation status and closer co-operation economically.[2]

But it was the Treaty of Rapallo which demonstrated that, in addition to the advantages of the diplomatic unity of the

[1] See A. A. Ioffe, *The Genoa Conference,* Gosizdat, Moscow, 1922, p. 16 (in Russian).
[2] See *Documents on the Foreign Policy of the USSR,* Vol. V, pp. 223-26.

Soviet republics, limitations on their opportunities in foreign policy would always exist, as long as there would only be federative ties between them without a closer union within a single state.

After additional talks the RSFSR delegation and the representatives of Germany in Genoa agreed that the scope of the Treaty of Rapallo would be expanded to cover the other Soviet republics. Both sides felt this to be to their advantage, because Germany wanted to develop economic relations not only with Russia but also with the Ukraine and the Transcaucasian republics, while for Soviet Russia the extension of the Treaty of Rapallo to cover the republics in union with it was a matter of principle, because it meant a considerable contribution to the diplomatic preparations for the formation of the Union of Soviet Socialist Republics and established a precedent for its subsequent *de jure* recognition by the capitalist countries.[1]

The talks between the RSFSR and Germany on the enlargement of the scope of the Treaty of Rapallo to cover the other Soviet republics were rather difficult, and continued for about seven months. It was only on November 5, 1922 that an agreement was signed extending the provisions of the Treaty of Rapallo to the Ukrainian, Byelorussian, Georgian, Azerbaijan and Armenian Soviet republics, as well as the then existing Far Eastern Republic which was shortly incorporated into the RSFSR.[2]

At the same time, British pressure to try and prevent the Central Asian and Caucasian republics from being included in the Soviet state, to tear them away from it, or at least not to recognise them as a part of the future Union state, as well as the claims and "special" interests of some circles within Germany itself as regards Georgia and the Ukraine, resulted in, first, the talks dragging out and, second, that the final agreement did not cover the Khorezm and Bukhara republics later incorporated in the USSR.[3]

---

[1] See A. A. Akhtamzyan, *The Rapallo Policy. Soviet-German Diplomatic Relations in 1922 through 1932*, Politizdat, Moscow, 1974, pp. 81, 84-85 (in Russian).

[2] See *Documents on the Foreign Policy of the USSR*, Vol. V, pp. 661-63.

[3] See A. A. Akhtamzyan, op. cit., pp. 85-94.

International Positions of the USSR
Are Strengthened

Thus, the diplomatic unity of the Soviet republics in Genoa based on a temporary agreement made it possible, on the one hand, to achieve great successes, but on the other, it demonstrated that only a single multinational Union state would be able to uphold the interests of all the Soviet republics in international affairs.

And it was only the formation of the single Union of Soviet Socialist Republics that enabled the Soviet republics to successfully withstand the tremendous pressure exerted at the turn of 1922 by a group of international oil monopolies which tried to retain their titles to the fields around Baku in Soviet Azerbaijan and Grozny in the Northern Caucasus, and to confront Great Britain whose Conservative government has begun issuing ultimatums to back its unfounded demands that the Soviet government recall its representatives from Iran and Afghanistan and that territorial waters be redefined to suit British interests unilaterally. In fact, a serious crisis erupted at that time between the Soviet state and the capitalist countries.

The Soviet state was able to overcome this crisis, to break the "oil blockade" and to resolve differences with Britain thanks to its strengthened position internationally as the result of the establishment of the USSR and the use by Soviet diplomacy and other Soviet agencies of all the ensuing advantages for the defence of the interests of the multinational land.

We will examine these events in more detail as they were crucial trials for the foreign policy of the Soviet state at the moment it established itself as the Union of Soviet Socialist Republics.

The export of petroleum products began again as the oil industry recovered. The first Soviet petroleum products which appeared on the world market in the autumn of 1921 did not yet worry the Western oil monopolies excessively because they did not take the Soviet state seriously as an exporter.

They even tried to profit from those occasional sales, offering ridiculous prices, sometimes as low as 60 per cent of the current world price, and demanding additional guarantees. Meanwhile,

Soviet oil exports were gradually increasing amounting to over 711,000 tons (75 per cent of the pre-war export) as early as the 1923/1924 production year.[1]

The Soviet state had suddenly become a very unwelcome competitor for the imperialist oil trusts. In November-December 1922, a group of Western oil monopolies and former owners of oil enterprises in Baku and Grozny, who belonged to the so-called united front against Soviet Russia, and demanded the return of their former property, decided on a total boycott of Soviet oil exports, and asked the largest oil monopolies—Standard Oil and Royal Dutch/Shell—to back them.[2]

The boycott of Soviet oil exports was announced with the tacit consent of the two oil giants, who hoped to be able not only to dictate the terms of oil sales to Soviet Russia but, if things turned out well, to be able to conclude a crippling agreement with it to again exploit the Russian oil industry.

At first, the "oil blockade" and the boycott of Soviet oil exports were effected rather consistently: Soviet foreign trade organisations began encountering difficulties in selling their petroleum products in a number of countries.

A major deal for the purchase by Standard Oil of a large quantity of petroleum and lubricants from the Neftesindikat of the USSR that seemed all sewn up, suddenly fell through. Just the day before the contract was to be signed, the Berlin office of Neftesindikat received a letter from the Standard Oil agent which read: "Please be advised that my U.S. principals have lost ... interest in Russian petroleum products... Further negotiations are considered to be unnecessary by the Americans."[3] In its turn, the Royal Dutch/Shell Group suddenly broke off negotiations in London for the purchase of 100,000 tons of kerosene from Neftesindikat.[4]

---

[1] See V. A. Shishkin, "The Formation of the USSR and Economic Relations with Capitalist Countries (1922-1923)", in: *Problems of State Structuring in the First Years of Soviet Power,* Nauka Publishers, Leningrad, 1973, p. 269; *Foreign Trade of the USSR from 1918 to 1940*, Moscow, 1960, pp. 45, 67 (both in Russian).

[2] See V. A. Shishkin, op. cit., p. 270.

[3] Quoted in V. A. Shishkin, op. cit., p. 271.

[4] Ibid.

But the inner contradictions of the Western oil monopolies and the USSR's astute and efficient oil export policy quickly led to a breach of the "oil blockade" and to the failure of the boycott attempts. Capitalising on the demand and desire of certain major independent oil importers in Germany, France, Italy and Britain to escape from the clutches of the international oil monopolies, Neftesindikat was still rather successfully exporting petroleum products in small quantities. Seeing that Soviet exports were not going to be curtailed completely, Henry Deterding, Head of the Royal Dutch/Shell Group, decided himself to make a deal with Neftesindikat. Royal Dutch/Shell offered to buy up all the available kerosene at extremely low prices on the condition that the USSR would not appear on the international markets for some time. The latter proposition was turned down and an agreement was finally reached on March 29, 1923—Royal Dutch/Shell would buy 70,000 tons of kerosene from Neftesindikat at the current world price and would be able to exceed this quantity to 200,000 tons. The British-Dutch trust evidently miscalculated in thinking that this kind of purchase could "remove" the USSR from the world oil market.

What it all meant in effect was that the "oil blockade" collapsed three or four months after it began.

The best evidence was the rapid growth of Soviet oil exports which exceeded the 1913 level by 50 per cent as early as the 1924-1925 production year.[1]

The key factor in the successful battle against the oil blockade was the correct policy of the Soviet state, which demonstrated that the definite course of the single multinational Union of Soviet Socialist Republics was far superior to the sporadic actions by imperialist oil monopolies. This battle led to the abysmal collapse of the "oil blockade" policy against the USSR. However, anti-Soviet campaigns were launched in some of European countries.

---

[1] See A. V. Shishkin, op. cit., pp. 273-74; *Foreign Trade of the USSR from 1918 to 1940*, pp. 45, 67 (in Russian); *Times*, No. 4. 1923.

The Curzon Ultimatum

The British government began taking openly hostile action. Lord Curzon, Britain's Foreign Secretary, sent a memorandum to the Soviet government on May 8, 1923 accusing the USSR of spreading anti-British propaganda in Afghanistan, Iran and India. He insisted that the USSR recall its diplomats from the first two countries, that apologies be made for their allegedly improper conduct, and that monetary compensation be paid for reprisals taken by competent Soviet agencies against British spies.

The British government claimed the right to interfere in the internal affairs of the USSR under the pretext of combating so-called "religious repression".

The Curzon memorandum seemed like an ultimatum and threatened to rupture Soviet-British relations. It caused an uproar in the USSR and among working people of other countries. Rallies and demostrations were held throughout the Soviet Union in protest against the British government's outrageous claims.

The working people expressed their willingness to do everything they could to defend the Soviet state.

A campaign called "Hands off Soviet Russia!" was launched again in the capitalist world, and as a result of the campaign by progressive forces in many countries, attempts to isolate the USSR again failed, and Lord Curzon was soon forced to resign.

Thanks to the consistent battle fought by Soviet Diplomats and trade representatives, the conflict produced by the Curzon ultimatum was settled in May 1923.

The Soviet government made some minor concessions to Britain in secondary matters, but rejected all British claims to interfere in the USSR's sovereign rights and affairs.

Fuelled by the Curzon ultimatum, however, the anti-Soviet tide which had rolled over many Western countries left its stains.

Vatslav Vatslavovich Vorovsky, one of the pioneers of Soviet diplomacy, a dauntless fighter for strengthening the political and economic positions of the Soviet state internationally, met a tragic death on May 10, 1923. He was a member of a joint Soviet delegation of the RSFSR, Ukraine and Georgia to the Lausanne Conference, where it upheld free merchant passage through the Black Sea straits, and actively opposed the attempt of imperialist powers to put this area under the control of their navy.

After the first stage of negotiations had wound up in February 1923, the Western countries decided to keep the Soviet delegation out of further discussion and did not invite it to participate in the concluding phase.

The Soviet government then decided that Vorovsky would go from Rome to Lausanne to try to get the Soviet delegation re-seated at the conference.[1]

He was met at the Lausanne railway station by M. A. Divilkovsky, a member of the delegation, and I. I. Arens, a correspondent of ROSTA (Russian Telegraph Agency), and they all went to the Cecil Hotel. On May 9, he reported his situation in neutral Switzerland to the People's Commissariat for Foreign Affairs: "...we are here as observers, but they want to force us to leave any way they possibly can. On Sunday, several young men headed by a pharmacist presented themselves at the hotel, and having declared that they were a delegation from a national organisation, were about to begin questioning my attitude to the Swiss government. I showed them the door... Now they are running around the city and yelling everywhere that they will thump us out of Switzerland by force, etc.

"We do not know whether the police are taking any measures for our security. There is nothing to be seen from outside. Someone else's deliberate hand, perhaps even a foreign one, can clearly be felt behind these hooligans... The Swiss government's behaviour is a shameful violation of guarantees given at the beginning of the conference, and any assault on us is possible only with the knowledge and connivance of the authorities in this super-orderly country. So let them take the responsibility."[2]

Some time after nine o'clock on the evening of May 10, Vo-

---

[1] *Documents on the Foreign Policy of the USSR*, Vol. V, pp. 245-46, 270-72, 285-86.

[2] *Documents on the Foreign Policy of the USSR*, Vol. VI, Politizdat, Moscow, 1961, p. 286.

rovsky, Divilkovsky and Arens had their supper in the half-empty restaurant of the Cecil Hotel. A man sitting nearby stood up suddenly, approached Vorovsky from behind and shot him in the back of his head almost point-blank. Then he fired several more shots at Vorovsky's two companions, wounding them seriously. Thus, the life of the outstanding Soviet diplomat V. V. Vorovsky came abruptly to an end. The assassin—a White Guard Moris Konradi—and his associate Arkady Polunin, a former tsarist army officer, had thought of killing G. V. Chicherin and L. B. Krasin shortly before this, and Konradi went to Berlin to do so. The indictment noted that Polunin had supplied Konradi with information about the character of Vorovsky and had made a special point of his outstanding qualities as a financial expert and diplomat who was well able to defend Soviet interests at the Lausanne Conference.[1]

The cantonal court acquitted the criminals, and the All-Union Central Executive Committee and the RSFSR Council of People's Commissars declared a political and economic boycott of Switzerland by a decree of June 20, 1923. The boycott lasted for four years.[2]

New Period in Relations with the Capitalist World

The assassination in Lausanne, which came at the time of the Curzon ultimatum, failed to stop the Soviet state from progressively consolidating its position internationally and on the world markets.

Chicherin said that the second half of 1923 began "a new period in our international relations" when political and economic ties with several capitalist countries were normalised. The principal result of this turning point in the international standing of the Soviet state, said Chicherin, was that "the capitalist world began adapting itself to the new relations and to accept

[1] See S. B. Chlenov, "Speech on the V. V. Vorovsky Assassination Case", Moscow, s.a., p. 10 (in Russian).
[2] Documents on the Foreign Policy of the USSR, Vol. VI, pp. 313-16, 356-57, 621.

the fact ... of the equality of the two economic systems".[1]

The formation of the USSR and the resultant political and economic consolidation of the Soviet state also affected its economic relations with the West.

Key to informing the business community in the capitalist world about real economic conditions in the USSR and its potential as a trade partner was the First All-Union Agricultural and Home-Industrial Exhibition held in Moscow from August 15 to October 21, 1923. It was a very important factor in finally overcoming the Western capitalist circles' lack of confidence in the possibility of good business relations with the USSR, and coincided with the beginning of a new stage in their relations.

In addition to demonstrating the achievements of the economies of all the republics that had just united into the Union of Soviet Socialist Republics, the All-Union Exhibition had the objective of "establishing ties with foreign markets".[2]

The Main Committee established to organise the exhibition had a foreign section with offices in 18 capitalist countries.

They spread information and materials about the exhibition, sent invitations to many companies and associations, and held talks with them. Altogether 401 companies from 20 capitalist countries were represented in the foreign section of the exhibition.

During and after the exhibition, the foreign section registered 456 agreements with exhibiting companies for purchases of products by the Soviet organisers.[3]

But it was not these specific deals which were most important in stimulating economic relations between the USSR and the capitalist world, but rather the profound impression which the exhibition made on all its foreign participants and on the many delegations from abroad[4] who had seen for themselves the dynamic growth of all the branches of the Soviet economy.

---

[1] G. V. Chicherin, op. cit., pp. 250-57, 266.

[2] *All-Union Agricultural and Home-Industrial Exhibition with a Foreign Section.* Materials and Documents, 2nd ed., Gosizdat, Moscow, 1923, p. 17 (in Russian).

[3] V. A. Shishkin, op. cit., pp. 282-83.

[4] 411 businessmen from 21 countries visited the exhibition just between August 20 and September 20 alone—see *Vneshnyaya torgovlya,* Nos. 37-38, 1923, p. 28.

Reports by Western businessmen, politicians and correspondents reflected their almost unanimous surprise at the progress the Soviet Union had made in so short a time, and made a point of the USSR's growing importance in the international division of labour. The US Senator Robert M. La Follette said, for example, that the exposition of machinery was a big surprise for him. "It could make a very good impression at any exhibition in the USA," he said. He also noted "its quite exceptional importance" for resuming economic relations between the USSR and the USA.[1]

Similar reports on the exhibition appeared in the German and American press. The Birmingham factory-owner, Ford, who had seen the exhibition shortly before it officially opened, told British newspaper men that Russia had made great progress in restoring its economy. He said he was ready to do business with Soviet organisations on a credit basis, and informed the reporters that he had signed a deal in Russia, opened an account at the State Bank, and was not at all worried about his capital not being safe.

The united economic front in relations with the capitalist world was closely associated with the formation of the USSR and with the political and economic consolidation of the Soviet state.

The great international success could hardly have come about so rapidly had all the Soviet republics not united in the USSR, thus transferring the principal functions involved in representation of the international interests of the Union state to the jurisdiction of its supreme authorities.

Under the USSR Constitution of 1924, all the functions involved in political and economic relations with other countries were assigned to the supreme authorities of the Soviet Union, including representation of the USSR in international affairs, the signing and ratification of treaties with other countries, obtaining loans and conclusion of concession treaties, the management of foreign trade, and legislation on the rights of foreigners. The formation of the USSR, as the Constitution stated, ensured

---

[1] See *Nakanune,* October 11, 1923; Central State Archive of the National Economy, stock 480, list 7, file 94, 160 (in Russian).

"the creation of a united front of Soviet republics faced by the capitalist encirclement".[1]

As the Constitution was going into force by decision of the Second Session of the Central Executive Committee in July 1923, the Committee Presidium issued an appeal "To All the Peoples and Governments of the World" setting forth the objectives and tasks of foreign policy of the Soviet Union.

The appeal said that "the Union state sets itself the aim of preserving peace with all nations... A natural ally of oppressed peoples, the Union of Soviet Socialist Republics seeks peaceful and friendly relations, and economic co-operation with all nations..."[2]

The unification of all the Soviet republics in the Union of Soviet Socialist Republics involved a considerable reorganisation of the bodies responsible for foreign relations. It was intended to centralise the diplomatic service, foreign trade operations, concession activities, and representation of the new state's industrial interests on the world market.

On July 23, 1923, on instructions from the Soviet government, G. V. Chicherin formally notified other countries that "from now on, the USSR will be responsible for international relations, including these of the republics it is composed of, through the bodies of Central Union power authorised for this purpose by the Fundamental Law."[3]

This meant that as of that moment, the People's Commissariat for Foreign Affairs and the USSR diplomatic missions abroad would represent the interests of not only Soviet Russia but of the entire multinational state as well, and international treaties and agreements would be concluded on behalf of the entire Union.

The activities of the state foreign trade bodies were also reorganised. After the USSR was formed and the People's Commissariat for Foreign Trade established, all the Soviet trade missions abroad were merged. A body of representatives of the

---

[1] *The Constitution and Constitutional Acts of the USSR, (1922-1936)*, pp. 41-42.

[2] *Documents on the Foreign Policy of the USSR*, Vol. VI, pp. 384-85.

[3] Ibid., p. 395-96.

People's Commissariat for Foreign Trade was established under each of the republic's Council of People's Commissars, and the representatives were to ensure that the interests of the Union republics and specific regions of the country were taken into account as much as possible.[1]

The new structure did not exclude the possibility of the Union republics being directly represented abroad when necessity demanded it.

Thus, foreign trade was completely centralised, and a unified trade policy of all the Soviet republics on the world market ensured.

The bodies dealing with concessional matters were also reorganised at the same time. Decrees of the All-Union Central Executive Committee and the Council of People's Commissars of the RSFSR, and a subsequent decree issued by the USSR Council of People's Commissars on August 21, 1923 established the Central Concessional Committee attached to the USSR Council of People's Commissars.

It conducted all negotiations on concessions, and supervised the execution of the contracts concluded.[2] Concession commissions were attached to the Soviet trade missions in Berlin and London in 1923 for preliminary consideration of propositions for concessions.[3]

Finally, in 1923, the Council of Labour and Defence decreed that foreign commercial operations such as imports and exports, should be allowed only to a specified number of state enterprises or their associations. Among them were Neftesindikat, Timber Export Bureau, Gostorg (national organisation for retail trade), Lnotsentr (Flax Centre), Khleboprodukt (Bread Products), and Textile Sindicate.[4]

This ensured that the principal producers or consumers of

---

[1] See *Statute of the People's Commissariat for Foreign Trade of the USSR of November 13, 1923*, Moscow, 1924 (in Russian).

[2] *Collection of Decrees of the RSFSR*, No. 20, 1923, p. 246; *Documents on the Foreign Policy of the USSR*, Vol. VI, pp. 413-16.

[3] *Report on the Activities of the AUCEC of the 10th Convocation in 1923*, Gosizdat, Moscow, 1924, pp. 24-25 (in Russian).

[4] A. Lyakhov, *Foreign Trade According to Current Law of Soviet Russia*, Gosizdat, Moscow, 1923, pp. 101-02 (in Russian).

various kinds of products—the domestic industrial enterprises—would enter foreign markets as exclusive sellers or buyers, thus creating the best possible conditions for transactions, quality control, etc.

Period of Recognition of the USSR

Most capitalist countries established diplomatic relations with the Soviet Union in 1924 and 1925. In his New-Year interview on January 1, 1924, Chicherin, People's Commissar for Foreign Affairs of the USSR, said that the USSR's relations with the bourgeois countries had entered a new phase and listed the principal reasons for the "sharp consolidation of the international position of the Union of SSR": the policy of peace and of politically resolving conflicts between countries pursued steadily by his government; the methodical development of close economic ties with other countries; the growth of the USSR's export potential, and the strengthening and consolidation of the Soviet state.[1]

Besides, while he had formerly called bread, timber and petroleum products only "arguments" in favour of promoting the country's role internationally when it just began to export, the Soviet Union's domestic economic growth, in Chicherin's opinion, was at that time the key factor for the increase of its influence and prestige in international politics.[2]

It would also be wrong to represent the expanding relations between the USSR and the capitalist world, begun in 1924, as the result of particular interest taken by the Soviet side alone, and its almost begging for Western recognition.

This point of view is sometimes expressed by bourgeois historians in their treatment of Soviet foreign policy in the mid-1920s.

Chicherin said time and again that "the establishment of long-term political and economic relations with us is brought about by the dictates of life itself, by objective necessity. . . .

---

[1] G. V. Chicherin, op. cit., p. 267.
[2] Ibid., pp. 220, 275.

The ruling circles' political rhetoric in regard to us and the façade of irreconcilability often conceal in reality the willingness caused by objective factors to agree after some bargaining to a long-term arrangement with us."[1]

The most substantial manifestation of the Soviet state's more solid international standing was its *de jure* recognition by several major capitalist countries of Europe and Asia, which resulted in the USSR taking its appropriate place in the system of great powers and in international politics.

While only ten—most of them small neighbouring European and Asian countries, such as Latvia, Lithuania, Estonia, Finland, Poland, Iran, Afghanistan, Turkey and Mongolia, and just one major European power, Germany—states had established diplomatic relations with the Union Soviet state at the time it was formed in 1922, in the one-year period from February 1924 to January 1925, the USSR was officially recognised by 12 countries of Europe, Asia and Latin America (Britain, Italy, Norway, Sweden, Denmark, France, China, Mexico, Japan, and others).

The Soviet government considered formal recognition of the USSR to be an objective need ensuing from the reality of the existence, alongside countries belonging to the capitalist system, of the world's first socialist state. By 1924 this state had already won solid political and economic positions internationally as a result of a long struggle, but a certain legal foundation was required for the development of normal relations with other countries. And both sides—the USSR as well as its partners—needed this equally.

"Many people are wrong to think," said Chicherin in January 1924, "that we require promotion to international rank. We do not want international rank. We do not think about a label. We are interested in *de jure* recognition only as a technical and practical step which facilitates our economic relationships. But this facilitation is needed not only by us, but by the other party to a contract as well."[2]

After February 1924, one country after another officially recognised the USSR. In the history books, this process was called

---

[1] Ibid., pp. 266, 327, 329.
[2] Ibid., pp. 273-74.

"the period of recognition". One Soviet newspaper of the time featured a typical cartoon showing Chicherin and representatives from many countries, trying to present him with their letters of recognition.

On February 2, 1924, R. M. Hodgson, the British representative in Moscow, presented the People's Commissar for Foreign Affairs G. V. Chicherin with the note of the official recognition by Great Britain of the government of the USSR "as a *de jure* government in the territories of the former Russian Empire, which recognise its power".

The Soviet Government expressed its satisfaction in a note sent in reply.[1] The resolution adopted by the Second All-Union Congress of Soviets on Britain's *de jure* recognition stated that the act reflected the consistency of the USSR's foreign policy of peace. "The Workers' and Peasants' Government of the Union of Soviet Socialist Republics, which emerged from the great revolution," the resolution said, "posed as a task of primary importance the struggle for peace, and has persistently striven to restore normal ties with all nations throughout its existence."[2]

It should be noted that Britain's first Labour government, led by Ramsay MacDonald, the government which established diplomatic relations with the USSR, wanted, as I. M. Maisky, the Soviet Ambassador to London, put it, "to sell recognition for some concessions on our part".[3]

The fact that the British government agreed to exchange only chargés d'affaires with the USSR until the problem of tsarist Russia's debts and other financial claims of the United Kingdom had been resolved, also served the same purpose.[4]

And although the talks on the problem finally resulted in the General and Trade Agreement signed in August 1924 by Britain and the USSR, where very complex and controversial issues had been resolved via compromise, the new Conservative government

---

[1] *Documents on the Foreign Policy of the USSR*, Vol. VII, Politizdat, Moscow, 1963, pp. 53-54.

[2] Ibid., p. 58.

[3] I. M. Maisky, *Reminiscences of a Soviet Diplomat. 1925-1945*, p. 22.

[4] *Documents on the Foreign Policy of the USSR*, Vol. VII, pp. 54, 98-100.

led by Baldwin refused to bring it to Parliament for ratification.

The result was that diplomatic relations remained on the level of chargés d'affaires, and economic relations were regulated by the temporary agreement signed between the RSFSR and Great Britain on March 16, 1921.

Negotiations with the Italian government, which later resulted in official recognition of the Soviet Union, began in the autumn of 1923.

The particular feature of these negotiations was that Italy, a country poor in natural resources, sought primarily to sign a trade agreement with the Soviet Union for its own benefit. While negotiating the trade agreement, the government also hoped to settle the issue of establishing diplomatic relations with the USSR. "Mussolini bases Italy's attitude towards Russia entirely on a commercial foundation," the well-informed Czechoslovak Ambassador to Italy, Dvořaček reported to his Ministry for Foreign Affairs. "The Italian government has accorded *de jure* recognition to the Soviet Union at the price of a trade agreement which would provide raw materials for the country, open the Russian market for it, gain industrial and agricultural concessions, and obtain Black Sea passage for its merchant fleet."[1]

Czechoslovakia's Foreign Minister was of the same opinion. He told the Soviet representative in Prague on January 3, 1924: "We will not follow the example of the blackmailer and extortioner Mussolini who wants to make you pay for recognition."[2] The Czechoslovak minister said that his country's recognition of the USSR was contingent on what Britain would do.

But an unforeseen incident befell Prime Minister Benito Mussolini at the concluding stage of the negotiations with the USSR.

Counting on Italy to be the first to officially recognise the USSR, Mussolini dragged out the negotiations in the attempt to wring as many concessions as possible out of the USSR for being the pace-setter.

After all matters had been agreed, Mussolini flirted with a proposal made my MacDonald at the end of January 1924 that

---

[1] *Archiv Federalniho Ministerstva zahraničnich věci*, Politicke Zprávy, Řim, 1924, No. 176, 16.XI.

[2] *Documents on the Foreign Policy of the USSR*, Vol. VII, p. 12.

it would be better for Italy to exhange only chargés d'affaires with the USSR.

Meanwhile London and Rome were discussing the matter through diplomatic channels, and Mussolini said that he was willing to abandon his former idea of exchanging ambassadors with the Soviet Union.

On February 2 he suddenly learned from the newspapers that Britain had fully recognised the Soviet Union.

After that any further delays by Mussolini were senseless. Ya. D. Yanson, a Soviet participant in the Rome talks, reported: "On the evening of February 6 . . . we were received by Mussolini. He was upset and absolutely furious; he cursed MacDonald, accused him of doubledealing and deception, and promised to expose MacDonald's policy with documents."[1]

On February 7, 1924 the USSR and Italy signed a treaty on trade and navigation, with the first clause providing for mutual official recognition and the establishment of diplomatic relations on the level of embassies.[2]

On February 15, 1924 documents associated with the act of official recognition of the USSR by Norway were signed, including a note from Minister of Foreign Affairs Mishle to A. M. Kollontai, the plenipotentiary representative of the USSR, and the Declaration on the settlement of controversial issues and the intention of the two sides to begin negotiating a trade agreement.

The interpretation of the text of the Declaration was made more precise by notes exchanged in February and March 1924.[3]

Austria followed suit on February 25; Greece on March 8; Sweden on March 15, and Denmark on June 18.

On May 31, 1924 an agreement was concluded on the general principles of resolving issues between the USSR and the Republic of China to provide for resumption of normal diplomatic and

---

[1] See in more detail about the recognition of the USSR by Italy: I. D. Ostoia-Ovsianyi, "On the History of the Establishment of Diplomatic Relations Between the USSR and Italy", in *Leninist Policy of Peace and Co-operation. Establishment of Diplomatic Relations Between the USSR and Capitalist Countries in 1924-1925*, Nauka Publishers, Moscow, 1965, pp. 94-100 (in Russian).

[2] *Documents on the Foreign Policy of the USSR*, Vol. VII, pp. 68-70.

[3] Ibid., pp. 107-09, 133-34, 163-64.

economic relations. There was not a single clause in the agreement which might make anything hazy about the borders between the two countries.[1]

The May 1924 elections in France brought the government of the so-called "left-wing bloc" to power headed by Edouard Herriot, the Mayor of Lyon and leader of radicals and radical socialists. Although the parties of the bloc had made official recognition of the USSR part of their programme, the cabinet was overlong in working out the formula of recognition and was careful to defend the interests of former French creditors of Russia.[2] Nevertheless, the French government declared in a note of October 28, 1924 that, true to the friendship binding the Russian and French nations, it officially recognised, as of that day, the government of the USSR as the government of the territories of the former Russian Empire where its authority was recognised by the people.[3]

The reply to the note was adopted by the USSR Central Executive Committee on October 28, 1924. It expressed satisfaction with France's act of recognition, expressed the willingness to begin immediate talks on a broad range of controversial unresolved issues, and underlined the "considerable benefit for both sides that would ensue from the creation of close and stable economic relations between them, which would promote the development of their productive forces and trade, as well as their rapprochement in the economic field".[4]

Soviet-Mexican negotiations on official recognition began in Berlin in February 1924 and ended on August 4 when the Mexican Ambassador to Germany, Ortis Rubio, presented a memorandum to the plenipotentiary representative of the USSR on the establishment of official diplomatic relations between Mexico and the Soviet Union.[5]

---

[1] Ibid., pp. 331-35.

[2] Yu. V. Borisov, *Soviet-French Relations (1924-1945)*, Politizdat, Moscow, 1964, pp. 38-39 (in Russian); *History of the Foreign Policy of the USSR*, Vol. I, pp. 204-05.

[3] *Documents on the Foreign Policy of the USSR*, Vol. VI, pp. 514-15.

[4] *USSR, CEC of the 2nd Convocation, the 2nd Session.* Verbatim Report, Gosizdat, Moscow, 1924, pp. 568-69 (in Russian).

[5] *History of the Foreign Policy of the USSR*, Vol. I, pp. 215-16.

Mexico was the first Latin American country to officially recognise the Union of Soviet Socialist Republics. The second was Uruguay, which established formal diplomatic relations with the USSR by an exchange of telegrams on August 21-22, 1926.[1]

The negotiations for normalisation of relations between the USSR and Japan were far longer and far more difficult. They had been held sporadically since 1923 and involved complicated military, territorial and economic issues. It was only on January 20, 1925 that several documents were signed, among them the Convention on basic principles of relations, protocols and declarations.

They formalised the provisions for the establishment of diplomatic relations, for leaving the Portsmouth Treaty of 1905, which was not to the USSR's advantage, in force, with a proviso made by the Soviet government that it "does not share the political responsibility of the former tsarist government for the conclusion of the said treaty", and for the intention of the two sides to resolve the problem of fishing in the border waters and to start talks on a trade agreement. The documents also contained a pledge by the Soviet government that it would provide oil and coal concessions for Japanese citizens in Northern Sakhalin and a pledge by the Japanese government to withdraw its troops from that part of the island by May 15, 1925.[2]

An official document issued by the Soviet government stated that the agreement with Japan "not only opens wide opportunities for further development of economic ties, but also is of great political significance both for the USSR and Japan, as well as for the entire Far East."[3]

Shortly afterward, on May 19, 1925, Northern Sakhalin, long occupied illegally by Japan, saw the Japanese flag lowered

---

[1] Ibid., pp. 216-17.

[2] *Documents on the Foreign Policy of the USSR,* Vol. VIII, Politizdat, Moscow, 1964, pp. 79-80.

[3] *Annual Report of the People's Commissariat for Foreign Affairs for 1924 by the 3rd Congress of Soviets,* Gosizdat, Moscow, 1925, p. 25 (in Russian).

and the flag of the USSR raised symbolising the restoration of its sovereignty over that territory.[1]

A key element in the USSR's international standing was that Soviet-German political and economic relations continued to develop successfully overall between 1923 and 1926 on the basis of "the Rapallo policy", which implied recognition by both sides of the historical necessity of peaceful coexistence as the norm in relations between countries with different social systems. Co-operation of the two powers was a positive factor that helped stabilise international relations, considering that during the period certain circles in the West tried to force Germany to re-orient its foreign policy and to set it at odds with the Soviet Union (the Dawes Plan, the Locarno accords).

Given that situation, the conclusion of an economic treaty with Germany on October 12, 1925, and of the non-aggression and neutrality pact on April 24, 1926 was a triumph for Soviet diplomacy.[2]

The USA remained the only major Western power which still refused to normalise political relations with and to officially recognise the Soviet Union. On December 16, 1923 Chicherin sent a telegram to the new US President, Calvin Coolidge, saying that the Soviet government was willing to begin negotiations with the aim of resolving all the controversial issues on an equality basis, including US Administration claims with respect to the debts of the bourgeois Provisional government of Russia, claims which amounted to the rather small sum of 187.7 million dollars. The Secretary of State Charles E. Hughes followed with a statement almost immediately. It was made in the Senate on December 18, 1923, and on the next day forwarded via the American ambassador in Tallinn to the Soviet plenipotentiary representative in Estonia.

The statement was in fact an ultimatum, rejecting any talks with the USSR and demanding that the USSR unilaterally abandon the basic principles of its domestic and foreign policy.[3]

There was no change in the US Administration policy on the

---

[1] *Izvestia,* May 24, 1925.
[2] *History of the Foreign Policy of the USSR,* Vol. I, pp. 224-28.
[3] *Documents on the Foreign Policy of the USSR,* Vol. VI, pp. 547-48.

"Russian question" in later years either. In December 1926, Chicherin stated in a telegram from Berlin to the People's Commissariat for Foreign Affairs: "The question of resuming diplomatic relations with America is hopeless, not a step forward has been made."[1]

At the same time, Soviet-American economic relations were expanding rather well. As certain US businessmen became increasingly interested in economic ties with the Soviet Union, a gradual evolution in government policy began as well towards removing obstacles to economic relations.

It is sufficient to say that in the 1924-1925 production year, Soviet American trade as well as American exports to the USSR were 300 per cent higher than the previous year. In terms of value, the USA was the USSR's biggest importer in 1924-1925.[2]

An important role in getting the US Administration to reappraise its former position in the undesirability of encouraging trade and economic relations with the USSR was played by the USSR's great progress in economic recovery and development.

A telling fact in this respect is a letter of September 22, 1925, sent by the representative of the All-Union Textile Syndicate (ATS) in New York (this Soviet organisation bought American cotton for the Soviet textile industry) to the ATS head office shortly after his return to the US from Moscow, reporting on a talk he had had with Herbert Hoover, the US Secretary of Commerce: "On the 19th of this month I had a long talk with Hoover. I spent an hour and 15 minutes with him instead of the 10 minutes specified beforehand. Hoover and I are old acquaintances, and have talked about the USSR several times. The first question he asked me was: 'Well, how did you find Russia?' He has absolutely no doubts about our economic recovery and, though still grumbling about communist methods, he admits that the USSR has taken a great economic step forward and is now a serious factor in the world economic situation. . . . I showed him current economic growth statistics. He did not question

---

[1] *Documents on the Foreign Policy of the USSR*, Vol. IX, p. 564.
[2] *Foreign Trade of the USSR. Collection of Statistics. 1918-1966*, Politizdat, Moscow, 1967, pp. 8-9; *USSR for 15 Years. Statistics on the National Economy*, Gosizdat, Moscow, 1932, p. 291 (both in Russian).

anything, but only grumbled all the time that 'they've done it in spite of themselves'. As far as recognition is concerned, he was very careful and always referred to official statements of the State Department."[1]

However, the US Administration's negative stand on formal recognition could not impede the USSR's growing international influence, its growing authority and prestige in world politics, and its expanding positions on the world market.

By the mid-1920s the Soviet state felt itself an equal and full member of the world community. Its representatives now had a multinational Union state behind them, which was growing stronger politically and economically, and whose power was steadily increasing.

An incident of the mid-1920s seems to be typical in this respect. It was told by B. I. Korotkin, one of Chicherin's secretaries: "Once the German Ambassador Brokford-Rantzau asked to be received urgently that same day. Georgi Vasilyevich [Chicherin— Ed.] was so overloaded with work that he was unable to find time for the unexpected talk, and asked me to notify the Ambassador that he would receive him the following day.

"The Ambassador still insisted on being received that same day.

"Then Chicherin asked me to inform the Ambassador that he could receive him that night, at 12 o'clock sharp. The Ambassador thanked him for the courtesy and agreed to the time specified.

"At midnight sharp, Chicherin went to his inner office and asked me to invite the Ambassador from the reception room but ... for some reason the Ambassador had not yet arrived. A counsellor of the Embassy apologized for the Ambassador and replied to my telephone inquiry that the Ambassador had been delayed, but was on his way. The Ambassador did arrive, but was 15 minutes late.

"When I informed Chicherin of the Ambassador's arrival, he answered calmly that he would soon come to his inner office and, having put his coat and hat on for some reason, took his

---

[1] *The Central Archives of the National Economy of the USSR*, Stock 7770 (VTS), list 3, file 38, pp. 111-12 (in Russian).

stick in hand, left the apartment via the back door, and returned only at about two o'clock that morning. The Ambassador was waiting patiently and, when I finally invited him into the People's Commissar's office, neither Chicherin nor the Ambassador showed by their appearances that anything unusual had happened and greeted each other warmly, taking their seats in the armchairs.

"Afterwards, some seven or eight years later, I once reminded Georgi Vasilyevich of that episode, saying that I was surprised that he made the German Ambassador wait for a good two hours in the reception lounge. Chicherin said smiling: 'I remember it very well. The point was that the Ambassador, who was annoyed at me for not agreeing to meet him that same day, strongly insisted on the reception. I decided to make the appointment for midnight, that is, neither today nor tomorrow. But the Ambassador had evidently decided to punish me for it by being 15 minutes late, though diplomats, and Germans especially, are extremely punctual. Well, because he punished me by 15 minutes, I decided to punish him by two hours."[1]

Development of Economic Relations

"The period of official recognition" of the USSR was also a time of several purely trade and economic agreements and treaties, most of them ensuing primarily from negotiations on diplomatic relations.

Between 1924 and 1926 alone, the Soviet Union concluded 15 economic agreements and treaties with various countries, among them the treaty on trade and navigation with Italy on February 7, 1924; a trade agreement with Sweden on March 15, 1924; one with Britain on August 8, 1924 but not ratified by its Conservative government; economic treaties with Germany on October 12 and Norway on December 15, 1925; credit and customs agreements, treaties on neutrality and the repudiation of participation in any economic or financial boycotts in 1926 with Germany, Greece, Lithuania, etc.

---

[1] Quoted in I. Gorokhov, L. Zamyatin, I. Zemskov, op. cit., pp. 191-92.

The Soviet Union maintained stable trade relations with almost 30 countries in the middle of the 1920s. In 1924 and 1925 Soviet foreign trade increased dramatically over 1923, with the respective figures of cost 1.8 times and 4.3 times respectively over 1923.[1] This level was later exceeded considerably. Foreign trade began to play an increasing part in completing the USSR's economic recovery, and then in its accelerated industrial growth.

Other types of economic ties were also developing. The year 1926 saw the greatest number of foreign concessions in the country's history: there were 101 concessional agreements in force, including agreements on technical assistance[2]. However, even at that time, when things were most favourable for the concessions, foreign concessions played a rather small role in the country's overall economic growth. The share they provided of investment in the economy and of industry came to no more than half of one per cent of the figures for the Union as a whole.

In general the Soviet Union's international standing in the mid-1920s was characterised by the undisputable consolidation of its political and economic positions and by its increased influence on the solution of international issues.

In evaluating the USSR's relations with the West, the 14th Congress of the All-Union Communist Party (Bolsheviks) (CPSU [B]), held in December 1925, noted the consolidation of the period of "peaceful cohabitation of the USSR with the capitalist states". "It provided," said the Congress resolution, "both the possibility of domestic construction and—thanks first of all to economic relations with foreign countries—certain benefits for accelerating this construction in the USSR."[3]

Thus, by the mid-1920s, the USSR was already a growing, united and strong multinational state both from the point of view of its domestic political and economic development and of its standing internationally. Its peoples had made their ultimate

---

[1] *Foreign Trade of the USSR,* Vneshtorgizdat, Moscow, 1954, pp. 165, 177 (in Russian).

[2] See V. I. Kasyanenko, *Achievement of Economic Independence of the USSR. (1917-1940),* Politizdat, Moscow, 1979, pp. 74, 89, 175 (in Russian).

[3] *The CPSU in Resolutions...,* Vol. 3, Politizdat, Moscow, 1970, p. 244.

historical choice. They chose the road of building socialism not separately, but by joining together in a voluntary alliance of equal sovereign republics—the Union of Soviet Socialist Republics—initiated by the great Lenin.

This road has resulted in tremendous accomplishments in social, political, economic and cultural life, making the multinational Soviet Union one of the world's most advanced and strongest industrial powers, a country of developed socialism.

It is a road that is still being followed today.

CONCLUSION

"The formation of the USSR was a direct continuation of the cause of the Great October Revolution, which opened up a new era in mankind's development; it was a practical embodiment of the idea of our great leader, Lenin—the idea of a voluntary union of free nations," said Leonid Brezhnev, General Secretary of the CPSU Central Committee.[1]

The solution of the national question—one of the most painful, the most dramatic questions in the history of human society —has occupied a special place in the history of the USSR.

Leading up to and during the October Socialist Revolution, the Communist Party was able to fuse the struggle of the proletariat for political power, that of the peasants for land, that of the working people as a whole for withdrawal from the imperialist war, and that of the liberation movements in the outlying ethnic regions into one powerful revolutionary current based on Lenin's nationalities policy.

Drawing on the support of the revolutionary and democratic elements in this movement and ingeniously combining the proletarian movement in the country's centre with the revolutionary-democratic liberation movement in outlying ethnic regions, the Communist Party rallied them around the banner of internationalism to fight for a new, socialist system.

The working people of all nationalities, led by the working

[1] L. I. Brezhnev, "The Fiftieth Anniversary of the Union of Soviet Socialist Republics", *Following Lenin's Course*, Progress Publishers, Moscow, 1975, p. 52.

class, were able to deal with and solve the fundamental problems of the socialist revolution like the establishment of the power of Soviets, the creation of a new administrative apparatus and the carrying out of radical reforms in the economy, politics and culture.

Initial documents, such as the resolutions of the Second and Third All-Russia congresses of Soviets, the Declaration of Rights of the Peoples of Russia, the Declaration of Rights of the Working and Exploited People, the first Constitutions of the RSFSR and the USSR, which were originated and adopted on Lenin's initiative, proclaimed the main principles in the solution of the national question in the era of the dictatorship of the proletariat.

All peoples—large and small alike—were granted the right to self-determination, and to the formation of national states; in this they received necessary assistance from Soviet Russia.

In dealing with the national question, Soviet power inexorably displayed respect for national sentiments.

Looking ahead to future relations between socialist nations, Lenin wrote: "The masses of working people, as they liberate themselves from the bourgeois yoke, *will gravitate* irresistibly towards union and integration with the great, advanced socialist nations for the sake of that 'cultural aid', provided yesterday's oppressors do not infringe on long-oppressed nations' highly-developed democratic feeling of self-respect, and provided they are granted equality in everything, including state construction, that is, experience in organising 'their own' state".[1]

The practice of creating national states during even the initial years of Soviet Power brilliantly confirmed Lenin's foresight.

The joint struggle against imperialism and domestic counter-revolutionary forces in the Land of Soviets to uphold the tremendous gains of the revolution showed the people that a solid military, political and economic alliance was necessary if the republic was to maintain its independent existence, especially as it was encircled by capitalist countries. At the same time the years of Civil War and foreign intervention (1918-1920) were

---

[1] V. I. Lenin, "The Discussion on Self-Determination Summed Up", *Collected Works*, Vol. 22, p. 339.

a crucial stage in the development of the unification movement to establish the USSR.

The history of the proletarian liberation movement was enriched by the experience of the federation of Soviet republics, which had emerged in the relations of the RSFSR with other Soviet republics and, within the RSFSR, with the nationalities, which had no state of their own before.[1]

December 30, 1922, the day the Union state was proclaimed, went down in Soviet history as a great landmark in the destiny of the working people of the Land of Soviets.

On the one hand, this event was an important result of the first five years of the power of the workers and peasants, who had prevailed in the gruelling battles against internal counter-revolutionary forces and imperialist intervention.

On the other hand, unification followed from Soviet experience in resolving the national question on the basis of a new, Soviet state system which brought the nations and ethnic groups of the multinational country to join together in a single state—the mighty Soviet Union.

The creation of the Union state was of exceptional importance for building socialism, for creating its material and technical base, and for equalising the economic, political and cultural level of different nations so that they could achieve genuine equality.

The material and technical base of socialism was created in the USSR through accumulating internal funds and mobilising the people's labour resources, since not a single major capitalist power provided loans to the Soviet state to enable it to create industry, build roads and develop its natural wealth.

The Soviet state could solve these problems only by constantly strengthening the alliance that had been formed between the working class and peasantry in the country's central and outlying regions.

It demanded a correct national policy, a solution of the na-

---

[1] Lenin regarded a federation as a transitional phase to more complete unity; he proved the necessity of a closer federative alliance and devised a plan for the establishment of a single Union state—the Union of Soviet Socialist Republics.

tional question which had emerged as a fundamental issue in building a socialist society. The Communist Party faced the crucial task of mobilising the peoples of the USSR on the basis of internationalist unity and of directing their efforts to build a new society.

Socialist industrialisation opened up the real possibility of radical changing the entire economy and of overcoming economic inequality.

This complicated problem was made even more difficult because many nations of Russia had not entered the stage of capitalism prior to the Great October Socialist Revolution due to the colonial policy of tsarism and the Russian bourgeoisie; they had no local industry, no proletariat and were economically and culturally underdeveloped.

It is enough to point out that at the time the USSR was proclaimed, the illiteracy rate in the Central Asian republics was 90 to 96 per cent, and 82 per cent in Kazakhstan.

The level of socio-political development in the Eastern outlying regions was far behind that of the central areas. Only under the Soviet system could the underdeveloped peoples move forward to socialism without going through the capitalist stage of development.

To do this, the proletariat of Russia came to the aid of working people of the outlying ethnic regions.

In 1921, the 10th Congress of the RCP(B) issued a directive to carry out "the planned implantation of industry on the outskirts through moving factories to the sources of raw materials."[1] The result of the directive was that many factories and plants were presented to the republics of Transcaucasia, Central Asia and Kazakhstan, and skilled workers, experts and engineers from other fraternal republics were assigned to work there.

During the First Five-Year Plan, the state laid great emphasis on correctly locating the productive forces and on bringing industry closer to the sources of raw materials; it coordinated this process in the best possible way with that of eliminating national inequality.

The directives of the 15th Congress of the CPSU(B) pointed

---

[1] *The CPSU in Resolutions...*, Vol. 2, p. 253.

out that particular attention had to be paid to economic and cultural growth in the underdeveloped outlying ethnic regions so that their backwardness could be gradually eliminated. To achieve this, swifter economic and cultural development rates were planned for these regions and their needs and requirements were closely coordinated with those of the rest of the Union.[1]

Therefore, a higher pace of industrialisation was envisaged for economically underdeveloped national republics than for the country as a whole. While fixed assets were to increase as a whole by 289 per cent over five years, the target was 494 per cent for the Central Asian republics, 549 per cent for Kazakhstan and 442 per cent for the Byelorussian SSR.[2]

The same policy was continued throughout the subsequent pre-war and post-war five-year plans. The result of 50 years of this policy was a 600-fold growth of industrial production in Kazakhstan, an over 500-fold growth in the Tajik SSR, over 400-fold in the Kirghiz SSR, almost 240-fold in the Uzbek SSR and over 130-fold in the Turkmen SSR. These republics have made great progress in agricultural development: Uzbekistan grows 120 times more cotton, and Turkmenia 90 times, while Kazakhstan now grows 30 times more grain than it did in 1922.

The more economically developed RSFSR and the Ukraine were the principal bases for industrialisation of the country.

Even though they assisted the other republics, they themselves have produced great economic and cultural accomplishments. The Ukraine's industry registered a 776-fold growth over the first half a century of the Soviet Union's existence. The Ukraine today has a highly developed and mechanised agriculture, outstanding scientific centres, and brilliant achievements in culture and the arts.

The Russian Federation—the largest and the most developed—has provided invaluable fraternal assistance to other nations. It built up industry in its main centres—Moscow, Leningrad, Gorky, Sverdlovsk—developed new sources of natural wealth, and raised the economies of the other peoples within its borders. Over the

---

[1] See *The CPSU in Resolutions...*, Vol. 4, Politizdat, Moscow, 1970, p. 45.

[2] See *The Five-Year Plan of Economic Construction of the USSR*, Gosizdat, Vol. 3, Moscow, 1930, p. 37 (in Russian).

first 50 years, its industrial output increased by over 300 times, while agricultural output doubled and trebled.

"History knows of no other state that has done so much in such a short time for the all-round development of nations and nationalities as the USSR, the socialist Motherland of all our peoples."[1]

Close observance of the interests of all nationalities, big and small, was a cornerstone of the Party and Government's national policy.

Based on five years of experience in dealing with the national question in the USSR, Lenin made this remark: "Our experience has left us with the firm conviction that only exclusive attention to the interests of various nations can remove grounds for conflicts, can remove mutual mistrust, can remove the fear of any intrigues and create that confidence, especially on the part of workers and peasants speaking different languages, without which there absolutely cannot be peaceful relations between peoples or anything like a successful development of everything that is of value in present-day civilisation."[2]

This idea permeates the entire practical economic and political course taken by the Union state for the entire country.

The budget expenditures of some Union republics were financed by subsidies from the Union budget for many years. Thus, in 1924-1925, only 10 per cent in the budget of the Turkmen SSR was covered by its own revenues, while the Ukraine financed as little as 40 per cent of its budget expenditures itself. It received 100,000 roubles from the Union budget in 1928-1929 and 16.9 million roubles in 1932.[3]

In 1928, the Council of People's Commissars of the USSR earmarked 8.3 million roubles from the Union budget for irrigation during the first quarter of the 1928-1929 fiscal year in the Transcaucasian Federation, Central Asia and Kazakh SSR.[4]

[1] Resolution of the Central Committee of the Communist Party of the Soviet Union on the Sixtieth Anniversary of the Formation of the Union of Soviet Socialist Republics", *Pravda*, 21 February 1982.

[2] V. I. Lenin, "Interview Given to Michael Farbman, *Observer* and *Manchester Guardian* Correspondent", *Collected Works,* Vol. 33, p. 386.

[3] See *Fraternal Community of Union Republics. 1917-1971,* Mysl Publishers, Moscow, 1973, p. 150 (in Russian).

[4] Ibid., p. 239.

The Party considered socialist reforms in the countryside, which were made difficult by the feudal and religious heritage, to be of great importance.

As Lenin said at the 8th Party Congress, the Kirghiz, the Uzbeks, the Tajiks and the Turkmens were then under the influence of their mullahs and, therefore, it was possible to overthrow exploiters there only after the differentiation of the proletariat from the bourgeois elements.[1]

In this connection, in 1921, so-called "*vakuf* lands" that had been expropriated earlier were returned to religious institutions; the courts of the *biis* and *kaziys* based on religious law and customs were restored, while religious schools functioned for several years. It was only in 1925 and 1926 that land and water reform was carried out in Central Asia, abolishing the landowners' estates and limiting the influence of the *bais* and kulaks. This reform won over farm labourers, the poor and peasants of average means to the side of the proletariat. The abolition of old forms of land-tenure facilitated the more rapid growth of the productive forces.

Collectivisation of agriculture was based on the stronger alliance between the working class and the peasants of the outlying ethnic regions. Financial assistance to peasants, teams of workers sent to the national regions from industrial centres, development of co-operatives and other measures ensured the triumph of the collective-farm system in both the country's central areas and the outlying ethnic regions. And the Party and state took the national-historical peculiarities into account in organising agricultural co-operatives in Central Asia, Kazakhstan, Transcaucasia and the North.

The resolution of the CPSU (B) Central Committee plenary meeting of November 1929 said: "The launching of collectivisation there entails the abolition of the vestiges of the feudal-tribal structure, which is bound to provoke fierce resistance by the kulak and semi-feudal elements who are waging a stubborn struggle against socialist construction under the guise of defending so-called "national interests".[2]

[1] See V. I. Lenin, "Eighth Congress of the R.C.P. (B.)", *Collected Works*, Vol. 29, p. 172.
[2] *The CPSU in Resolutions...*, Vol. 4, p. 358.

Socialist industrialisation and collectivisation of agriculture eliminated the gap in the levels of economic development of the national republics, consolidated the alliance of the working class and collective farmers throughout the USSR and within each nation, and eliminated cultural backwardness by introducing higher forms of economic organisation and culture.

The triumph of socialism in the USSR was marked by the rise of the literacy rate, by the emergence of the people's intelligentsia, and by the development and mutual enrichment of national cultures.

Cultural inequality was eliminated, with illiteracy throughout the multinational country almost totally eradicated by the late 1930s. While in 1926, the literacy rate was 63.6 per cent in the Ukraine, 60.9 in the RSFSR, 59.7 in Byelorussia, 3.8 in Tajikistan, 11.6 in Uzbekistan, 14.0 in Turkmenistan and 16.5 per cent in Kirghizia, the country's overall literacy rate in 1939 was 87.4 per cent with very slight deviations from this level in the individual republics.[1] The Central Asian republics and Kazakhstan now have 100 per cent literacy. And in the Uzbek SSR alone there are now more graduates of higher-educational establishments and secondary technical schools in the labour force than there were working in the entire USSR in the late 1920s.

In his report on the 50th anniversary of the formation of the USSR, L. I. Brezhnev said: "Soviet culture is socialist in content, in its main trend of development, is varied in national form and internationalist in spirit and character. It is thus an organic fusion of the spiritual riches being created by all the Soviet nations."[2]

The triumph of socialism in the USSR was marked by further growth of Soviet national statehood, which is now represented by 15 Union republics, 19 autonomous republics, six autonomous regions and ten national areas. It was the development of national statehood in its various forms which facilitated the establishment of new, socialist relations between the peoples within the Union state as a whole and in each individual republic.

---

[1] M. I. Kulichenko, *National Relations in the USSR and Their Development Tendencies*, p. 349.

[2] L. I. Brezhnev, *Following Lenin's Course*, pp. 72-73.

Social and political activity of the Soviet citizens grew as the country developed. The American politician Campbell, who visited several cities of Soviet Russia in early 1929, wrote about "the astounding activity of the nation". This was also typical of the other national republics and regions. While only 40 per cent of the voters came out to the polls when Soviets were elected in Azerbaijan in 1925, the percentage increased to 72.5 in 1929. The turnout was 82 per cent in the election of rural Soviets in Byelorussia in 1934 but later, when city Soviets were elected, 92 per cent of voters turned up. And there was an almost 100 per cent turn out for the elections to the Supreme Soviets of the USSR and of the republics in 1937 and 1938.

The nations of the USSR built the foundations of socialism within a single Union state. This was formalised by the USSR Constitution of 1936.

The greatly strengthened friendship of peoples of the USSR was one of the key reasons for the Soviet Union's victory in the Great Patriotic War of 1941-1945. And the whole world knows that the nazis were certain that Soviet state system would collapse like a house of cards.

Meanwhile the united Soviet state, based on the friendship of its peoples, grew immeasurably stronger as national and state sovereignty developed.

"The most convincing expression of the Soviet people's unity," said Leonid Brezhnev, "was the heroic exploits in defence of the socialist Motherland. The union and friendship of all the nations and nationalities withstood the grim trials of the Great Patriotic War, during which the sons and daughters of the Soviet Motherland not only succeeded in safeguarding with honour their socialist gains, but also saved world civilisation from the barbarity of fascism, thereby lending powerful support to the people's liberation struggle."[1]

After the war, the Soviet peoples' friendship and mutual assistance created the foundation for the rebuilding of the war-ravaged economy by the late 1940s and for considerable strides forward in equalising the economic growth levels of the republics by the late 1950s.

---

[1] L. I. Brezhnev, op. cit., p. 73.

By the turn of the 1950s the USSR had built a developed socialist society. A new historical community of people—the Soviet people—had evolved in the USSR. "This community," Leonid Brezhnev noted, "is based on the deeply-rooted objective material and spiritual changes in the country's life, on the emergence and development in our country of socialist nations which have established a new type of relations among themselves."[1]

Socialist property, which draws nations together, is the economic basis of this community. Even when socialism in the USSR was still in the emerging stage, the country's economy was fused into a single organism based on the common economic goals of the Union state as a whole, on the objectives and interests of all nations and ethnic groups, as well as on the interests of each.

The alliance of the working class, collective farmers and people's intellectuals is the social basis of this community. They are socialist classes and social groups fused together by common goals—improving socialist society, and building communism.

The Soviet people are an internationalist community made up of over 130 nations and nationalities, and based on the principles of socialist internationalism. The leading role in this community is played by the working class—by its very nature the most internationalist class, which is playing the decisive role in bringing all the nations and nationalities of the Soviet Land together.

People of many nationalities work side by side in industry in the Soviet Union, and the more intensive the social and economic growth of any national republic, the more distinctly the internationalisation of its entire life can be seen.

Some people drew an erroneous conclusion from the fact that the Soviet people had emerged as a new historical community, and suggested that a concept of one single Soviet nation be introduced into the Constitution, that the Union and autonomous republics be abolished altogether, their right to sovereignty limited, and that they be deprived of the right to secede from the USSR and to enter into foreign relations.

Pointing out the error of these suggestions, Leonid Brezhnev said: "The Soviet people's social and political unity does not at

---

[1] Op. cit., p. 70.

all imply the disappearance of national distinctions. Thanks to the consistent pursuance of the Leninist nationalities policy we have, simultaneously with the building of socialism, successfully solved the nationalities question, for the first time in history. The friendship of the Soviet peoples is indissoluble, and in the process of building communism they are steadily drawing ever closer together and their spiritual life is being mutually enriched. But we would be taking a dangerous path if we were artificially to step up this objective process of national integration. That is something Lenin persistently warned against, and we shall not depart from his precepts."[1]

Soviet socialist culture, one in spirit and content, and which contains the most valuable features and traditions of the culture and daily life of every nation of the country, is characteristic of the Soviet people as a new historical community.

It is developing on the basis of the mutual enrichment of national cultures, and the common, internationalist features are becoming increasingly distinct. In this way the foundations of a new, communist culture, unfettered by any national barriers and meeting the interests of people of labour, are being created.

The total triumph of socialist social relations embodied in society of mature socialism has led to the state of the dictatorship of the proletariat evolving into the state of the whole people. "The Soviet Union today is a natural, inevitable stage in the development of the state born of the October Revolution —a stage characteristic of mature socialism."[2] The tasks of government bodies, their structure and functions, as well as their administrative procedures, have to correspond to the stage of development reached by society.

This is the reason why the Supreme Soviet of the USSR adopted a new Constitution for the country in 1977. This Constitution continues the ideas and principles of the first Soviet Constitution of 1918, of the 1924 Constitution and of the Constitution of 1936.

The achievements of the Soviet Union in the 60 years since

---

[1] L. I. Brezhnev, *Our Course: Peace and Socialism. A Collection of Speeches*, p. 143.
[2] Ibid., p. 153.

the single Union state was formed are the result of the profound organising activities and inspirational strength of the Communist Party of the Soviet Union.

The Communist Party is the organising and guiding force, which paved the way for the formation of the USSR and which has directed its development throughout all these years. A party of internationalists by ideology and policy, composition and structure, it has been able to turn internationalism from an ideal of the class vanguard—the Communist Party—into the profound convictions and norms of behaviour of millions and millions of Soviet people of all nations and nationalities.

This radical change in the socal consciousness of millions of working people was ensured by socio-economic and cultural reforms, and by the Party's irreconcilable struggle against all digressions from the Leninist nationalities policy and against deviations in the sphere of national relations.

Lenin fought unrelentlessly against any manifestations of nationalism or great power chauvinism among the Communist Party membership.

He strove to get the Party to pursue its policy "through Soviet administrative bodies, in the framework of the Soviet Constitutions."[1]

This principle was formalised in the USSR Constitution of 1977, too. It says that the Party functions within the framework of the Constitution, in other words, it pursues its course through Communists elected into Soviets and working in state administrative bodies.

Concern for further development of socialist democracy is one of the major tasks of the CPSU.

All the 60 years of experience of the single Union state confirms that its strength lies in the unbreakable unity of the Party and the people, and that this is the source of the further flourishing of socialist democracy, and of all the accomplishments of the Soviet people in their struggle to see communism truimph.

The significance of this experience is not simply *historic,* confirmed by the path which the Soviet people have already travelled, but also *international,* in the sense that it influences the

---

[1] *The CPSU in Resolutions. . .,* Vol. 2, p. 77.

liberation struggle for social and national emancipation from the fetters of imperialism.

The Communist Party must always maintain relations between nations in Soviet society in its field of vision. These relations are still a reality even in a developed socialist society, and demand constant attention.

The 26th CPSU Congress, held from February 23 to March 3, 1981, provided clear directives for further strengthening the fraternal friendship of all the peoples in the Soviet multinational state, for consistently expanding the material and spiritual potential of each republic, and using this in the best possible way for the harmonious development of the country as a whole.

The Congress gave notice that the Party would continue to combat chauvinism and nationalism, and nationalist aberrations such as anti-Semitism and Zionism.

"We are against tendencies aimed at an artificial obliteration of national identities. And, to a similar extent, we consider their artificial inflation inadmissible. It is the Party's sacrosanct duty to educate the people in a spirit of Soviet patriotism and socialist internationalism, to foster a sense of pride in belonging to the great integral Soviet Union."[1]

Soviet people are marking the 60th anniversary of the Union of Soviet Socialist Republics, a red-letter day in the life of the nations of the USSR, with new successes in all fields. They are putting their backs behind the tasks set in the plans of communist construction worked out by the 26th Congress of the CPSU. Guided by the decisions of the Congress, the Party and the people are working hard to eliminate the threat of war and to strengthen world peace.

---

[1] L. I. Brezhnev, *Report of the Central Committee of the CPSU to the XXVI Congress of the Communist Party of the Soviet Union and the Immediate Tasks of the Party in Home and Foreign Policy,* Novosti Press Agency, Moscow, 1981, p. 76.

SUBJECT AND GEOGRAPHICAL INDEX

A

Afghanistan—201, 270, 273, 281
Akmolinsk region—116
Alash—14
Alash-orda—14, 75
Algeria—16
All-Russia Railway Workers' Union (Vikzhel)—47, 48
Altai—263
Ankara—206, 207
Arkhangelsk (city, province)—152, 177, 214
Armenian SSR (Armenia)—14, 26, 29, 34, 88, 124, 157, 179, 189-91, 204, 206, 208, 209, 212-15, 219, 224, 228, 244, 261, 269
Astrakhan—67, 154, 211
Austria, Austria-Hungary—26, 85, 86, 154, 160, 186, 198, 265, 284
Azerbaijan SSR (Azerbaijan)—14, 26, 29, 31, 34, 125, 138, 145,157, 179, 189-91, 203, 204, 206, 208, 209, 211-16, 219, 224, 228, 244, 245, 249, 254, 255, 258, 261, 269

B

Baku—26, 31, 74, 135, 154, 202, 224, 254, 270, 271

Baku Commune—74
Baltic area—23, 33, 68, 115, 152, 155, 161-63, 165, 166, 170
Baltic Sea—84-86
Bashkir ASSR (Bashkiria)—14, 125, 181, 214, 244
Batumi—190, 206, 207
Bendery—73
Belgium—80
Berlin—80, 265, 275, 285, 288
Bessarabia—73, 88, 152, 244
Black Sea—84-86, 170, 190, 205, 245
Brest (Brest-Litovsk)—84, 85, 93, 152, 154
Britain (Great Britain)—10, 38, 79-81 83, 86-88, 91, 93, 117, 150, 152, 190, 193-95, 206, 207, 246, 265, 270-73, 281-83, 290
Bryansk—254
Bukhara province (Bukhara, Bukhara SPR)—136, 181-83, 208, 209, 232, 242, 243, 269
Bulgaria—85
Buryat autonomous region (Buryat-Mongolia)—14, 214
Byelorussian Rada—14, 68, 162
Byelorussian SSR (Byelorussia)—17, 30, 34, 68, 115, 138, 155, 157, 158, 160-62, 165, 166, 172-76, 179, 188-93, 208-10, 212, 213, 216, 219, 222, 224,

NAME INDEX

A

Agamali-ogly, S. A.—219
Akhtamzyan, A. A.—269
Aleks-Angarietis, Z.—103
Alexeyev, M. V.—153
Antonov-Ovseyenko, V. A.—35, 154, 156, 161, 171, 172
Anvelt, J. J.—69, 162, 163
Arens, I. I.—274, 275
Armand, I. F.—110
Atatürk, Mustafa Kemal—206, 207
Avanesov, V. A.—55, 103, 127
Averin, V. K.—162
Azizbekov, M. A.—74

B

Babushkin, E. A.—204
Bailey, F. M.—204
Bakh, A. N.—262
Baldwin, S.—283
Balfour A. J.—87, 153
Barthou, Louis—266
Bartold, V. V.—263
Beksadyan, A. A.—208
Belyakov, N. K.—85
Berzin, R. I.—84
Bobinski, S. Y.—103
Bogolepov, D. P.—50
Bonar Law, A.—194
Bonch-Bruyevich, M. A.—263
Bonch-Bruyevich, V. D.—40, 199

Borisov, Yu. V.—285
Bortnowski—103
Bosh, E. B.—72
Brezhnev, L. I.—7, 147, 293, 300-03, 305
Brokford-Rantzau—289
Buachidze, S. A.—73
Bubnov, A. S.—50, 112, 260
Buchanan, D.—47, 78, 79, 80
Buinaksky, U. D.—73
Bukharin, N. N.—28, 167

C

Cecil, R.—87
Cecil Harmsworth—194
Chaikovsky—81
Chamberlain, A.—197
Chaplygin, S. A.—263
Chervyakov, A. G.—55, 103, 162, 219, 228, 232
Chicherin, G. V.—194, 199, 201, 206, 208, 265-67, 275, 276, 278, 280-82, 287-90
Chlenov, S. B.—275
Chubaryan, A. O.—87
Chugayev, D. A.—31, 115
Churchill, W.—197
Clemenceau, G.—87, 165
Coolidge, C.—287
Curzon, George—194, 197, 273, 275
Cychowski, K.—103

313

315

316